I0667642

Praise for *Ditch the Act*

"I love a book that is entertaining and engaging. But, it also has to teach me something. *Ditch the Act* delivers the goods! As an expert in customer and employee loyalty, I found lessons to help people create loyal relationships with people they haven't met yet, digitally that is. Foland and Kim's concept of revealing your whole self with candor will help you drive loyalty with the masses."

—**SHEP HYKEN**, customer service/experience expert and *New York Times* bestselling author of *The Amazement Revolution*

"One of the key elements to making valuable connections in your life and in business is embracing the power of authenticity. *Ditch the Act* is the playbook you need to follow to execute a winning game plan to embrace being genuine and establishing trust to thrive each and every day."

—**LOU DIAMOND**, CEO of Thrive, bestselling author and international keynote speaker

"At Zoom, we know the power of human to human connection. In a world where there is more digital connection than ever before, a reminder to be more human when on digital platforms is highly valuable. In *Ditch the Act*, Foland and Kim dive deep into how to showcase your real and whole self, both online and offline, in a way that builds trust by being truthful."

—**ERIC YUAN**, founder and CEO, Zoom

"I'll admit that I wasn't the most vulnerable leader for most of my career. In fact, I was given feedback by someone on my team years ago that I was 'prickly to get to know.' I focused too much on being 'polished' and didn't share much about who I was outside of work. While I made some subtle changes in response to the feedback, I was still holding back. And I knew it. Well that changed when, a few years later, our six-month-old son was diagnosed with stage 3 neuroblastoma. I was scared and simply couldn't hide it. In fact, I decided to not even try. I shared what was going on with my team and that I would be away from work often while he went through his treatment over the coming months. I shared with them how I was feeling along the way, how we were coping as a family with two other kids in the home, and how when I couldn't sleep I decided to start writing about my family's journey. They embraced me and my family in ways I couldn't have imagined. My vulnerability allowed us to become very close as a team. They supported me greatly professionally and delivered some of the best results that team had ever achieved. That mask I took off, I've tried to leave behind for good. I try to be vulnerable often about what I know, what I need help with, and who I am. It's liberating. I think it encourages others to do the same and allows them to do their best work. That team taught me that. Btw, my son is now seven and completely healthy!"

—**KAMAU WITHERSPOON**, SVP operations, Target

"As someone who specializes in helping companies grow leaders, retain top talent, and develop employees, I believe that *Ditch the Act* outlines the fundamentals that an organization requires to enable employees to connect to the company brand and turn their employees into brand advocates."

—**MICHELLE TILLIS LEDERMAN**, author of *The Connector's Advantage*
and *The 11 Laws of Likability*

"Being vulnerable is essential to innovation, but very few know how to actually do it in an authentic way. *Ditch the Act* is the most comprehensive guide I've seen that provides a step-by-step actionable plan on how to get started now."

—**JOSH LINKNER**, five-time tech entrepreneur, *New York Times* bestselling
author, and founder/former CEO of Detroit Venture Partners

"*Ditch the Act* shows that the time is NOW to expose our own humanity to achieve not just success, but LONGSTANDING IMPACT. When I coach individuals to tap into that humanity, they gain a surefire foundation to achieve their full potential."

—**DR. AVIVA LEGATT**, The Ivy League Executive Coach; TEDx speaker;
Forbes contributor; and affiliated faculty, The Wharton School
at the University of Pennsylvania

"Authenticity cannot be contrived and passion cannot be faked. Ryan and Leonard share valuable stories and methods for getting out of your own way and getting to the real you. And that is a sustainable business strategy."

—**TRACY HAZZARD**, *Inc.* and *Authority Magazine* columnist,
host of four podcasts, and CEO of Podetize

"As a chief marketing officer who specializes in inbound marketing, I see *Ditch the Act* as not only a practical guide, but quite tactical as well, to not only take an individual and turn them into the face of a brand, but to rally large teams at companies to do the same. I will be implementing these practices at my company with all our employees."

    —**RYAN BONNICI**, chief marketing officer at G2, former Hubspot,
      Salesforce, and Microsoft, Forbes top 50 CMO

"In *Ditch the Act*, Kim and Foland's radical authenticity is not a strategy that we're used to seeing from thought leaders who generally rely on a guise of perfection to amass influence. And that's why it's so effective. The authors show that in our airbrushed culture, aspiration is less effective than vulnerability."

    —**TINA MULQUEEN**, CEO of Kindred PR, *Forbes* contributor,
      nonprofit founder, and technology ethics speaker

"*Ditch the Act* is one of the best books I've ever read. Ryan and Leonard's stories are both relatable and inspiring, demonstrating the power of showing your true self to the world. Their stories, lessons, and insights will encourage you to take off your mask and become the authentic leader you're meant to be. Lots of tips in here to get you to your next level of success, impact, and difference-making. If you find yourself hiding in the darkness, as I and many others have, this book will help you step into the light. Read it."

    —**JEFF DAVIS**, author of *The Power of Authentic Leadership* and
      international keynote speaker

"I LOVE the 'Exposure Résumé'—the idea made a lot of intuitive sense, and also effectively challenges the conventional wisdom of résumé crafting/polishing. There's a ton of 'personal branding gurus' out there. What makes Leonard and Ryan different (and 100 times better)? First, they have ultra-successful personal brands (with hundreds of thousands of followers and more), so they actually walk the talk, and second, their message of authenticity isn't just some 'hack'—it's a philosophy of how we can become more human as entrepreneurs, experts, etc. If you're a bit jaded about personal branding (like me), this book could very well change your mind."

    —**IAN CHEW**, founding executive at Seminal

"*Ditch the Act* isn't about creating a personal brand; it's a step-by-step guide to articulating your story, identifying the wisdom in your wounds, and sharing them both with the world. Foland and Kim demonstrate that in a world of carefully curated online identities designed to impress, the true key to connection isn't making people say, 'oh wow! That's amazing'; it's giving people the opportunity to say, 'oh my God, I thought I was the only one afraid, hurt, and hiding.'"

—**DREW DUDLEY**, internationally bestselling author of *This Is Day One*

"When it comes to getting your dream job, you must learn to balance sharing both your expertise and the experience that has actually made you an expert. In *Ditch the Act*, Foland and Kim teach readers how to use their failures and mistakes to build out an Exposure Résumé that helps tease out the learning lessons that make you unique and relatable. Read this book and you will discover your true and authentic brand."

—**DAVID RODRIGUEZ**, cofounder and CEO, CornerJob

"Our personal brand is critical in the age of knowledge work and collaboration. Ryan and Leonard provide the *must know* advice on how to build our personal brand value successfully. Learning my lesson from the book, don't be ideal, be real! Start your journey to prosperity by reading this book!"

—**NEIL SAHOTA**, United Nations advisor, University of California at Irvine faculty, and author of *Own the A.I. Revolution*

"'True Self' is the new 'Best Self.' We are conditioned to only putting our 'Best Self' forward in relationships and professional settings, and social media is making things worse by driving new levels of imposter syndrome and self-doubt. *Ditch the Act* offers concrete steps to overcome fears and grow into who you want to be. Professionally, this book offers tremendous advice on self branding. Personally (and perhaps more importantly) this book generates a road map to self-acceptance."

—**MIKE BUSH**, founder, Nomad Communications

"If you are ready and have the courage to be authentic, transparent, and relatable in business and in life, *Ditch the Act* will walk you through a pragmatic, clear, step-by-step blueprint. Leonard and Ryan walk us through a proven formula to look in the mirror and unlock the strength of seeing all of you—not just the strengths and accomplishments, but the mistakes, warts, and vulnerabilities. In being honest and sharing yourself fully, you discover your secret sauce, your key differentiators, what makes you stand out."

—**MARIA DIAZ**, MBA, chief leadership and impact strategist, founder and CEO, The Elixir Edge

"Many people look great on paper, but few know how to translate that to real relatability. In fact, the more success you find, the more unrelatable you can become (without even realizing it). We live in a world where people crave authenticity. *Ditch the Act* shows you how to be more comfortable with yourself, and shows the value in sharing the struggles that built your success. Doing so helps others see themselves in your story, and that is what creates real connection in an authentic way."

—**DAVID MELTZER**, CEO and cofounder, Sports 1 Marketing

"It's amazing how you shine when you take the polish off. *Ditch the Act* is a timely user manual on how to turn your awkward vulnerability into a powerful brand asset."

—**PARK HOWELL**, founder of Business of Story

"As the founder of BNI (Business Network International), I can tell you that the most powerful element of each member of any group is their ability to share their own story. In *Ditch the Act*, you will learn how to share stories around the most compelling topic of all, yourself."

—**IVAN MISNER**, *New York Times* bestselling author

"*Ditch the Act* is exactly what people need to do to be more authentic. It's all eloquently explained with examples by the authors. I predict this book will be seen as powerful as the book *How to Win Friends and Influence People* by Dale Carnegie. If you want to find your authentic self and allow that self to be seen and heard by the world, *Ditch the Act* is your key to success."

—**NATHAN GOLD**, The Demo Coach

"In *Ditch the Act*, Leonard and Ryan have done a superb job of giving us permission to not only show up and share our more authentic selves, they've also included numerous thought-provoking, step-by-step exercises to blast through our fears and achieve a much deeper relationship with our online and offline audiences."

—**MARI SMITH**, premier Facebook marketing expert, social media thought
leader, and author of *The New Relationship Marketing* and
coauthor of *Facebook Marketing: An Hour a Day*

"In *Ditch the Act*, Leonard and Ryan teach readers how to turn their biggest weaknesses into their greatest strengths. They show you how transparency and vulnerability can make you stronger, not weaker, and how you can go from fearful to fearless. They provide an easy-to-implement guide that includes highly effective exercises that help you cut through the nonsense and noise and establish a bold and honest brand."

—**JONATHAN ALPERT**, psychotherapist, performance coach, and
author of *Be Fearless: Change Your Life in 28 Days*

"The key to building a good brand is to be raw and authentic with your audience. Leonard and Ryan jump right into showing you who they are with candid examples and backstory to develop exactly how they have been able to achieve success with their brands. *Ditch the Act* helps to strip down your barriers through engaging stories, data and homework to truly find who you are and how you can achieve more from yourself. It may be the cheapest therapist you ever engage with."

—**JOE MARTIN**, VP of marketing at CloudApp, formerly known
as Adobe Joe

"From presidents to superstars and the biggest brands, I've assisted thousands of clients to build their personas and connect them to their audiences in the social graph. In *Ditch the Act*, Leonard and Ryan have highlighted the most important quality that resonates with large audiences: to be human. Their unique approach should help you break through hubris and allow your human, vulnerable self to be expressed, all in hopes to build a more suitable Social Organism for all of us!"

—**OLIVER LUCKETT**, 10x entrepreneur, founder of HausMart and
author of *The Social Organism*

"Leonard and Ryan have written a transformative book that brings forth not only why we need to be online, but how we can create and spark

impact in our communities, build sustainable relationships, and pay it forward to others. This book brings forth applicable best practices that can empower executives, educators, and young professionals entering the workplace. *Ditch the Act* needs to be added to your bookshelf and course reading lists!"

—**KAREN JUNE FREBERG**, University of Louisville associate professor in strategic communications and chair of Cannes Lions Educators Summit

"No one is perfect, and *Ditch the Act* helps you move past your imperfections to craft and create your own narrative. In today's world of highlight reels, Leonard and Ryan share bravely and openly their ups and downs, while providing a framework to uncover our own stories. This must-read not only shares the tools but also gives us the courage to move past our fears and embrace vulnerability."

—**ALISSA CARPENTER**, MEd, keynote speaker and facilitator at Everything's Not OK and That's OK

EMBRACE THE GOOD AND BAD

DITCH
THE ACT

DITCH
THE ACT

Reveal the Surprising Power of the Real You for Greater Success

LEONARD KIM AND RYAN FOLAND

New York   Chicago   San Francisco   Athens
London   Madrid   Mexico City   Milan
New Delhi   Singapore   Sydney   Toronto

1 2 3 4 5 6 7 8 9   LWI   24 22 23 21 20 19

ISBN   978-1-260-45437-6
MHID   1-260-45437-1

e-ISBN   978-1-260-45438-3
e-MHID   1-260-45438-X

Library of Congress Cataloging-in-Publication Data

Names: Kim, Leonard, author. | Foland, Ryan, author.
Title: Ditch the act / Leonard Kim and Ryan Foland.
Description: New York : McGraw-Hill, [2020]
Identifiers: LCCN 2019028633 (print) | LCCN 2019028634 (ebook) | ISBN
   9781260454376 (hardcover) | ISBN 9781260454383 (ebook)
Subjects: LCSH: Success in business. | Self-disclosure. | Self-realization. | Success.
Classification: LCC HF5386 .K4835 2020 (print) | LCC HF5386 (ebook) |
   DDC 650.1—-dc23
LC record available at https://lccn.loc.gov/2019028633
LC ebook record available at https://lccn.loc.gov/2019028634

McGraw-Hill Education books are available at special quantity discounts to use as premiums and sales promotions or for use in corporate training programs. To contact a representative, please visit the Contact Us pages at www.mhprofessional.com.

CONTENTS

Worksheets   vii
Foreword by Keith Ferrazzi   ix
Acknowledgments   xiii
Introduction   xv
Disclaimer   xix

PART I

YOU DON'T HAVE TO BE ANYONE BUT YOURSELF

Chapter I
   Own Your Whole Story   3

Chapter 2
   Don't Be Ideal, Be Real   11

Chapter 3
   When You Speak, Speak Your Truth   25

Chapter 4
   Run Farther with Imperfect Friends   41

PART 2

LET YOUR FEARS GUIDE YOU

Chapter 5
   Your Brand Is Who You Are   59

Chapter 6
   Your Brand Precedes You   75

Chapter 7

Put Yourself Out There   91

Chapter 8

Ditch the Act and Be Yourself   107

PART 3

REVEAL YOUR WHOLE SELF

Chapter 9

Step One: Positioning Is an Art Form   129

Chapter 10

Step Two: Discover What Makes You Stand Out   161

Chapter 11

Step Three: Overcome Fear and Share   185

Chapter 12

Step Four: Focus on Form, Not Force   213

Chapter 13

Step Five: Make Eye Contact with the Camera   231

Chapter 14

Step Six: Be Consistent with Content   243

Chapter 15

Step Seven: Keep It Social   255

Chapter 16

Step Eight: Sequential Steps Create Success   269

Chapter 17

Your Success Is Half the Story   285

Notes   293

Index   295

WORKSHEETS

Chapter 5

Rapid Reflection Discovery Process Worksheet   65–71

Chapter 7

Exposures Ranked by Level Worksheet   94–98

Chapter 8

Exposure Résumé Worksheet   109–117

Chapter 9

The Exposed and Authentic Bio Worksheet   132–147

Personal Branding Positioning and Strategy Worksheet   152–159

Chapter 10

The 3-1-3 Challenge Worksheet   164–179

Chapter 11

Overcoming Fear and Sharing Worksheet   190–194

Story Creation Worksheet   201–208

Chapter 12

Amplify What Is Working Worksheet   223–227

Chapter 14

Content Calendar Worksheet   247–251

Chapter 15

Ditch the Act Peer Group Charter Starter Worksheet   261–263

Chapter 16

Success Stacking Worksheet   273–276

FOREWORD

When I host dinner parties at my house, I like to bring together complementary people whose interests and expertise may have some overlap, but who will also bring new insight and perspective to the group. I'm a strong believer in the wisdom of the group, and I like bringing those groups together. I also like bringing together these curated groups because I hate small talk and want each person to bring their uniqueness and authenticity to share with the rest of us. That way everyone leaves my dinner parties feeling like they've nourished their minds as well as their bodies.

It was at one of these dinners that I hosted on September 12, 2015, that Ryan and Leonard first met. I wanted to have a dinner for the rising entrepreneurial stars, and that night, after my short introduction, my guests broke off to different tables based on the numbers below their plates where, serendipitously, Leonard and Ryan, who had just met for the first time, decided to build a company together.

Because I like connecting good people, it's not uncommon for someone I haven't seen in years to reach out and say thanks for an introduction that changed the course of their career. That is exactly what happened two years after that initial event that Leonard and Ryan attended. I had sent Leonard a connection request on LinkedIn, and a few days later, a message showed up in my inbox, thanking me for connecting him and Ryan.

He then explained that they had been promoting and elevating my brand in the articles they were writing for various major publications. It wasn't, he wrote, just a way to say thank you—the spirit in which I had held the dinner party that night had become a foundational component of their business. Of course I was grateful to hear this, but the gratitude we now shared for each other went a step further.

As a measure of their thanks, they offered to help me promote my third book, *Leading Without Authority*, which is on a concept I created, called co-elevation. The offer made perfect sense. The three of us were practicing and had proven the strength of that very thing. Co-elevating is a new level of showing up at the office—and in life—with a shared commitment to the mission and one's teammates. It's an attitude that says, "Let's do this together. I care about your success, and I'm committed to making sure you succeed, too, as we work toward this shared mission in our partnership." Leonard, Ryan, and I were operating as a co-elevating team, and the results have lifted all of us up further.

Back in my early career I was a bow tie guy. Whenever I would go to events, I'd put on a bow tie to make an impression. It often sparked conversations that led to great connections. When I met Ryan at my house that first night, he was, fittingly, wearing a knitted bow tie. He made an immediate and lasting impression on me and continues to stand out in the crowd today. Outgoing and charismatic, and he understands communication in a unique way. When I was working with Ryan through his 3-1-3 Method, which you will learn about in this book, he challenged the way that I position myself and my company. The resolution we reached was a small but significant change that is already paying dividends.

I believe that there is nothing more powerful than candor when building relationships. Leonard is a master of implementing the lessons of his truth and experiences—both the ups and downs—that come with success and failure. What sets him out from the crowd is his bravery in sharing through an unfiltered lens not only what has worked, but more importantly what has not. I consult with some of the biggest brands in the world, and what I constantly see lacking in executive leadership is the candor to let their authentic selves shine through. To accept that we all have flaws, that none of us know everything and, most importantly, that our team doesn't expect us to. What Leonard teaches his clients, myself included, is how to position your "not so good moments" into teachable lessons that make you more approachable and, frankly, more human.

As you will see with the section on Leonard and Ryan's Exposure Résumé, they have broken down their process of turning the moments from which you're hiding into moments that define your strongest brand. These are the moments when you show your strength, resilience, and bravery by sharing your own moments of weakness and insecurity that led to greater understanding. Their authenticity, reliability, professionalism, and creativity come to life in the pages of *Ditch the Act*. You will enjoy their candor and approachability from the first page.

Let me finish off with this. If you're scared of what it may mean to expose yourself, this is all the more reason to read this book. You'll quickly realize that your real power—as an individual or as a company—is not in being picture perfect but in being vulnerable and honest. And Leonard and Ryan can show you how—precisely because they were once just as scared and skeptical as you might be right now.

—Keith Ferrazzi
New York Times bestselling author of
Never Eat Alone and *Who's Got Your Back*

ACKNOWLEDGMENTS

This book is dedicated to the millions of readers and all our friends we made along the way, who have not only believed in us, but helped us get to where we are today (especially you). From the conversations that have helped us get over our personal struggles, to the support that is derived from the love of human connection, to the opportunities that we would have never imagined possible.

To Donya Dickerson, Maura Teitelbaum, Brent Cole, and Sara Bliss, for their immense help in believing in us and helping us put this project together, in order to share this way of life with the world.

To the bosses who have taken a chance on us, supported us in all that we do, and brought out our best selves, Michael Dennin, Iain Grainger, Christopher Bazin, and Jeana Rettig.

To a few of our close friends we have made through this journey, Michael and Bonnie, Catheryn Chen, Tone Loc, Iman Oubou, Ben Landis, Kim Orlesky, Josef Cheng, Winnie Sun, Aaron Orendorff, Daniel Egan, Keith Ferrazzi, Joseph M. Bradley, Cheryl Snapp Conner, Hai Truong, Michael Simmons, Nathan Gold, Brian MacMahon, Kenneth Artery, John Lim, Tiffani Bova, Erin Paige Law, Nathalie Salhi, Alexandre Laulhé, Sol Orwell, Daniel Midson-Short, Evan Duning, Philip Wong, Alexander Ali, Brian D. Evans, Dorie Clark, Kent Jacobs, Blake Jamieson, Ian Chew, David Mack, Kameka M. Dempsey, Allen Han, Rachel Pedersen, Dan Bennett, Dennis Yu, Deep Patel, Aj Agrawal, Vivien Pham, Christa Pecikozic, Celine Petrossian, Jessica Stafford, Miguel and Rosario Dias, Kelly Hrudey, Sean McKeon, Daniel and Chelsea and Caleb Vantol, Hadari Oshri, Joan McLane, Kevin Huie, John Bates, Josh Linkner, Kevin Stockdale, Angie Sarabia, Barbara Whitmore, Lauren Carpio, Paul and Emma, Jen and Jesse, Dave and Daniele, Brian Nowak, Mark Deppe, Cameron Brown, Rahfeal Gordon, Levi Eastwood, Louise Story, Tommy Sanders, Daniel Kim, Daniel Marlin, Dr. Zeev Neuwirth, Arden Kaisman, Noelle

Chang, Suzanne Brown, Alissa Carpenter, Mark Wilcox, Mary Dacuma, Joseph Davis, Rhett Power, Deirdre Breakenridge, Jennifer Aaron, Jeff Spenard, Simon Thompson, Nari Hwangpo, Ulyses Osuna, Hunter and Taylor Decker, Jonathan Alpert, Jay Kim, Robyn Stevens, Ryan Bonnici, Kyle Ellicott, Adam Stone, Robin Humbert, Sovanara Ker, Johnathan Grzybowski, David Braun, Kevin J. Ryan, Karen June Freberg, Chris Agos, Myla Morhun-Le, Dean Van Dyke, John Boitnott, Tara Jaye Frank, Stephanie Lee, Dr. Aviva Legatt, Marsha Collier, Dr. Diane Hamilton, Mike Wood, Arka Sengupta, Erica Rheinschild, May Busch, Allen Ortega, Nicolas Cole, Joe Martin, Dr. Michael Johns, Dr. Maria Nelson, Dr. Karla O'Dell, Dr. Jay Lieberman, Dr. Steven Giannotta, Dr. Jonathan Russin, Dr. Mary Samplaski, Dr. John Lipham, Shawn Copeland, Matti Owens, Frank Dumas, Deinis Matos, Chris Strub, Holly Ridings, Rob Balasabas, Justin Keltner, Derin Cag, Danny Moon, Ann Hoy, Christine Cavalier, Mitch Jackson, James Bae, Rebekah Radice, Katelynn Fetterly, Fanny Chavarria, Albert Chen, Andrew Smith, Suzie Nguyen, Laura Gassner Otting, Zainab Reda, Viram Lodhia, Adam Indrayana, Jonathan Beltran, Julia Arthur, Deb Shufelt, Michael Koerbel, Laura Rubinstein, Monica Padilla, Alecia Li Morgan, Stephen Panus, Scott Hansen, Tina Mulqueen, Mary C. Long, Stacey Boehrns, Colin McGuire, Mimi Zheng, Guy Woods, Jason Chen, Michael Roderick, Michael Schein, James Altucher, Nicole Jansen, Byron Hsu, Dr. Linda F. Williams, Leo Bottary, Brian Fanzo, Annie Crawford, Charles Hughes, Julia Malacoff, Fabiola Torres, Sensei Paul, Yuri Kruman, Nicholas Smith, Eugene Hong, Sangita Dube, Brett Miketta, Paul Shepherd, Jonathan Trejo, Jonathan Beltran, Chris Harvey, Laurena Huh, and the countless other amazing people who have taken time to touch our lives.

A special thanks is made to our significant others, Angie and Cyn, and the family members that have supported us, both in their lifetime, and long after their deaths: Robert L. Landis, Hyang S. Landis, Katherine Choi, Woo C. Park, Jihwa Park, Ron Foland, Joanne Foland, Robert Knowles, Grandma Nell, Terri and Stan Salstrom, Leonard and Angie's chihuahua, Roo, and Ryan and Cyn's stuffed animals, Cow and Freckles.

INTRODUCTION

Ditch the Act demonstrates how revealing your failures and weaknesses is an essential element in building and sustaining a viral personal brand to help propel your relationships, your career, and/or your business. In this book, we'll show how ditching your act and getting vulnerable creates a unique and somewhat ironic combination of differentiation and like-mindedness with your audience.

As marketing and communications experts in the corporate, academic, and start-up world, we understand both the reality and the pervasiveness of failure, weakness, and frustration. According to the U.S. Bureau of Labor Statistics, about 50 percent of new businesses survive five years or more, and only one-third survive more than ten years. Failure is not just relegated to business, though. Around 50 percent of marriages end in divorce, which is to say nothing of interpersonal relationships. Aside from failure, all of us suffer from fears, exasperations, or perceived shortcomings. While these are common experiences, however, our natural tendency is to hide the skeletons in our closets—not just the things we've done but the things done to us—and construct facades of perceived strength. This is how most people build their brands. The trouble is, facades and false images hide who we really are and block true, authentic, and meaningful connection with others—and ourselves.

We live in a world that rewards experts, gurus, and thought leaders. We've been told that the way to join their ranks is to share your success stories, offer practical advice, and thus convince others of your value. This, we are told, is why people return. The value you offer them. The problem is that it becomes extremely difficult to stand out when thousands if not millions of others are making the same play. It's also only half the story of who you really are.

What if you came at it from another angle? An angle that's not based on your ability to build yourself up and convince others to put you on a pedestal. An angle that's based instead on your ability to be real and show others that you're, in fact, not better than they are but rather a lot like them.

In *Ditch the Act*, we share our own stories of failure and weakness, and show how vulnerably exposing those stories helped us connect with others and cultivate large, authentic, trustworthy personal brands. We share how Leonard's naïveté and arrogance—his *narrogance* as he calls it—led him from failure to failure early in his career. It's quite pitiful actually. Believing success would be easy, and arrogantly refusing jobs that he felt were beneath him, he eventually found himself alone and broke, reevaluating his life and whether it would be best to just end it all. Only in his rock-bottom moment could he objectively evaluate his failures. In that evaluation—and perhaps as a last-ditch effort to convince himself of his own value—he began to expose himself through his writing. Through his exposure, Leonard was shocked to find an empathetic, loyal, and growing fan base.

Ditch the Act demonstrates how exposing your failures and weaknesses is an essential element in creating an authentic personal brand . . . We'll show how ditching the act and getting vulnerable is the best way to differentiate and grow your brand, while cultivating brand loyalty.

Likewise, we share Ryan's story, how he experienced his own series of setbacks. Bullied as a kid, he struggled to achieve in an effort to prove his worth. He dove into martial arts and hockey to show his tenacity and toughness. After college, he did what he could to get ahead, trusting others who promised him an easy path to success, wealth, and popularity. It didn't work. Ultimately, Ryan and his business partner at the time were investigated by the Federal Trade Commission (FTC) in connection with his partner's activities. After settling with the FTC and coming through the darkness of that period, Ryan set out to learn how manipulation, poor communication, and betrayal had swept him into a string of failures and an FTC investigation. Through the process, he too began vulnerably sharing his story and the lessons he learned from it.

Eventually, we'd meet at a dinner party thrown by entrepreneur and *New York Times* bestselling author Keith Ferrazzi. There, Keith asked us to pair up and share one area of need or vulnerability in our own lives. Having never met before, the two of us paired up and began exposing ourselves. We discussed setbacks and legitimate areas of need and ultimately discovered we each had something to offer the other. We discovered, too, that our unique abilities and areas of expertise grew from a commitment to vulnerability and surprising honesty. Over the following months, we'd partner in creating InfluenceTree, a personal branding and professional recognition company, to share our expertise with others, an expertise centered in our mutual commitment to transparency and vulnerability.

Readers, clients, and customers connect to human stories, stories of those who've overcome failure or weakness and have learned lessons in the process. Yet when it comes to our own lives, how many of us are able to ditch the act and be that transparent? How many of us are afraid to be vulnerable with others for fear that they will judge, stereotype, or misunderstand us?

Facades and false images hide who we really are and block true, authentic, and meaningful connection with others—and ourselves.

Ditch the Act shows you why exposure is important and how it helps cultivate connection and grow personal brand loyalty better than any polished persona can. It also teaches you what to expose through the development of a personal, proprietary "Exposure Résumé," which strategically prompts you to list your most valuable failures, setbacks, or perceived weaknesses and then clarify the key lessons that can be shared with others. Once those lessons are understood through the creation of your new résumé, *Ditch the Act* leads you through a practical eight-step process we use with ourselves and all our clients that is designed to help you use the fresh exposure and lessons to drive brand differentiation and growth:

1. Craft your unique bio, personal brand positioning, and strategy.
2. Find what makes you unique and identify the problem you are best suited to solve.

3. Create stories and insights based on your Exposure Résumé.
4. Speak your truth and give your stories an audience and then spend time, effort, and marketing dollars where you see performance.
5. Extract key content pieces to turn into video scripts you will post, share, and embed in content you've already published.
6. Nourish streams of content to stay top of mind.
7. Foster camaraderie in new relationships.
8. Stack your successes.

Ditch the Act is an important, unique book for all who are tired of trying to build and manage their brand by fostering a polished persona that others might admire but that you know is at least partly made to fit the standard of society, yet may not be true. It's a book for those who are ready to ditch the act and stop working so hard to be something they aren't. *Ditch the Act* is for those who want to harness the power of vulnerability and authenticity to build a better, more believable, more profitable personal brand—whether in their relationships, in their career, or in business—and enjoy a clean conscience while doing it.

DISCLAIMER

In *Ditch the Act,* the ideas and methods outlined will go against what you think you should do. Your entire body and mind will reject the idea of sharing some of the experiences that you have faced in life that you have hidden out of shame, regret, or fear of being judged. You may have deeply buried some of these stories and hidden them from the world, aside from a few confidants. We will talk about these parts of your life and walk you through different levels of exposure to ease you into being able to share these dark moments, while storing the most difficult stories for when you can muster up the courage to share them. The sooner you can accept you for who you are, as a result of all your experiences, the sooner you will be able to take off the mask, ditch the act, and reveal who you are as the truly authentic person you have always been, both digitally and in real life. Ditching the act and exposing yourself is not a gimmick or a tactic you implement here and there to draw upon success—it's embracing a lifestyle that you fully incorporate—in both your in-person and digital relationships.

Ditch the Act contains tactical advice that will teach you, step-by-step, exactly what you need to do in order to build an intentional personal brand. Much of the tactical advice is delivered through worksheets. If you prefer to print out the worksheets or edit them on your own device, visit https://ditchtheact.com/resources and enter the password DSAyourfearstoDitchTheAct to access the files.

PART I

YOU DON'T HAVE TO BE ANYONE BUT YOURSELF

CHAPTER 1

OWN YOUR WHOLE STORY

I walked into Keith Ferrazzi's house like I owned the place, put together and wearing a confident smile. By all accounts, things were going well. I had a growing personal brand. I was writing articles for large publications like *Inc.* and *Entrepreneur*. I was making more money than I'd thought possible after declaring bankruptcy just a few years earlier. I'd reinvented myself, and though I wasn't living some rags-to-riches story yet, I was on my way. My résumé, my growth, my trajectory—all of it justified my invitation to this exclusive networking dinner party thrown by a *New York Times* bestselling author and entrepreneur. But as I stepped through the front door of his Hollywood Hills home, the truth was that I didn't feel like I belonged. I felt like a failure in so many areas of my life. And I was fresh off a breakup.

I was dressed as a successful and somewhat eccentric entrepreneur in a dark suit with tasteful sparkling flecks and a red velvet bow tie. I mingled with the dinner party guests, sipped scotch, and enjoyed a spectacular view of the valley from

Ferrazzi's hillside deck. It was a party with up-and-coming entrepreneurs living in the Los Angeles area, a group of individuals who'd created strong differentiated personal brands, and we were all playing the part. I didn't know any of the others, and they didn't know me. Still, we knew what we shared: we were climbing the ladder of success. We were the badasses of the business future. It's why we'd been invited.

Before dinner, Keith called us together and offered some welcoming comments. He asked us to turn our cell phones off and refrain from taking any photos or videos. Satisfied that all phones were off, that all distractions had been minimized, he then told us this was a different sort of dinner party than we probably expected. It was a networking event, yes. But tonight we'd network around the themes of vulnerability and candor. I don't know about the others, but I felt the discomfort start to rise . . .

Until Keith led the way and shared his own current struggles. He shared about a very real, daily challenge in his own business that had been keeping him up at night. Some surprisingly raw stuff. His candidness opened the door with a level of vulnerability uncommon in the entrepreneurial circles I'd become accustomed to. It was an unexpected move and a moment in which Ferrazzi revealed that while he was a little older and more experienced than us, he was a lot more like us than we thought.

When he finished sharing, he set the parameters for the evening. Just like any other networking event, he said, many of us had come to his party with our personas and profiles intact. We'd come wearing masks of success and were ready to play *that game*. We were probably good at it too. But the truth, he said, was that none of us had all our stuff together. None of us was as put together as we'd liked everyone to believe. We all needed help. Right then and there.

"So," he continued, "over dinner, share with someone near you. But when you introduce yourself, don't share what you do. Instead, share where you need help, an area you're struggling with or not getting right."

This was a simple enough task, I thought. I'd had plenty of personal setbacks over the years and had grown my personal brand by sharing those setbacks with my readers. I'd learned to connect with others through exposing my shortcomings, and that led to my being named a Top Writer on Quora for two consecutive years and attracting over 50,000 social media followers, before even attending this party. And sharing those shortcomings was what I was already teaching to others who asked me for mentorship (or were studying from a bird's-eye view of how my writing reached over 10 million reads). I looked across the table to the person I'd be sharing with over the next hour. There sat the only other man wearing a bow tie, his knitted and green.

"Ryan Foland," he said, and I introduced myself. Without skipping a beat, Ryan shared how he was a communications expert who managed an entrepreneurial incubator at the University of California, Irvine (UCI). Through failed business partnerships, including one that subjected him to investigation by the Federal Trade Commission, he'd learned hard lessons about the value of truth, candor, and clarity. He used those lessons at UCI and helped his students learn to clearly communicate their vision with investors and business partners. Reaching beyond his students, though, had proved to be challenging. He struggled to get his ideas out. He had to scratch and claw to get free speaking gigs, and though he was a good writer, he wasn't able to solidify a solid platform. Worse, when he landed a gig, he had to constantly explain the FTC investigation that he'd settled because of his public past. He couldn't seem to get much traction in light of the negative publicity of his past.

After he spoke, I shared how I'd built a successful platform through writing but still struggled to connect with people in person and even more when speaking on stage . . . and that I'd also recently lost my girlfriend.

Ryan listened carefully. When I was finished, he cut to the chase. "I can help you connect with people," he said, "if you can help me build my platform." It was a straightforward comment, an obvious solution. And right there, on the spot, Ryan Foland became my client and I became his.

Over the months that followed the dinner party, I worked with Ryan to grow his platform. Starting with a meager 200 followers across all social networks, we worked together to expand his reach. He began sharing about his own failures and weaknesses—details he'd naturally hid until then—and how he'd learned from them. In a year, he grew his platform to over 100,000 followers and landed several articles in major publications.

Throughout the process, Ryan and I became friends and discovered that our skill sets complemented each other. I understood the power of print and knew how to grow his social media following. He had an in-person charisma, the kind that was natural on video. We'd also both learned the power of vulnerability in building our own brands. By recognizing our unique strengths and weaknesses and our common belief in the power of vulnerability, it was apparent what happened next. I asked Ryan if he'd consider partnering with me in InfluenceTree, a personal branding and marketing company. Without a second thought, he agreed.

THE BIGGEST BRANDING MISTAKE THAT MOST PEOPLE MAKE

We live in the age of branding, both corporate and personal. The reality is, all people have a personal brand whether they realize it or not, and though it is true that your brand might encompass your résumé, your skills, and your expertise, there is so much more to it that people don't realize. The executive of a Fortune 500 company, the upstart entrepreneur, the teenage dishwasher who wants to work hard and become the restaurant chef— each projects a certain image, a way of being seen by others. This way of being seen, the way you carry yourself with friends, coworkers, prospective employers, and clients, is the essence of your personal brand.

Yet the image most people portray isn't the real thing. It's only their good side. This is the biggest branding mistake you can make.

In our work as personal branding experts, Ryan and I have seen so many people try to grow their brand by projecting only their better angles, only beauty, confidence, and success. They've perfected the art of putting on professional masks, and write and speak as if they have it all together. They tout their credentials on their curriculum vitae and have become master name-droppers. They avoid talking about their failures— the time they were fired from their first job, or their pending divorce, or that time they were investigated by the Federal Trade Commission. They minimize the areas where they might need a little help—the trouble they have translating their thoughts to the page or their inability to connect with others from the stage. They minimize, spin, and shade around the truth of their own areas of need, then wonder why their brand isn't quite connecting with others. And though highlighting your competencies is important in promoting your brand, what good is all that expertise if others can't relate to you?

Our clients so often wonder why their expertise fails to connect with their audience. The secret to connection, we tell them, is simple: ditch the act and expose yourself, your whole self. It's by far your best, broadest strategy for connection.

The truth is, we've all experienced failure, fear, and weakness, in both our personal lives and our business pursuits. We've all been bullied, been on the brink of losing a job, or been in hot water with a significant other (or the law). We've all made mistakes; we've all needed a little help along the way. Because of our own struggles, we're instinctually primed to connect with those who've shared similar struggles and are willing to say "me too." We're less inclined to connect with those who project perfect confidence and success. *In fact, we're actually more prone to disconnect* with those who seem to project they are above us, are better than us, or have it together more than we do. It makes no sense—from a personal standpoint or a business standpoint.

THE SURPRISING ATTRACTIVENESS OF OPENING UP

Exposing your whole self is about more than cultivating human connection. So much of our unique expertise and skill grows from those failures, fears, and weaknesses we've overcome. By removing our masks, ditching the act, and sharing vulnerably, we demonstrate the authority behind the lessons we've learned. We give a more authentic, relatable basis for our expertise. We simply say, "We've been there too, and here's what we've learned. Maybe it can help you." We differentiate ourselves from those who share their expertise without revealing the raw realities behind it.

Exposing yourself also helps you take control of your narrative. It allows you to get in front of negative publicity and mitigate the venom from it. As we'll show, particularly through Ryan's story, you don't have to be afraid of someone exposing the skeletons in your closet if you've already dragged them out yourself and put them on display.

REWIRING YOUR BRAIN AND YOUR SOCIAL PLATFORMS

Even with all these benefits, though, exposing yourself isn't easy. It's a little scary at first. It brings out discomfort, and we worry that it'll lead to ridicule. We worry that others will discount or misconstrue what we have to say. It is true, exposing yourself is a risk. But if we've learned one thing in growing our own personal brands and in helping so many others do the same, it's this: vulnerable, authentic brands attract the most loyal clients, fans, and partners; vulnerable and authentic brands are the only ones that gain cult-like followings.

There's not a more powerful brand-building tool than exposing yourself. In this book, we'll show you why it is important and how it promotes differentiation that drives brand growth. We'll help you create your own Exposure Résumé, highlighting those failures and weaknesses that give you a unique perspective and authority. We will walk you through different stages of exposure, such as Level 1, which could be sharing how you have a pimple you are embarrassed about before walking up on a stage to give a speech, to help you ease into the vulnerability process. Then we will teach you how to progress to Level 4, which includes sharing events that will probably scare you, like a tumultuous event of hardship that reshaped your life—perhaps when you lost your career, or when you lost sight of who you were, or when your life began to fall apart. We will discuss Level 5 exposures, when vulnerability can be taken too far. We will also touch upon the Exposure Bank, where you can store the stories that you are too scared to share today, but will work up the courage to share through your personal branding journey. Finally, we'll teach you the tricks of our trade. We'll show ways you can harness the power of your Exposure Résumé to create immediate brand loyalty through your relatability and gain the respect of others.

GET READY FOR YOUR LIFE TO CHANGE

If you're still skeptical of the power of exposure, if you wonder whether the principles in this book can change the course of your brand and make you more influential with your own audience, consider the results of Ferrazzi's vulnerability. Had he not shared about his own setbacks, the places he needed a little help, Ryan and I would never have taken off our networking masks. Ryan would not have shared how he needed advice in building his writing platform, and I would not have shared my own inability to connect with others in person. We would not have become each other's client, and we would not have unlocked the secrets that led us to create InfluenceTree, our personal branding company. Ultimately, we'd have never experienced the power of vulnerability in rapid, reliable brand building, and you definitely wouldn't be holding this book.

Ferrazzi's unexpected exposure opened the door to a set of possibilities we'd never considered before. It changed the course of both our businesses and launched a new partnership that has become very successful. It also pointed us to a better way to succeed by being our truest selves. No more smoke and mirrors. No more personas. No more spin. Is there any wonder why we're both so loyal to Ferrazzi's personal brand?

Exposure works.

I don't know about you, but I haven't always been authentic. I might have said I was, even convinced myself and others I was. But I know the truth . . . for most of my life I tried to keep my skeletons hidden and only expose the "acceptable" stuff—or make it up if it didn't exist. It's a horrible, exhausting way to live, to be perfectly honest. It's also much more difficult to sustain a brand that way. You're always on guard, and always detached from your real life and the deeper matters that are in your heart and mind. I'm grateful that's all changed.

While I haven't always been authentic, I do know I have always been drawn to authentic people. Now I've learned how to become one; and not only that, but Ryan and I have learned how to use that realness to help people like you build a better brand. I'm not just talking bigger numbers. I'm also talking about tangible results like more media coverage, more clients, more business. This isn't hyperbole. It's been happening for our clients time and time again. You'll hear some of their stories in the pages to come. And you'll also hear the dirty details of ours too. You'll see that we're a lot more like you than you realize. We're both train wrecks who got back on track despite the damage because we stopped trying to act like the wrecks didn't happen . . . or won't again. We can both tell you with a high degree of certainty that this one change has been the most liberating career move we've ever made. It's also been the most lucrative by far.

We're inviting you to ditch the act along with us. We're inviting you to grow your personal brand by exposing your whole self. If you follow the tips in this books, we believe you'll be well on your way to developing your own cult-like following. It won't take as long as you think. Authentic exposure yields results almost immediately.

CHAPTER 2

DON'T BE IDEAL, BE REAL

Ditching the act and exposing yourself is not just a personal branding hack or something you just do online; it is a lifestyle that is incorporated into both your digital and real-life networks. As this book progresses, we will teach you everything that you need to know to follow our Expose Yourself Process to help deepen your relationships, build trust and camaraderie with others, create impactful influence, and ignite your career onto the fast track of success. Before we get to that, both Ryan and I will ditch the act and lead with our personal stories of how we got to where we are now. These stories will set you up with a foundation for structuring your own stories and show you how being vulnerable, open, and real will allow you to create a bond so strong with others that when you implement the Expose Yourself Process in your life, others will be attracted to you and want to help you further succeed in your career and life.

LEONARD'S STORY

SEARCHING FOR SHORTCUTS

I grew up in a loving home with my grandparents, whom I thought for the longest time were my parents. My grandfather did everything in his power to show me how much he loved me, from telling me stories while I sat on his lap, to taking me out to get ice cream, to spoiling me with toys and video games. My grandmother was the stereotypical tiger mom. She reprimanded me for the things I did wrong, maintained a stern personality, and ensured structure in the household. Whenever I would face being disciplined by my grandmother, I would cry and run into my grandfather's arms for comfort. It was their version of good cop, bad cop.

As a student, I enrolled in the gifted and talented education (GATE) program, but besides keeping up my GPA, I sucked at everything else. By fourth grade, I was the last one picked for basketball at the Boys and Girls Club and spent my time as the benchwarmer for years. I also tried playing baseball, but never could hit, throw, or catch a baseball if my life depended on it. My piano lessons were a bust, and even though I spent years practicing, all I can play to this day is the first line of Beethoven's Für Elise. It was no different when I tried to learn Korean or went to art school.

By eighth grade, there was nothing I was really good at, and I knew it. One time, my grandmother asked me what I wanted to do when I grew up. My response was that I didn't know. Saying that I didn't know was a common theme throughout my life, and my grandmother absolutely hated hearing it. She would tell me that I couldn't say "I don't know" and that I always needed to have an answer.

Since I didn't know what I wanted to be, my grandmother made a few suggestions for me. She asked if I wanted to grow up to join the army or become a police officer or a firefighter. When I replied no to every suggestion, she then asked what I really wanted to do, in hopes of hearing a different response. Instead, I turned to her and said as loud and as passionately as possible, "I want to do nothing!" Looking at where I am today, I might have spoken the most honest words of my life. I wanted a cushy life, but I didn't want to work hard to get it because I loved how my grandparents were retired and didn't have to work. Because my passions have always revolved around lying in bed, watching television, and hanging out with my friends, I wanted to do nothing and get everything. Later I found something I was quite good at doing and enjoyed, then learned to build plug-and-play systems that work on autopilot, but we will get further into that in the Expose Yourself Process.

LOSING MY FOUNDATION

In my early teens, I spent most of my time at home playing video games, since I was a loner and didn't have many friends. My grandmother forced me to go to church, where I tried to make friends, but instead I would often be picked on and made fun of. Sometimes, even beat up.

At home things weren't any better. By junior high school my grandfather was diagnosed with Alzheimer's and started to experience symptoms of forgetfulness and memory loss. As the disease progressed, my grandfather was unable to care for himself. He soon had his leg amputated, was forced to live life in a wheelchair, and eventually forgot everything and everyone, even me. Even though our bond had been so strong, it wasn't a match for Alzheimer's.

My grandmother made a decision to move to Fountain Valley, where I started at a new school in ninth grade. I knew no one and couldn't fit in, but this was nothing compared with the pain I felt because of my grandfather's condition. When my grandfather couldn't remember who I was, my heart was broken. He was more than a father figure to me. He raised me as if I were his own son. When he died, I couldn't cry. I couldn't feel the pain because I already felt so much pain from his forgetting who he was, who I was, that I became disassociated. I blocked my emotions out completely. With the limited resources I was given, it was the only way I knew how to cope.

I couldn't really communicate how I felt with my grandmother because I knew she was suffering even more than I was. On top of that, in the Asian culture, therapy isn't really thought of as an option. Instead, the expectation is to deal with a tragedy and move on. If you have tried this, you know it's a temporary fix; ultimately it leaves us with deep-rooted scars that shape the people we grow up to become. I wish at that time my grandmother had brought me to therapy so I could have understood how to better deal with the situation, forgive myself for forgetting my grandfather, and come to peace with the death of my role model. But instead, I started to lash out.

At the age of 16, I started hanging out with a different group of kids at school and picked up habits like smoking cigarettes and drinking coffee. This then led to leaving school early to go smoke weed and drink with my neighbors who lived two blocks away.

Without my role model, my lashing out only got worse. I lost my consideration and respect for everyone. Things were so bad that one day when I had asked my grandmother to borrow her car, a gold Toyota Corolla, she turned me down, but I stole her keys and took the car anyway. I had the nerve to go hang out with my friends for two days. On the second day I tried to show off in the car by taking a turn at 55 miles per hour. The car fishtailed, and I hit a tree, totaling my grandmother's precious car.

That was the last straw. My grandmother felt she could no longer raise me, so she disowned me and sent my mother to pick me up. I felt so much shame and disappointment. And what's worse was that this wasn't the first person who abandoned me. First, it was my father when he divorced my mother, and then my mother when she left me to live with my grandparents. Then my grandfather when he passed, even though that wasn't his fault. Now I was losing my grandmother too.

THE DOWNWARD SPIRAL CONTINUES

When I lived with my grandparents, my mom used to visit me on my birthday and on holidays. Even though I knew she was my mom, our relationship wasn't that of a typical mother and son. She would sneak me into the back of the movie theater at Universal Studios; and at Tommy's Burgers, she would pull out 10 cans of soda and stuff them in her purse. She would buy me cigarettes and alcohol starting at age 16.

During the day my mom ran a toy business at the local swap meet, and at night she tended a bar. Since she spent so much time working, she bought me a 2001 Toyota Camry so that I could take myself back and forth to my eleventh grade classes at Buena Park High School, then later Los Angeles High School. Instead, I missed school, slept in my car, and went to house parties where I drank. I also spent as much time as possible chasing girls, not only to have fun but with hopes to one day find true love. I started to get pulled into a group of people who did drugs, drank heavily, broke laws, and had no concern about society, just themselves.

The one thing I did love was writing. I wrote poems about my life, plans for the future, and stories I was passionate about in journals and on Word documents on my computer. I remember one night wanting to impress a girl and pulling out a notebook at a party to write a poem. A guy grabbed it, read it with total mockery, and then tossed it in the trash laughing. This incident, along with always getting Cs in English, really crushed my dreams of ever writing. I equated writing and creativity with total vulnerability, but not in a good way.

Most people would be scared or embarrassed to bring up moments like these to even their closest friends. In Chapter 7, we will help you identify low- to high-level exposures, so you can work on developing the courage to share the moments that scare you, which in reality are the moments that will drive instantaneous connection to your intended audience.

My mother wasn't a stable foundation for me. She ended up falling into debt, and we had our cars repossessed and had to sell all our possessions, including the furniture. All we could afford to eat was rice, egg, and soy sauce once a day. I needed a way out, but how was I going to achieve it? Instead of indulging in debauchery, I knew that this was a moment in my life where I needed to go back to focus on earning money. I just wasn't sure how.

NARROGANCE

One day, I was online messaging a friend whom I hadn't seen for a long time. She brought up a business opportunity to me and said she wanted to meet at this venue in Hacienda Heights. When I arrived, there was a speaker who talked about how he retired at such an early age and how he worked because it was his passion, not because he needed to. As he talked about how he changed his life, I could picture this being the opportunity to change mine.

After the seminar, I had an overwhelming sense of naïveté, mixed with arrogance, or what I call "narrogance." I fully believed that this was the opportunity I needed to change my life. So when I went home, I did everything in my power to convince my mom to let me start this venture. For some reason, she told me to give it a try. I began to make goals to become rich and successful. I started spending a large amount of time studying how to earn money from the company, trying to get others involved, and building out my team that would make me millions. But who really listens to a 17-year-old when it comes to business? Let alone one that is working in a multilevel marketing company.

Instead of earning millions, I spun my wheels and went nowhere. It took me months to earn back the initial investment, and my friends who decided to join me ultimately ended up cutting me out of their lives when the company went bankrupt.

Expectations were extremely high because of cultural pressures, and so even though I got Bs in school, they weren't seen as good enough by my family. Because of that, I figured that the best thing for me to do was take shortcuts to get ahead. Instead of looking at traditional four-year universities, I picked a trade school to learn electronic business, which I was led to believe was a program that would teach me how to be the manager of a digital business. But I didn't learn anything about online business. Instead, I learned how to network computers, use Microsoft products, and learned the very basics of C++. Instead of school helping me get ahead, I felt it was even harder to achieve the goals I wanted, so I made a decision to quit.

Around this time, I met a woman whom I wanted to start a relationship with, but she would always point out how broke I was. I thought that if I could shower her with gifts, she would give me a chance. She basically told me I needed to earn six figures. So I was inspired to work at Macy's at the Beverly Center selling women's shoes. My first few months, I crushed it, and since my mother paid the bills at home, I could use my entire paycheck for anything I wanted. I was even able to buy this woman gifts, even though those gifts didn't change how she felt about me.

After being at Macy's for over a year, my mom said we needed to talk. She told me I would be responsible for paying all the bills. For our car, the apartment, electricity, and everything else. She was going off to Hawaii, and I was supposed to stay in Los Angeles and cover all the expenses. I started to do the math on my earnings, then quickly realized I wasn't earning enough money. Something had to change, or I would lose everything that my mom had pushed upon me.

So I went online and started asking all my friends how much they were earning at their jobs. A friend, John, told me he was earning $4,000 a month at Manhattan Beach Toyota. I did the math and figured that was more than I needed to pay for all the bills, and so I applied for a job there. The first two months, I couldn't figure out what I was doing, so I ended up earning minimum wage while eating as much free popcorn as I could out of the machine next to the receptionist. My boss told me I was going to get fired if I didn't turn things around. Then something magical happened. I finally got it. I understood the exact science behind what it took to sell cars—I made around $4,000 my third month. But the more successful I was, the more I began to change.

I started to get cockier. More arrogant. I felt like I could do anything in the world I wanted. I tried managing two relationships at once, both of which blew up in my face. One was with the woman whom I tried to woo while working at Macy's; the other with my former best friend. As I started to rub my success in the faces of my peers, my friends began to resent me.

Then as I embarked on a life of being addicted to drugs, my career and success slowly began to wither away. I was fired from Toyota. When I was fired, I took a hard look at my bank account and saw how much I was spending on drugs, so I quit immediately, knowing that I couldn't afford them any longer—financially, emotionally, or physically.

I told everyone that I quit working at Toyota to pursue a business, but the truth of the matter was, of course, that I was fired. I was left with no other choice than to try to run a music business like iTunes. After running myself into debt, I started to lose everything else that I held precious in my life. I had my car repossessed, and I didn't know what to do to get out of the mess. The depression led me back to using drugs again.

When you look at most biographies of people on their résumés, digital profiles, and websites, more often than not, there is no mention of their childhood or their early careers. Yet these are absolutely essential moments of your life and include the building blocks of who you are today. We will teach you how to integrate these components into your own personal brand in Chapter 9.

ATTEMPTING TO GET RICH QUICK AND FAILING

In 2008, my friends were making a small fortune in real estate, so I decided to give that a try. But by the time I got into the business and worked up the documents to close a few deals, Bear Stearns, a mortgage-heavy investment banking company, went down in a fire sale, and I couldn't get my deals funded. Those commissions went up in smoke with the entire mortgage industry. From there, I thought the next logical move would to be to get into the stock and investment industry, but that fell apart immediately afterward.

After those two failures, it was difficult for me to get out of bed. I was dead broke and discouraged, and each failure made it harder to imagine myself ever being successful. At the beginning of 2009, a colleague I worked with told me he was starting up a lead generation company with a few other people out in Fontana and asked me if I wanted to join. Eventually he convinced me to join. I worked there for nearly a year. Shortly after, that company went under.

At this time, I no longer had the energy or courage to stand up and continue trying. Each failure made it tougher to get the energy to move on. I began getting panic attacks and spent days on end in bed, without ever getting up. I faced my darkest demons, and failure looked like it was about to hit me hard and take away everything I had.

Looking back on my work history, I started to notice a theme. I was constantly working for frauds who had no ethics. I didn't even feel I had ethics at the time either, because all I cared about was money and would do anything to get it. I was as narrogant as possible, and it was causing my life to crumble more. My life had fallen apart to such an extent that I had no choice but to go from start-up to start-up, experiencing failure after failure.

By this point, since I no longer had a car, I applied for jobs around my surrounding area. AXA Equitable wanted to hire me on salary for $4,000 a month to sell life insurance, but I didn't have the money to take the tests. So I had to take another job, raising money for political causes part-time and earning $10 an hour.

The depression set loose, and I could do nothing but fall further and further behind. Instead of spending money on taking the required tests I needed to get the better job selling financial services, I spent every last dime on cocaine and alcohol to wash away the pain that I was feeling. It took me months to finally save up enough to take the first test; then when I took it, I failed.

ROCK BOTTOM

There was no choice left for me. I didn't pay my electricity bill for months. I was living on food from 7-Eleven. I was struggling to find money to pay rent. Then all of a sudden, my lights in my home went out. I had gone six months without paying the Los Angeles Department of Water and Power and had to begin showering in the dark, carrying my microwave into the lighted apartment hallway to heat food, and sitting for hours on end charging my phone in an outlet in the hallway. This continued until I could no longer pay for rent and was served an eviction notice.

I hit rock bottom. I called my mom and told her my plans to live under a bridge. In a panic, she called up my grandmother and explained the situation to her. My grandmother called me and told me that she was going to come with my cousin to pick me up and that I could live with her. I was saved from homelessness. And my mother figure, who once disowned me, welcomed me back into her family.

It wasn't all smooth sailing from there though. The first few months, I experienced alcohol and drug withdrawals while I spent my days playing video games. My grandmother yelled at me, telling me that I needed to find a job and start contributing. I saw my window for moving ahead becoming nonexistent.

I was so ashamed and embarrassed of who I was, so I wore a mask where I portrayed myself as the successful salesman that everyone once knew. I did everything I could to hide my truth from others. I lied to my friends when they asked me how I was doing and told them that everything was great. I was holding onto my act to the point where I was living a complete lie.

I was embarrassed. I used to carry an aura of success, wearing Versace suits and Ferragamo shoes. People looked up to me. How could I ever tell anyone that I was living with my grandma, that she forced me to find a job, and that I took a job at the first place that would hire me, a start-up that paid me $2,600 for six months of work? How could I shatter that reputation that people had placed upon me? Couldn't I just keep lying about why I couldn't hang out with the people I knew because of how busy I was?

TELLING THE TRUTH

Then one day I broke down. I couldn't hold onto my act any longer, no matter how hard I tried. I started to tell people about what was going on in my life. Instead of them looking down on me as I expected, they offered to help drive me to Los Angeles so I could hang out with them. I saw quickly that sharing the truth brought me closer to the people in my life, instead of pushing them further away. It was the opposite of what I expected and a welcome relief. The moment I received support from my friends to spend time with them, regardless of how far I had fallen, was one of the first moments that opened my eyes to just how powerful taking off the mask, ditching the act, and exposing myself truly could impact the future of who I would become.

Regardless, I knew that I couldn't spend the rest of my life living with my grandmother. I knew I needed to stand on my own again, so I borrowed a few hundred dollars from a friend, moved back to Los Angeles to live on a sofa in a living room that everyone walked through daily, and started to look for work. My friend Deinis helped me get a job at

American Honda earning $16.24 an hour answering phones for customer complaints. I thought I could work my way up there until I became a director, then retire.

That plan didn't go as expected. Before the end of 2011, my first year there, I tried a few other ventures on the side that failed. My former girlfriend was playing games with me about whether or not we would get back together. This other girl I was seeing kicked me out of my hotel room and ordered a love kit to rub it in my face. I just felt so defeated, that I made a decision to end it all. I wrote a note to two people whom I confided in and said goodbye.

I kept running situations through my head until I finally figured out the perfect way to kill myself. Then, on the morning of the day I was about to implement my plan, my phone rang. It was one of the two girls I dated. She met with me and told me how stupid and selfish I was and that I needed to make a decision to live. She asked how I could do that to my family, how I could not value my life and who I was.

After hearing her out, I made a decision to continue to live, but I didn't know what I was living for.

BANKRUPTCY

A judgment for the car I subleased was issued against me. Since I already had $50,000 of credit card debt and repossessed cars, I figured that it wouldn't hurt to just file bankruptcy. And I was left with nothing, except my student loan debt that decided to follow me.

A few months later, I was out and got beyond drunk. Earlier that day, my keys had fallen out of my pocket while I was on the bus, so I asked my roommate if I could use his. When I got home, I forgot I borrowed my roommate's keys, so I tried to hop the fence in front. The first attempt, I landed on the wrong side of the fence. The second attempt, I landed wrong, fell to the ground, and heard a snap. I tried to stand but fell straight back to the ground. I lay there for 10 minutes until I crawled up two flights of stairs to collapse on my sofa.

I had a broken ankle and was bedridden for three months. During those months, I started to really think about where I was in life. I'm a firm believer that where you are today is exactly where you are supposed to be. And I was exactly where I was supposed to be: dead broke, miserable, and alone. But how did I end up like this?

I started to reflect on my life and every decision I made. I began to see the patterns and how when the girl I was trying to impress kept saying she wanted to see me earn six figures, it made me feel I needed to continue taking shortcuts. Through all the self-reflection, I finally came to understand that I was so hurt by the loss of my grandfather, that I forgot how he raised me. In fact, I lived the exact opposite life he tried to teach me. While he lived his life with love and compassion, I lived my life being self-centered and selfish.

I had to make a change, but how was I going to do it?

WRITING MY WAY BACK

While working at American Honda, I had hopes that I could accelerate my career. That I would no longer have to ride a subway and two buses to work. That I would no longer have 30-minute lunch breaks where I could only afford a $1.64 quesadilla. That if I was two minutes late to the bus stop home, I wouldn't have to sit around for 30 minutes to an hour to wait for the next bus.

Two years into my role, I ended up becoming sick and tired of being sick and tired. I couldn't afford anything after a healthcare tax was implemented, causing an additional $80 to be taken out of my paycheck. Those $1.64 quesadillas for lunch were gone.

I knew that I had to do something, or I'd be stuck forever. I tried applying for hundreds of jobs within Honda and outside the organization. I received three calls back and wasn't hired anywhere. I tried going back to school, but that ended up taking years and there was no immediate reward. Then my friend sent me a post by James Altucher on Quora on what it felt like to lose a lot of money quickly. I refused to read it, saying that I wasn't a reader and that it was too long, but he asked me what else I was doing with my life. I knew I was doing nothing, so I read it.

After reading Altucher's piece, I was shocked at how similar his life was to mine, but how he made and lost so much more money than I ever did. I dove into his posts about the power of failure and reinventing yourself after things go south. I was inspired to take a stab at reinventing myself after my string of failures. I needed to be authentic. I needed to be vulnerable. And most importantly, I needed to share my story with others so they could prevent making the same mistakes I did.

I mustered up all my courage and wrote my first post. But when it came time to click "publish," I went back and forth for 30 minutes about whether or not I could let this part of me out into the world. I had those same fears of being judged, mocked, and ridiculed that prevented me from opening up to my friends when I was living a lie. But I remembered the empathy and goodwill they showed me after I ditched the act and exposed myself, so I finally closed my eyes and clicked "enter."

My first post had 102 reads within a month. I was especially excited when someone liked my post so much that the person shared it with over 1,000 people. That spark was what I needed to continually write multiple posts a day.

I had no plan in mind when I began writing, I just wanted to share my past failings and explore the lessons I learned. In fact, if you had asked me on the first day of writing, whether or not I would have thought that within a six-month time frame, people would value my content, that I would have 3,000 new social media followers and 2 million reads, and that I had built amazing friendships with people all across the world, I would have laughed. How could I ever imagine something like that happening?

CONNECTING

By the end of 2014, after I had been writing for 1.5 years, I had 10 million reads. As my readership grew, I built connections all around the world with people whom I never thought I would ever connect with in my previous life. I was talking to lawyers, venture capitalists, successful CEOs, people who graduated from Ivy League colleges, McKinsey consultants, and so many other people whom I deemed successful.

I built solid relationships, while changing my world picture by taking a more global perspective to expand my culture. I ended up getting paid to write for the first time in my life, even though I didn't know what I was doing, making $75 an hour on a project. I was asked to do a photo shoot with Will Ferrell for *British GQ*. Jason Chen, a Quora user whom I became friends with, let me stay at his home in New York when I went to go visit James Altucher, my virtual mentor at the time. Jason also offered to invest in a company if I wanted to start one. I became friends with May Busch, who was the chief operating officer of Morgan Stanley Europe. One year, she flew in from London to bring me cupcakes on my birthday. I met Michael Simmons, who was an entrepreneur that was personally recognized for his entrepreneurial accomplishments by Barack Obama, was heavily featured in many publications, and was known for writing deeply insightful articles that went viral and were read over 100,000 times each. He hired me as a consultant to help him gain more traction on Quora, while teaching me the ins and outs of the publishing industry. Thousands of people sent me messages, asking if I could mentor them. I went from earning $16.24 an hour to being offered thousands of dollars per project for work that would take a few short hours of my time.

My network, relationships, income, career trajectory, respect . . . everything changed. I created real friends, real connections, and real clients all across the world. What I didn't realize is that I had unlocked the secret to cultivating a strong personal brand.

Then one day a friend told me that I should apply for a position to do social media for the University of Southern California's medical enterprise, Keck Medicine of USC. When the recruiter called me asking if I was interested in the position, I asked him how much it paid. He told me a number that was almost 2.5 times more than I was earning at Honda. I got the job.

In Chapter 15, we will teach you how to foster camaraderie in new relationships so you can follow an exact method to achieve the same type of compounding success I had unexpectedly accomplished.

I took a quick trip to San Francisco before work started. Then when I came back, I had my invite to be on the exclusive guest list for Keith Ferrazzi's party where I first met Ryan Foland. I had achieved so many qualitative results up to this point. But could they grow even more?

Little did I know that this party would be the moment where my career and personal life would hyperaccelerate, while bringing in many more quantitative results to come . . .

CHAPTER 3

WHEN YOU SPEAK, SPEAK YOUR TRUTH

SET UP FOR NERDINESS

My story starts in Huntington Beach, California, where I was raised by my father and mother, who were both educators. My parents were teach-ers, then principals, then administrators. They were loving, thoughtful, and always encouraging, but always expected that I would do my best, especially with school. I lived with my brother, Rob, whom I never grew close to, and my sister, Chelsea, whom I am close to now but used to fight with all the time. For the school year, I was a latchkey kid, spending afternoons solo while my parents were working and my siblings were at their athletic classes or hanging out with their friends.

In my house, getting good grades and doing well in school wasn't an option—it was a requirement. Starting in the third grade, since I was nerdy and super grade-focused, and the other kids at school knew my parents were school administrators, I wasn't just an outcast; I was treated like an enemy of the state. Luckily, my only saving grace was that my parents weren't principals at *my* school. If they were, my life would've been a complete nightmare. However, there was a positive that came with being raised by educators; our family would be able to spend summers jumping onto our boat and enjoying months on Catalina Island, where I would go wakeboarding, lobster hunting, and scuba diving with my dad, while going on hikes with my mom. Catalina Island became home to many of my favorite childhood memories, and it is core to who I am today.

HOOP DREAMS

All I ever wanted to do in school was fit in, but instead, I was picked on, bullied, and beaten up. In fifth grade, at Harbor View Elementary School, I wanted to play basketball with my fellow classmates, but no one would ever pick me. I just wasn't cool enough. I didn't have the Jordan shoes. I didn't have the cool gear. On top of that, other kids didn't like me because I looked weird thanks to freckles and a bowl cut. It wasn't like I wasn't picked because there were too many players either; kids actively sought to exclude me by playing half-court games with a half team just because they didn't want me to play.

As you can imagine, I became pretty sullen. It's always been difficult for me to share my feelings. Even as a young kid I would internalize how I felt and just go on with my business. However, mom knew something was wrong and would get the info out of me.

Much like how my mom pushed me to share my emotions, even though it was uncomfortable, and how Leonard pushes me to share my emotions to this day, we will be pushing you to ditch the act by sharing your feelings too. As you will see, it's how breakthroughs are made.

My mom, a natural problem solver, heard my story of not ever getting picked to play and said, "We're going to Sport Chalet right now. I'm buying you a basketball so you can play on your own team." I hoped it was the answer.

At the store, I was immediately drawn to a white basketball with Michael Jordan on it. I thought to myself, "This is the coolest thing ever; everybody is going to love it." At home, I awkwardly dribbled it on the wood floors, annoying my family to no end.

I remember bringing it to school, all excited, until I realized that basketballs don't fit in backpacks. I found myself walking around with this white basketball, without any idea what to do with it. I was aware of my limited basketball dribbling skills, and I wasn't going to even attempt it and make a fool of myself. So I just awkwardly carried this ball around until recess time came. I yelled to no one in particular, "I got a ball!" And asked, "You guys wanna play?" They said, "No, we already have a ball. Thanks though." Having a ball didn't solve the problem; all it did was make me look even more awkward while I carried it around.

MORE MIDDLE SCHOOL HUMILIATION

The only advantage of being so publicly humiliated is that sometimes people notice and try to help out. One of my sixth grade classmates, Eduardo Neary, saw that I was constantly excluded from events. He took me under his wing and taught me some cholo words (Mexican slang words), and I started to adopt his sense of fashion. Some of Eduardo's friends wanted to use my basketball for soccer. I agreed, but I didn't know how to play soccer, and I didn't like running around either, so I would just sit and watch as they played. I was in with his group, but literally on the outside just watching.

Plus, even with my new group of friends, the bullying didn't stop. The guys from basketball snuck up on me a few times and gave me gnarly wedgies. I became increasingly paranoid and went around like I had my head on a swivel.

The torment didn't just happen at school. Two doors down from my home lived a kid who went by the name of Dane-O, a red flag if there ever was one. Since we lived so close, it made sense for us to play together, but whenever we would play a game like cops and robbers, he would want to *actually* fight me. This later turned to harassment, as he threatened me. One day, Dane-O was chasing me down the street trying to beat me up, so I ran into my garage to take refuge, but he came in and threatened to beat me up anyway. I tried to hold my ground and exclaimed, "You can't trespass. This is America, and this is my property!" His response? To kick me in the balls. I ended up collapsed on the floor, ego totally deflated.

THE BREAKTHROUGH

One day, when Dane-O bullied me so bad, I locked my bedroom door, turned on "Don't Worry Be Happy" by Bobby McFerrin, and bawled my eyes out. My father noticed that I locked my door, something that was not allowed in our home, so he forced his way in. When my dad entered, he saw that I was a mess, and in his serious dad voice, he asked what happened, listened, paused, then told me that I needed to learn martial arts and play a sport. I chose karate and ice hockey. That decision changed everything for me.

Karate helped me overcome the bullying by teaching me how to defend myself, while being a goalie at hockey became an obsession that I thrived at. One of the most exciting days of my life was when my brother took me to a Los Angeles Kings game. At the game, I snuck down past everyone and ran into Dave Taylor, a defenseman, who took me into the locker room to see Kelly Hrudey, the goaltender whom I idolized. Kelly signed my shirt, and I was able to hang out with the entire team. It was the coolest thing ever. My brother, on the other hand, was super worried that I just vanished, but when he saw me with Kelly's autograph, he couldn't help but be excited about the experience.

MAKING CHANGES

I didn't know it at the time, but these early events in life transformed me internally. I became obsessed with being socially accepted. I wanted friends. I began making a conscious effort to be more outgoing and was bent on being "cool" while maintaining my straight As to keep my parents happy. My parents pushed me to take a test that identified me as GATE like Leonard, which meant that my reading, writing, and math were above my grade level. More often than not, in your life people will try to label you in a certain way, either for better or for worse.

In Chapter 5, we will introduce you to the Rapid Reflection Discovery Process Worksheet that will teach you how to control your own narrative by utilizing both what others think of you and what you want to be known for.

To pursue the GATE program, I would have to go to a school that was farther away, but I decided to make the move and transfer. I was exhausted from the constant bullying but was hopeful that I might meet new people who would accept me; maybe I'd even make some friends.

Talk about another bad decision, because now I had abandoned the very few people I had made friends with, while I had to make new friends with those who just saw me as a newly transplanted nerd at their school. My assumption that like-minded nerds would serve as a supportive environment was completely false; they cared more about their already-formed cliques.

Tom was a leader of a group, and he made it a point to make my life miserable by threatening to beat me up, oftentimes chasing me off campus. I would call my mom crying from the pay phone a mile away. She wouldn't be able to pick me up, so my grandpa had to come. Talk about being embarrassed. This was after being at my new school for a year in seventh grade. I couldn't handle the situation anymore, so when eighth grade started, I went back to my former school.

It took a few years, but by my sophomore year in high school, I began to find my inner cool kid. In addition to playing club hockey, I got involved in school sports (wrestling and pole vaulting), and my network of friends changed too; I had nerd friends, but I also had cool friends. We skateboarded, played hockey, and had fun. A nerd friend of mine from calculus class, Danielle, started to push me to join student council, which ultimately landed me in the position of senior class president. Once I was president, I did things that were absolutely unheard of at my school, such as instituting a "Battle of the Sexes" week to raise money for a senior walkway (until the activities director shut the battle down), and organizing a car smash where local junkyards donated cars for us to sledgehammer. Needless to say, none of those events ever happened again, but I got a confidence boost that was invaluable.

DISCOVERING MY PASSION

After high school, I knew I wanted to go to a college by the beach, so I chose the University of California, Santa Barbara. I was thrilled to go there, but when the time came to choose my first set of classes during freshman orientation, I freaked out. I couldn't decide what classes to take, and it was so stressful that I asked my mom to choose. I didn't even look at her choices until the first day of class and noticed that the first class was Introduction to Dramatic Arts. I balked.

When I read the lines in my first audition, everyone laughed. I thought I messed up, and so I ran out, got my skateboard, and cried on the way home. It was a miserable day—until I got that callback the following day. They were laughing because I was good.

The following quarter, I got the lead role in William Mastrosimone's *Bang Bang You're Dead*. Coincidentally a school shooting happened around the same time, and the play took on a whole new meaning. It was the first time that I truly understood the impact of human connection, as hundreds of attendees in the audience laughed and cried at the same time. What was even more rewarding was when people came up to me after the show and told me how they related to and found meaning in their lives through the performance.

LONDON CALLING

In my junior year in college, I went to the University of Reading just outside London, and I studied both economics and theater. There was a moment when I was standing in the Globe Theatre, where Shakespeare's plays were originally performed, and I had this moment of seeing exactly what I wanted to do with my life. I thought, "The world is a stage, and I can make an impact. I can share things with people through a medium that can affect them and get them to think differently. This is it! I'm meant to make plays and movies and be a film producer." I didn't want to act; I just wanted to be a director and put everything together. I ended up graduating a year later with honors, holding a double major in business economics and dramatic arts.

HOLLYWOOD DREAMS

I thought I was on my way to be a kick-ass TV producer. I applied for grad school to get my master's in film, but the problem was that I had no portfolio. None of my plays were documented, because this was before there was digital technology and cameras were built into every smartphone. And it did not occur to me, as a theater major, that I could have or should have worked with a videographer to document our plays. Every place that I applied to go to grad school for film rejected me. It was crushing.

I saw a way in through the internship route. I landed one at ABC by sending applications everywhere and contacting all my friends and friends of friends until I found out someone had a sister who worked there; then I asked her to help me get my foot in the door, and later she had me work for her. I used the internship at ABC as a reference and credibility point to position myself into working with David E. Kelley on the set of *The Practice*.

In Chapter 16, you will learn how to "success-stack," which is leveraging one accomplishment to get another accomplishment and so on. When used properly, success stacking has a compounding effect that propels careers exponentially.

However, a concerning theme kept popping up. People would say, "Hey kid, you seem like you've got great energy. I'm excited to see what you do in 30 years." I'm like, "What do you mean 30 years?" They'd say, "Well you're at the bottom here; you have to earn your way as you go. You can't just all of a sudden make creative decisions. You've got to put in your time." For a 23-year-old eager to make my mark, this wasn't what I wanted to hear. I thought, "I don't want to put in any time. I'm ready. I want to produce! I want to direct! I want to create and make an impact!"

Even worse, I also had enough people say, "You are a dime a dozen. You will go nowhere, son." There were so many people who were working on set already for 30 years, never achieving their dreams to produce and direct. Meeting the more experienced employees on the totem pole led me to believe that this could ultimately end up being my fate too.

I also met all kinds of famous people who were disappointing in real life, including William Shatner. I was supposed to take him to the set, and I took him to the wrong spot. I've never seen someone so irritated with me. I had the most awkward elevator ride up returning to where we started so I could double-check where he needed to be delivered. That was a moment where I was like, "If I'm rich and famous, I'm not gonna be like William Shatner."

Despite big dreams and a serious work ethic, I literally went broke from working for free and driving hundreds of miles up to Los Angeles and back, trying to get my foot in the TV industry. I finally took a look at my bank account and my prospects and decided I needed to pivot fast.

RAKING IT IN

Looking for my next move, I focused on a friend who was making all kinds of money selling mortgages. I decided to drop everything and shoot for a different career. I needed money, and my friend was making it. I found this mortgage company that was looking for inexperienced, highly motivated individuals to hire. The people at the company promised that they would teach me everything I needed to know to be successful there, through an intensive two-week training program. I left my dreams of Hollywood behind and headed to work in the mortgage industry in Irvine. At this sales job you start out on the lowest rung possible, and you only get one lead per week. And if you don't close your leads, you don't get more leads.

So you're stuck with these leads that are not that great, and it forces you to make things happen.

I quickly learned how to do sales and started to see success, but I needed the loans I was closing to fund faster so I could get more leads. I came up with ways to win over my coworkers, like creating Friday snack hour and bringing salami and cheese for everyone in the office. I would have special sausages, special crackers, and special chips only for processors. Then I started to draw stick figures on my submissions that had to do with things that the processors liked. I'd walk by a processor and say, "Hey, here's another submission!" and she'd look over and see a stick figure drawing that was holding a big cupcake or something; then I'd throw it up on the top of the stack. She'd grab that, get a giggle out of it, then start processing mine immediately.

By drawing stick figures on the cover sheets and building relationships with the processors, I was able to get my deals through faster, and then because I was able to do that, I was able to close more loans and get more leads. I went from the lowest person on the totem pole to the president's club, to the chairman's club, which featured the perk of all-paid quarterly adventures to exotic locations. When I learned that the company would reimburse higher education, I entered into an MBA program and started working toward my graduate degree.

I started earning double-digit-figure checks and bought a house and multiple cars and was living the high life. I remember I got a check for $16,000, and I couldn't believe it. But with more money came more stupidity. I bought ridiculous things like remedy red matching 22-inch rims for my Range Rover and a private knife collection that I thought was really cool but didn't have a use for. Then I spent a bunch of money on alcohol, cocaine, and partying. Now, looking back on the situation, I should've just paid off my student loan debt.

LOSING IT ALL

I thought I was making good money until I realized that the mortgage company was making *real* money. I thought I could get a broker's license to do the same thing I was already doing, but earn well over 10 times what

I was earning as an employee. It took six months to study and pass a test to get the license, and to celebrate, I took a two-month vacation to Costa Rica and didn't tell my coworkers that I was going. When I came back, my desk was moved and all my stuff was in a box, so I took it as a sign that I needed to make my move. I left and decided I was going to open up my own mortgage company. I landed my first client and closed my first loan, getting a sizable commission from the bank. I felt incredible for about three months. Then the market crashed in 2008, and I was out of business just as soon as I started.

I was drinking heavily at this time, and one night I was out in Laguna Beach partying until about three or four in the morning with my friend Tommy. I thought I was being responsible, because we decided to sleep in my car rather than attempt to drive. But it's uncomfortable sleeping in a sports car, so we foolishly decided to drive home. I stopped by a Del Taco near my home, and like an idiot, I was opening and closing the convertible top in Sally, my champagne Mercedes SL 500, laughing like there was no tomorrow. When I left the drive-through, I burned out and took a left-hand turn at 65 miles per hour, and there was a cop waiting for me. She turned on her lights, and I was going so fast that I thought I could outrun her. But then I flinched, knew I was done for, and pulled over. I blew a .21. I was going to jail.

I wasn't able to drive for a year. I felt like a complete failure. I was so ashamed that I tried to hide it, even from my family. But it's very hard to hide a DUI from your family and friends. I only told one of my friends, who tried to help drive me around, but the shame I felt from the entire event turned me into a hermit. I felt like it was a scarlet letter and that whoever found out would lose all respect for me.

Bottling up and keeping this huge secret made me feel like a fraud. I was putting on this front that I was doing fine. I wanted to do things myself. I have always had this mentality that asking for help was a sign of weakness. Because of my hockey goaltender mentality, I'll jump in to help anybody, but if I need something, I'll go to the brink of bankruptcy before asking for help from my parents. When I let the goal in, it's my fault. That was my thinking, and it led to terrible consequences.

Feeling like a fraud comes in many forms. Sometimes, it comes from bottling things up and not sharing our truth with others. Other times, it happens when our ego gets in the way and we try to talk up who we really are and what we are doing. The reason the feeling prevails in these situations is because we are hiding our true selves from others. When shame, embarrassment, or ego prevents us from speaking up about what truly happened in our lives, we end up closing out any opportunity for others who care about us to help us get out of the situations we are in. And what we ultimately do by hiding our truth is hurt ourselves even further, which usually causes a downward spiral of despair and loss of both friendships and material possessions.

Things started to go downhill fast. I had no income. I was burning through cash fast. I was not finished with my MBA, and I decided to start taking out student loans, and instead of enrolling in the classes I needed, I started using the money to try and maintain the lifestyle I had. The loans totaled $70,000, an amount that still plagues me to this day, as I still owe the debt. My roommate and I were going to fancy restaurants, drinking, and doing drugs with money we didn't have. Then one day, my roommate came home without a car, so I let him use mine, and he paid me what he could each month. Then I came home one day, and all his stuff was gone. He had stolen my Mercedes, which I never got back. It was impounded, and I didn't have the money to take it out of impound, let alone make the payments. So it eventually ended up as a huge judgment against my credit.

I had to foreclose on my home, but then short-sold it for a third of what I bought it for. I moved back into my parents' home and began to lose everything else I had, from my material possessions like my other car, the Range Rover. I even lost the girl that I was dating at the time, who wanted the Escalade, a couple of children, and the Orange County house-wife lifestyle. Everything I had worked so hard to attain was gone, and I had nothing to show for it.

ASKING FOR HELP

I needed to get out of this situation, so I began working at a boiler room selling stocks and chasing down private equity deals. It wasn't as glorious as movies like *The Wolf of Wall Street* depicted it. I hated it. I didn't make any money from the ventures and knew that my only way out was to file for bankruptcy. The cheapest lawyer I could find cost $375, but I couldn't even afford that.

Desperate, with no options left, I finally opened up and became vulnerable with my parents about my situation. They loaned me the money so I could file, and I hired the attorney, filled out all the paperwork, and was in charge of putting the documents in the mail. A few days later, I checked the mailbox, and my bankruptcy package was there in my own mailbox with a return to sender label because I was 32 cents short on postage. I took this as a sign that I needed to just suck it up and move on. I tore up my bankruptcy application right there in front of the mailbox. Then I felt bad for littering and cleaned it up.

While all this was happening, I still needed to earn an income. So while I was living with my parents, I started teaching karate on the side, and I tried to pivot into selling construction loans for a home remodeling company. The whole loan process failed miserably, but because I was in the office anyway and customers would come in, I coincidentally became very good at selling bathrooms, but was extremely embarrassed about doing it.

Another person who was affected by the mortgage meltdown needed a job, so I helped him get a position at the company where I was selling bathrooms. Every day, he would be in my ear talking about a new special program that would help people erase their debt. It sounded too good to be true, but since my identity was so dissociated from who I was because I felt absolutely miserable selling bathrooms, I figured what could I lose? It couldn't be much worse than selling bathrooms.

This colleague and I saved up a few thousand dollars and then started up a company in the same building as the home remodeling company, to help people who were losing their homes restructure their lives and save what they had—or so I thought. One day, I found out my partner was spending company money for personal use. He said he wouldn't do it anymore, but a few months later, I was updating the domain server, and in there, I saw emails that proved he was embezzling money and building a multimillion dollar home in Texas. At this point, I reported him to the Federal Trade Commission, but the folks there weren't interested because they didn't think it was a big enough case for them.

That night, I took off the mask, ditched the act, and called my closest friends to tell them what happened. They helped me move everything out of my office. The next day, I went to a lawyer and notified my business partner that I was leaving the company.

FINDING LOVE AND SUCCESS

During this time, I also met Cyn, who has since become the love of my life for over 10 years. The first day we met, I told her that I was broke, that I didn't own anything, and that my financial life was falling apart. To this day, she continues to tell me that my honesty was proof that I wasn't like the typical California guys she met before. That honesty was the determining factor for the foundation of our relationship. She knew I would never lie to her. I didn't think it was possible, but that moment of exposing myself led me to create a bond and trust that is absolutely irreplaceable. In Chapter 7, we will teach you why ditching the act and being vulnerable creates that irreplaceable bond, and in Chapter 8, we will teach you how to identify the key moments in your life that cultivate this bond.

I went back to teaching karate to pay the bills and began looking for a way to move ahead. I needed a job, so I applied everywhere. My first interview at the University of California, Irvine, turned out to be a bust. But my second one for the UCI ANTrepreneur Center went well. I came in hot, touted my accomplishments in the start-up world, and was hired to lead the undergraduate entrepreneurship program on the UCI campus.

Things at UCI were great. I helped 2,400 college students start companies my first year and built a mailing list of 15,000 people. My bosses had my back and supported me. But one day, when I was with them, a man who looked weirdly out of place with hardly any hair, and a particularly odd limp, came to our office and served me with a lawsuit from the Federal Trade Commission. My mistake from years before was coming back to haunt me. The decision to trust my former business partner at the debt relief company caused more problems down the line, and they were catching up to me.

My boss called me into his office, and I was certain I was about to get fired. But I opened up—again ditching the act and exposing myself—and told him exactly what had happened. Instead of being fired, he supported me in my role, and at that point I knew that in order to maintain or grow in life, I needed to be who I wanted to be, who I could be. I needed to build a personal brand. I was sick and tired of having to reinvent myself when something went wrong, like when I was told I would never get into film school, or when I was told that I wouldn't make it in Hollywood, or how I had to start over after the mortgage meltdown, or how I had to take on roles that embarrassed me like selling bathrooms, all the way to selling products that ultimately didn't work.

I was tired of being known as the guy who helped people get out of debt, then failing at that. I hated that I lost the credibility of being a successful entrepreneur when the business failed. I was sick of reinventing myself time and time again, and I knew that the only way out of this was to build my own reputation so that no matter what happened in the market, what went wrong in the world, and what fell apart, I could still make it through all the turmoil, stand strong, and take control of my narrative and own my own story.

I wanted to build credibility in the entrepreneurship and business space, so I did everything that I thought I was supposed to do. I put all my effort into everything I was doing. I started writing everywhere and wrote 50 articles in three months. I focused heavily on growing my Twitter following by tweeting multiple times a day, but ended up with 200 followers. I started to message every event organizer I could think of and offered my services for free, because I wanted to be on the big stage, but I was still being turned down.

Everything I was doing ended up being unsuccessful. Then I had even worse news. My boss called me into his office again. I knew this time for sure that I was about to be fired. It was all about to be over. I was about to have no more job. On top of that, I had no social media following, I had no personal brand, and I was stuck without any hope or direction.

A funny thing happened in that meeting. I wasn't fired, but was told that what I was doing to try to not lose everything was impressive. I was put in charge of social media for over 20 programs on campus. Then one day a colleague of mine who worked at Microsoft was invited to an exclusive party at Keith Ferrazzi's house. I was jealous and I felt it was another missed opportunity that I deserved. But my friend couldn't make it, so he called me and asked if I wanted to go in his place. And that's how I was able to get on the list to Ferrazzi's dinner party, where I was about to meet Leonard Kim and totally change my life.

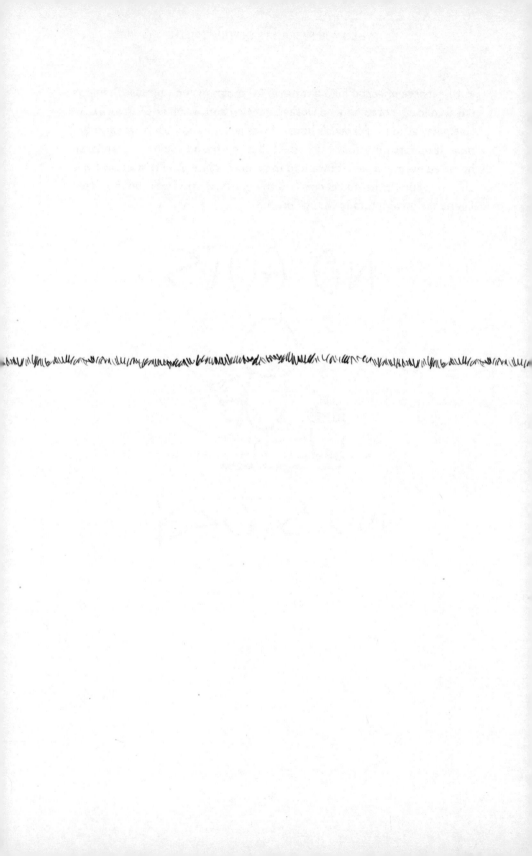

CHAPTER 4

RUN FARTHER WITH IMPERFECT FRIENDS

The morning after he left Keith's house, Ryan looked me up online and began to dive deep into my content. He didn't find what he expected. Most of my articles showed my true, authentic, vulnerable self—which as you know involved lots of failures and struggles and flaws. He didn't know what to think. When he read my post about impostor syndrome (more about the syndrome below), he turned to his girlfriend, Cyn, in disbelief and said, "This article says he is a fraud, and he wrote it?" Even though Ryan was surprised by the level of candor in my content, he decided that if I could get the results he was looking for, he was willing to ask for the help he needed.

IT'S LEONARD

The first assignment I gave Ryan was to have him write out everything that he wanted to learn how to do. I immediately saw that Ryan knew all the right stuff but was doing it in the wrong order. He wrote numerous articles, but he didn't even have his bio listed anywhere! It's like what many of us do when we try to build our personal brands—we take the insights we learn, and we go out there and do everything right—but not in the right order, we will teach you how to write your own Exposed and Authentic Bio.

The funny thing about experts and specialists is that we all know how to do exactly what we do—and we do it extremely well. At the beginning of my career in teaching personal branding, it was difficult to share the exact process of what to do in the proper order. But when put on the spot by having to explain the science of what I was doing to Ryan, a paying client who was depending on me to help him build his personal brand, I was able to dissect the process with each individual component laid chronologically.

By organizing the material in my head and putting it down in a structured format, I was able to pull my expertise and place topics into multiple buckets so we could go and build Ryan's personal brand the right way. Ryan became the test pilot and case study for our new company, InfluenceTree, as we both homed in on building his brand. As we began to get traction and Ryan's articles started to get read, he started to see more social media followers and began landing more speaking engagements. Our client relationship evolved into a partnership. After a few months of seeing traction, Ryan had the realization that he wanted to dive deeper into these concepts of being vulnerable and help teach others how to cultivate the same success he was achieving. I also needed a business partner to help me create video content for the course material, so it was just natural for both of us to decide to work together.

LAUNCHING, QUITTING, AND OVERCOMING HURDLES

In December 2015, we wanted to see if there was a demand for what we were doing, so we built out a mock website on a landing page and wrote three articles about the company in *Fortune, Inc.,* and *Entrepreneur.* Then next thing you know, we had over 1,000 visitors to the site and 100 people ready and willing to pay us for the courses we were advertising.

There was demand. People wanted our product. Now, the only problem was that this was a test to see if people were interested in knowing our formula on how to build a personal brand. We didn't have the course material built yet. So Ryan and I locked ourselves away for months to build the course that so many people were waiting for. We sought out a partner to help us build our email campaign, but that didn't go as expected. Our courses were taking us longer to build than we thought they would. We both became so frustrated about not getting anywhere with the company even though people wanted what we had, that Ryan and I both got to the point where we cursed at each other at low points. We questioned the whole idea of our company. We worried that it was not worth going through tons of stress to not earn any money, and we both mutually made a decision to walk away.

We told our silent investor that we were quitting, and he asked us what we were going to do about the client we landed. I texted Ryan and asked, "What in the world, we have a client! What are we supposed to do? Can we really quit and let this person down?"

We knew we couldn't walk away. We took it as a sign to continue onward. A month or two later, I decided that it was best to be transparent about our business, so I went on Facebook and shared the experience of our fight and how we stayed together because of our first client. A different client thought we were talking about him and felt honored about the situation! It made him more connected with our company. The entire experience also made us feel more invested in our business. People were depending on us; we had a mission bigger than ourselves.

PARTNERSHIP: IT'S NOT EASY

Most of the time, Ryan and I were each other's biggest support system. We would encourage each other when our days were tough and feed each other motivation to continue to move forward as we were seeing results, but at other times we were each other's worst enemy. We would also be at each other's throats, cursing, arguing, and saying how much we hated each other. That drama continues until this day, but we hash it out and get back to the objectives at hand of growing the business.

Through building InfluenceTree, Ryan and I both made a decision that we would continue working at our day jobs at our respective universities—Ryan in his role at University of California, Irvine, and me in my role at the University of Southern California's medical enterprise, Keck Medicine of USC—while growing the business. One of the main objectives we focused on for the business was to build out the course.

Ryan and Leonard had a choice to let their employers know about what they were doing on the side. By being transparent, both of their bosses bought into their vision and encouraged them to pursue their dreams. When they would face struggles in their business or had arguments, they would be transparent and share their frustration with each other openly.

If you are an employee and you want to go and do something on the side, whether it's dancing, writing a book, starting a side business, or doing any other new type of project, let your employer know and be fully transparent. Give your boss a chance to buy into what you are doing. You might be surprised at your boss's enthusiasm for your project.

If you are having struggles at work that are causing you to face frustration head on, whether it is a conflict with your business partner or the completion of a project within your business, share what you are feeling so others can come to help you overcome the situation or offer to help with your project.

We tried to make videos, but we sucked at it. We just set up a camera in front of us at Expert Dojo in Santa Monica, pretended we knew how to use microphones to capture our audio, then put together course material each weekend. But we could see that we weren't where we should be. We invested in better equipment. We worked on our editing. As with any business, the struggles and complications were exhausting, and yet we pushed through. Looking back, I can see that the first videos we did were absolutely atrocious, but somehow they worked because together we brought different, but complementary, perspectives to the table.

SIDE HUSTLE SUCCESS

While maintaining our day jobs, we both sought out opportunities that could fit in with what we were doing in our business that would complement what we were doing at our day jobs. Ryan looked for speaking opportunities on campus at UCI, and I wrote about stuff in the medical field that was related to my work. Most people hide their side hustles from their employer in fear that they will be fired for what they are doing, but Ryan and I knew that the right thing to do was to be completely open and honest by sharing exactly what we were doing with our direct supervisors. We had to be consistent with the message of honesty we were trying to teach. Surprisingly, both of them were completely supportive. Ryan's boss, Iain Grainger, told him that he would have his back for any project, while my boss, Christopher Bazin, allowed me the opportunity to use my lunch breaks to work on business-related ventures or to take time off to speak at events.

Ryan's boss started to identify events where Ryan could speak on behalf of UCI, and Ryan was so appreciative of his boss's support that he worked harder at his job. To this day, Ryan and his boss have a strong sense of camaraderie, while my relationship with my boss evolved into a friendship where my boss and I talk weekly about our personal lives. Christopher even invited me to be a part of his wedding. If you are scared to share your side hustle with your boss, don't be. When you are transparent with your boss, you give your boss the opportunity to get to know you for who you truly are. Real leaders want their employees to be real with them. There is a way to position your desire to build your personal brand or side hustle that not only makes your boss look good, but makes your company look good.

SPINNING NEGATIVES INTO POSITIVES

As Ryan's personal brand continued to grow, he began landing media features in national media publications, like *Huff Post*, *Inc.* and *Entrepreneur*. His social media followers began to grow to the hundreds of thousands.

He even became verified on Facebook, Twitter, and Instagram. It wasn't easy to achieve these results, but the case study worked, and Ryan was living proof that it was possible to go from having nearly no digital presence to being a true leader with a personal brand that others respected. Ryan utilized those successes and accomplishments as a brand halo to support UCI, while UCI supported him, leading to a promotion from the chancellor to work directly on building the personal brand for the vice provost for teaching and learning, Michael Dennin. While Ryan was building his own personal brand, he used that experience and insight to figure out best practices in brand building for the university and Michael. The relationship grew seamlessly, as the investment into growing one area of Ryan's own personal brand allowed him to utilize those same tactics to help Michael continue to establish his influence as well.

It wasn't all sunshine and rainbows from that point forward though. Struggles still came our way. When Ryan landed one of his first major media features, someone had left a comment on the article, calling out Ryan's incident with the Federal Trade Commission and stating that he was a fraud.

The fear of being called a fraud is valid, whether we are one or not.

The last thing anyone wants is to be called a fraud. Some of us have troubling pasts where we have done things that were not right and are scared of having those issues resurface. If you have done anything that you are not proud of, do not let anyone use that against you or manipulate your story to put your career at risk. Instead, get ahead of it and control the narrative rather than let someone else control your narrative in the future.

For others, we feel like we do not deserve our accomplishments we rightfully earned because we don't feel like we are good enough. That feeling is called the "impostor syndrome," which is another form of feeling like a fraud. Many successful actors, such as Tina Fey, Don Cheadle, and Denzel Washington, along with numerous business leaders, professors, engineers, authors, entrepreneurs, and other high-achieving professionals, have suffered from impostor syndrome in their careers. If you feel like you are not good enough and that someone will one day discover that you don't deserve your position, here's a hard wake-up call for you. You earned everything that you have for being the exact person that you are.

Many of us are stricken with impostor syndrome, while others of us have troublesome pasts like Ryan and me. Ryan was so overwhelmed by the incident that he called me and told me that if I felt that I couldn't be a business partner with him anymore for what happened in the past, he would understand and we could move on, going our separate ways. More than anything, I felt that if Ryan had been open and honest about the incident with me from the very beginning, then we could have completely avoided the situation from ever happening.

We chose to face it head on as a team. When I publicly stated facts about what happened as a comment on the article, Ryan had to resist the urge to say anything because it could come out the wrong way. We let the facts clear the air, and others came out of the woodworks to defend Ryan as well. This situation could have left both the author of the article and Ryan in heaps of trouble, but the transparency after the fact helped cool things down.

At this point, I knew that in order to prevent this situation from ever happening again, we would need Ryan to own the situation. To make it a part of who he is. To accept the consequences of his fate and incorporate it into his story. We worked to ditch the act and expose Ryan by redoing his bio and including the Federal Trade Commission as an integral part of his story. We live in a world of transparency. We may think we have secrets, but with how much information is readily available, those days are over.

Ryan made the mistake of not getting ahead of something he did, and it came back to bite him in the butt. If you don't get ahead of something that you may have done, the same thing can happen to you. As we progress through the book, we will teach you how to share these Level 4 exposures and how to get in front of what you are ashamed of so it can never be used against you.

PROOF THAT DITCHING THE ACT WORKS

This incident became an eye-opener for Ryan. He knew it was time for him to get a little more vulnerable. He knew that he had to open up more. He started to discover his past and how relevant the past incidences of bullying were to his current life, and how he was not just bullied by his classmates, but by former bosses and business partners who used him.

Ryan incorporated the authenticity into his speaking style, and it resonated. The results started to come in. Ryan became an MC, then became known as the Ginger MC. He started 1 Million Cups in Irvine, which allowed entrepreneurs to share their start-ups with the community. He became the cofounder of OC Tech Happy Hour, which was the fastest-growing meetup in Orange County with over 6,000 members. He started to be seen in the right light. He held events at the university, creating a double-brand halo while raising both the university's and his own reputation. The university's radio station, KUCI, gave him a radio show. He knew he couldn't do all this on his own because he wasn't earning money, so he depended on the university for its help, and UCI gave him the support he needed. Soon Ryan began getting paid to speak around the world, and after submitting 12 applications, he achieved a milestone he thought was once impossible—landing a talk on the red carpet of the TEDx stage.

Ryan continued to support his job while supporting his own personal brand, and he started to attend conferences. One confusing moment for him was when he was named the top speaker at Social Media Marketing World, even though he wasn't a speaker. This happened because he had created so much engagement through his hashtagged tweets, or what he calls a "Tweetnado," that he continued to be placed on the top lists of the event. When Ryan was invited to China to speak, he spoke about the 3-1-3° Method, which we will get more into later in Chapter 10, but since he created another Tweetnado at that event, he was asked by Huawei, the biggest phone retailer in Asia, to become a Key Opinion Leader, which is a part of Huawei's influencer program. Ryan continued to be featured on podcast after podcast, so he made his own podcast called *The World of Speakers*. Then he began teaching classes at UCI, while holding social media lunches and continuing to develop the brand halo both ways.

When you let your employees have the freedom to build their personal brands, they will share their expertise with other employees. Ryan suggested going to a conference to learn best practices in social media, and said that he would put on a workshop at work to teach his colleagues what he learned. This idea not only was approved, but sparked a regular workshop series that now attracts people from all parts of the campus. Also, as Ryan tested strategies with his brand, he was able to implement the ones that worked at UCI.

As Ryan's brand continued to grow, we started to get big clients for InfluenceTree. We landed Fortune 100 executives, *New York Times* bestselling authors, venture capitalists, and entrepreneurs of multimillion dollar companies as clients. They all came to us as inbound leads, meaning that they sought us out; we didn't look for them. Ryan then began holding workshops at the Orange County Transit Authority, and now he even has a teaching position at Cal State Fullerton.

Ryan and I both use the work we do with clients as testing grounds for new ideas to see how well they do. Once they hit and perform well, we both incorporate these ideas to elevate the university brands with our own respective employers. In a world where everyone looks the same and is doing the exact same things, we push ourselves, our clients, and our employers to get braver, share deeper stories, and get those harder stories to share out there in the world.

We have learned the difference between growth and community and how a follower count means nothing if you are not engaged with your audience. Ryan now has a network of people across the world that not only respect him, but love him for who he is and have his back no matter what. At the end of the day, Ryan became more than just a case study of how far a personal brand could grow—he became a person who has made and will continue to make a positive impact in the lives of people across the world.

MEANWHILE, LEONARD IS STILL OVERCOMING OBSTACLES

On the other hand . . . I was still living with my mom and just started my brand-new job at Keck Medicine of the University of Southern California. I had just passed the initial phase of my first TEDx application at the University of California, Los Angeles, and was about to get on a call with the organizer. On that call, I completely blew it. I stumbled over myself and did so horribly at answering the questions that I never heard from them again.

Even though I had a solid personal brand, there were some things that I wasn't able to do. In the past, getting a job interview would have been nearly impossible. But my personal brand got me into the running for a position as an associate director of social media at USC, and I made it to the second round of interviews, but was disqualified by human resources since I didn't have the bachelor's degree that was required for the position. My social media began to grow quickly like Ryan's, going from the 50,000 followers I had at the time I met him to well over 600,000 as of writing this.

My life was anywhere from perfect—in fact it was still full of struggles. I dated a woman who was abusive and treated me like I was worthless. She went back and forth about whether or not she should be with me and if I should meet her parents. Truthfully, it felt like she kept me in limbo because she couldn't figure out what she wanted. She would pull me in and give me attention one moment; then the next, she would strongly express her feelings of doubt and push me away. She wasn't just verbally abusive; she would also pull back her arm when I tried to hold her hand and actively avoid kissing me. One time when we went to the Veuve Clicquot Polo Classic, all I could do was take slight glances at her while a look of disgust radiated out of her eyes. I honestly believe she was repulsed by me.

We broke up a few times, once on a horrendous trip to Seattle and another time on Thanksgiving, when she told me to never message her again. I felt defeated and worthless afterward. I was so devastated and broken from losing my girlfriend, that I just wanted to get in my car without a seat belt on and drive straight into a wall at 70 miles per hour, crushing my body into a pancake.

This wasn't the first time I felt defeated and wanted to end it all either because of someone I was dating. Because ditching the act and exposing myself became an integral part of my lifestyle, I turned to my friend Myla to tell her about the situation. She talked me out of doing something crazy and then told me that I needed to share the story with others so they would know that they aren't the only ones who felt this way. So I did.

Even though I shared my story and people responded with support, I was still so miserable that I had to find a therapist to share my pain with just to get by. All the while my former girlfriend continually tried to come back into my life, yet still played mind games with me and flake on the dates we were scheduled to meet.

In February, a week after I got back from a vacation in New York, we agreed to meet on a Sunday for brunch. A few days before, I saw my therapist and told her that maybe things were going to work, but I didn't really know. It was three months since I had seen my girlfriend, but she called me and we talked for hours about a concern she was having in her life and how she was sorry for leaving me the way she did. She said she panicked and freaked out.

I forgave her, and we decided to meet. I put on my best outfit, did my hair, and did everything I could to look put together. I drove out to the city of Orange, parked my car, and went into the restaurant. When I sat down, I asked the waitress for a bloody mary and began to wait. Thirty minutes passed; no one was there. I called her. No answer. Then the cycle repeated. After two hours, I gave up and decided to leave. My waitress comped my meal since I barely ate; then I got into my car. Instead of going to UCI to see Ryan's TEDx Talk where he mentioned me, I felt so broken that I decided to drive home instead. The song "Worst Day" by Calvin Harris began playing in my car, so I put it on repeat for the entire ride. A few hours later, she called me and apologized.

When I told my therapist what happened at my next session, she asked me a question. I don't remember exactly what I told her, but she misheard me. Then my therapist said, "Leonard, there is no way in the world that she loves you. You can't believe that!"

I should've taken my therapist's cue and let it all end that day, but I let my former girlfriend string me along for a little longer . . . Until, one day, when we finally met up again and she treated me so horribly, I decided I no longer wanted anything to do with her. I knew it was time to let her go and move on—or I would be forever held down in my own misery of trying to impress someone who didn't want to do anything but continue to string me along.

PERSONAL BRANDING LEADS TO DREAM OPPORTUNITIES

Businesswise, I was experiencing more success. I began landing media features by the hundreds and even having appearances on television. I was able to afford decent vacations where I could stay at a four star hotel for an entire week instead of vacations where I pinched pennies the entire time. One vacation that shifted everything for me was the first time I stayed at the Le Méridien New York. I had an in-room massage, went on a helicopter ride over the city, and was put onto the guest list at some of the coolest clubs. It was a great experience to see what the other side of life was like—the lifestyle I never really got to experience before.

I didn't just grow my own personal brand though. I worked tirelessly at incorporating my learnings into our company's digital accounts at Keck Medicine of USC. With the help of our amazing team and the trust of my boss, Christopher, we were able to grow the social media following from 10,000 to over 250,000, while increasing monthly unique pageviews on the website from 100,000 to 450,000 and getting 150 media syndications into major publications like *Forbes*, *Time*, *Medical Daily*, and more. I started to get recognition for what I was doing. My superiors trusted me to create new tactics to continue to grow the organization's digital presence.

As my brand grew, I was invited to be the host of my own radio show on the Influencers channel of VoiceAmerica, called *Grow Your Influence Tree*. The TEDx organization at the University of California, Irvine, reached out to me and invited me to do my own TEDx Talk. It was so satisfying to have the opportunity to be on the red carpet, especially after originally being shut down completely by the TEDx organization at the University of California, Los Angeles.

My talk. "Why You Should Let Your Fears Guide You," became internationally recognized as a top TED Talk by Forbes, Inc., Mashable, and many other outlets. I felt so much fulfillment and self-worth from all my successes, that I thought the rest of my life would be smooth sailing.

FINDING TRUE LOVE

When you try to bury your emotions and don't face them head on, they don't go away. They stay in your subconscious and start to eat away at your soul. One night, when I was driving, I was listening to the song "Attention" by Charlie Puth, on full blast. A car pulled forward and almost hit me as I was driving 50 miles per hour down the street. After I swerved out of the way, I broke down and started bawling my eyes out. In that moment of translucency, I knew that I needed to face my demons or I would never be able to move ahead. So for the next few days, I faced what had happened and forgave my former girlfriend for leaving me. Slowly afterward, I began to realize that life is good and that forgetting about something and moving on doesn't work. Instead, I had to own up to what happened and to my part in continuing the cycle of being tormented, and then I could reclaim my life.

After I began to find my confidence once again, I ended up in another relationship. A few months into it, I realized that she had absolutely no respect for me. Instead of trying to win her back like I tried with my former girlfriend, I knew that I didn't deserve to be treated like this anymore—that I was worthy of love and that I deserved to be happy. So on my thirty-third birthday, I broke up with her and we went our separate ways. The next week, I went out with friends, and on the flip of a coin, we made a mutual decision to go to a music festival called Countdown. After the first night of Countdown, a nurse from New York named Angie flew in with her chihuahua named Roo. I was exhausted and didn't want to talk about healthcare with her, even after all her attempts to strike up a conversation. That night, we acknowledged each other, but we did our own things.

Ryan and I were picked to be on a television show called *Break Through the Crowd*, where we consulted with the two finalists and helped one of the teams raise over two million dollars on its crowdfunding campaign. Just before we were to fly out to New York City to film the show, Ryan got a call from the producers, as they discovered his past trouble with the Federal Trade Commission. Ryan almost lost his spot on the show; however, since he had owned up to it long beforehand in his bio, the television network saw how strong his character was and kept his spot intact.

On that visit to New York to film for the television show, I randomly reached out to Angie to see if I could borrow her Tupperware so I could bring back an artichoke pizza for my friend in Los Angeles. She agreed, and we met. That night, we grew super fond of each other; then we began talking on the phone daily. Within a month, we knew we wanted to be together.

On March 17, 2018, Angie and I took our relationship a step further and started dating. We rode horses, went to basketball games, and spent hours upon hours on FaceTime with each other, completely ditching the act and opening our souls to each other. By April 18, 2018, we went off to El Matador Beach in Malibu for a ceremony, and next thing you know, I was married to the love of my life. Each month, my wife and I would put all our worries away as we flew out to see each other. We maintained a long-distance relationship until we could set ourselves up financially and handle all our prior obligations, and in July, she moved to Los Angeles.

Things weren't all smooth sailing from there. Angie and I struggled to get to know each other's quirks and learn how to coexist in the same household, all while outside stressors caused us to hurt each other's feelings in the first year of our marriage. As difficult as those times were, we continued to learn how to love and support each other. Angie has been a rock to me and is essential to making me a better person each and every day, while constantly reminding me of the importance of spreading love throughout the world and being a beacon of hope to others. She is the cornerstone of who I am, and I will always cherish her with all my heart.

USING OUR SUCCESS TO BUILD YOURS

To this day, Ryan and I are still working together at InfluenceTree, teaching people just like you and companies that want to survive in this new digital age how to take off the mask, ditch the act, and leverage the art of the personal brand to create greater success. Ryan and I complement each other because we are both great at different things (I focus on writing, and Ryan's gift is speaking). Now we're mutually seen as top experts in multiple categories, from marketing, to personal branding and communication, by not just top publications, but also people and companies across the world. *New York Times* bestselling author Sara Bliss reached out to interview me and showcase my story and InfluenceTree in her book *Take the Leap: Change Your Career, Change Your Life*, along with 62 other amazing individuals who changed their lives, and so did Dr. Diane Hamilton in her book *Cracking the Curiosity Code: The Key to Unlocking Human Potential*.

We've spoken side by side, earned money together, created an impact together, been on the big screen together, and landed clients together. And most importantly, together we are spreading our vulnerabilities and shortcomings with people just like you. Our self-exposure has helped us create a deep connection with you, and we are continuing to build authentic, growing personal brands, not just for ourselves and our clients—but for someone incredibly important to us, the reader of our book, you. We hope through this book, we will teach you to do the same thing too.

YOUR BIGGEST INVESTMENT IS YOU
- WINNIE SUN

PART 2

LET YOUR FEARS GUIDE YOU

CHAPTER 5

YOUR BRAND IS WHO YOU ARE

Like the rest of us, you have a personal brand, even if you don't know it. That brand is framed by the way people understand your story, for better or worse. More often than not, the image we believe we are portraying is the exact opposite of the message we are sending into the world.

PERCEPTION VERSUS REALITY

Before I evaluated my life, I had no idea how others perceived me. I assumed that I was well respected by my peers and that I had all the answers when it came to business. I assumed that my prior experience through my sales roles and my work in the start-up ring gave me the skills I needed to get ahead in life. And I assumed that I would be able to take massive strides forward and achieve anything that my heart desired.

Reality did nothing but prove to me just how wrong I was. After all, it's what led me from failure to failure, until I no longer could afford to keep the lights on in my home. It's what caused me to move back to my grandmother's house. It's even what held me down at an entry-level position at American Honda for two years, without earning a single raise.

How wrong could I have been about everything? Looking back today, I see it so clearly. I projected a brand of naïveté and arrogance, or "narrogance." That narrogance didn't work in my favor either; it's what stripped away everything that mattered to me and left me stagnant in not just my life, but my career as well, without any way to move ahead. It pushed people away from me and left me broke, miserable, and alone. My narrogance held me exactly where I was, like shackles that were chained to my feet and hands, preventing me from ever breaking free.

And before Ryan resolved his issues with the Federal Trade Commission, his brand was like mine—and quite clear to others. He was a fast-talking salesman who was out for a quick buck. People were on edge around him and kept their distance because they were scared he would take their hard-earned money or sell them on an unachievable dream. Just like I was unable to move forward, so was Ryan. He was working as hard as he could to get out of his situation and move forward, but he was stuck like a sailboat with no wind and getting nowhere.

Imagine where Ryan and I would be today if we never took a hard look at our lives and saw ourselves for who we truly were and how we were portraying ourselves to others. How long do you think we would have continued to live like this? Months? Years? Our whole lives? Would we be where we are today, where we are able to share our insights with you to help you move ahead in your life?

Probably not.

Luckily, when Ryan and I got sick and tired of being sick and tired, we took a hard look at our lives and began to take a look at our stories. That's when we discovered what our own brand weaknesses were and what was holding us back from achieving the success we were looking for. We can do the same for you.

WHO NEEDS BRANDING

Building a personal brand isn't just limited to one specific type of person. It doesn't just work for me. It doesn't just work for Ryan. It doesn't just work for our clients either. The process of taking off the mask, ditching the act, and exposing ourselves works no matter who you are.

Do you *hate* your job? It's okay. You have what it takes to build a powerful personal brand that will help you find the career you always wanted.

Do you *love* your job? That's great. You can build a personal brand that will allow you to continue to grow and move forward, long after you outgrow your current position.

Are you an entrepreneur? Awesome. A personal brand will be the cornerstone of the growth of your company.

Are you a mother, or do you have a family? Great. Those differentiations could be driving factors that make you stick out as you build your personal brand. When you take your dynamic perspectives into the office or share them with a wider audience, you are able to relate to many other parents who understand the importance of instilling balance in both the home and work environment.

If you don't have a job and are looking for one, you will find that a personal brand is absolutely essential in landing your next role.

No matter what category you fall under, listed here or not, you still have a personal brand. And your personal brand is the intersection between what you want to be known for and what people think of you.

Throughout the rest of the book, you will read examples of how following our Expose Yourself Process has helped people just like you, across various careers, live their dreams—from the employee with no direction who found her dream job, to the financial advisor who became one of the most sought-after money managers in the United States, to the budding writer who took on his dream role of editor in chief of Shopify Plus, to Miss New York US who took it upon herself to chase her dreams and become the founder of one of the biggest media companies for business-minded women, to a bank robber who repositioned himself into a growth hacker, along with many other people, some whose names you may have already come across.

WHY YOU NEED A PERSONAL BRAND

Now you may be asking yourself, why should I build a personal brand? Let me ask you a better question. Why shouldn't you build a personal brand?

If you're looking to stay in the same position at the same employer for the rest of your life, then you don't need a personal brand.

If you want to struggle because you have to compete against hundreds of other applicants when you make career changes, then you don't need a personal brand.

If you are fine being overlooked internally for promotions garnered by outsiders who have an established track record of success, then you don't need a personal brand either.

If you do not want to make deep connections with your employees and colleagues in the office, then you don't need to have a personal brand.

If you have to reenter the job market in the future or if you've been laid off or fired after dedicating decades of your life to a company and you want to spend months, if not years, trying to land a new job, then you too don't need to worry about that personal brand.

A personal brand is only effective if you are a person who wants to be a leader who has a deep connection with your team and is able to move ahead in your career, whether by getting a promotion at your company, paving your way up to the C-suite, being sought out by a competing company for better pay, landing the job of your dreams, or making sure that your career becomes recession proof. On the last point of being recession proof, there is one type of candidate who is always sought out no matter how bad the economy gets. And that's the one who is well respected as a thought leader in their space.

CHANGING HOW OTHERS SEE YOU

It's up to you whether you want to leave your company or grow with it. That's a decision that you have to make. But no matter what you do, you have to know this: The old way of professional development where you built face-to-face relationships worked well in the 1980s, but in this new world, you can't just please your internal stakeholders—you need to create a digital footprint as well.

Do you want to leave your company or grow with it? After asking himself this question, Ryan quickly found out how UCI and his boss supported him on his journey. When I asked myself that question, I saw how USC and my boss Christopher could support me as well. Even though we may have outgrown our roles, we made decisions to stick with our employers because they stuck with us. However, if your job doesn't help you, it may be time to find a new job.

If you're an employer, or part of your human resource team at your company, you need to ask yourself a very important question. Do you want the people you employ to stay at your company? If you answer yes, you need to support your employees' efforts to build their brands, or they will leave you for another employer that will have their back. The biggest benefits you will see are happy, engaged, loyal employees who are helping you broaden your digital reach, as your employees work toward building out their digital presences.

Pansy Lee, director of product and design at Maple Leaf Sports and Entertainment Partnership, and former senior product manager and principal design researcher at Intuit, has managed teams for over a decade. When employees come to her stating they have a desire to do something outside of work in their personal life, she gives them her full support. She even encourages her employees to come and talk to her about their goals and ambitions. As counterintuitive as it may sound, when Pansy shows her support to her employees, she increases their retention and work ethic because her employees feel that they are working in an environment that supports their goals.

Before we go any further, you have to understand that your brand is who you are. But it's not just your own interpretation of what your brand is. Remember, this is what Ryan and I had done, and we were both wrong when we looked at ourselves from our own perspectives. You have to know how others interpret your brand as well. What is the real image you are projecting? Are you seen as authentic and vulnerable or as shy and awkward? Is your unintentional projection as bad as the perspectives that Ryan and I held of ourselves, as narrogant, easy-money hustlers to be avoided at all costs?

Your personal brand is the gap between how you see yourself and how others see you. There are two ways to discover this. The first is through introspection, which could take years of reflecting on past events to understand exactly how you got to where you are today. Most of us do not have time to go through that entire process. Luckily, there's an easier way. And that's with Post-it Notes.

Ryan loves Post-it Notes and always has one stuck to his computer— and has a folder full of them with things he is working on or with quote ideas to draw as stick figures. He has them in his car, saves then in his laptop bag, and always keeps them in his pocket at conferences. He has also been harassing 3M for a couple of years to get the company to sponsor him. I have made fun of Ryan for this multiple times. But the more I give him a hard time, the more he seems to get energized about it.

When we were beginning to work on the foundation of his brand, I asked him make a list of qualities and traits that he liked about himself. Then we could work into his brand positioning. With a smile, Ryan pulled out a stack of his beloved yellow semi-sticky friends.

Ryan turned the task into what we now call the Rapid Reflection Discovery Process. And now it is time for you to work through it. No matter where you are in the branding process, taking the time to complete this activity is worth its weight in gold. Since your personal brand is the intersection between what you want to be known for and what others already see you as, we have a way for you to discover this intersection . . . with Post-it Notes!

Here are the steps in the Rapid Reflection Discovery Process Worksheet.

Rapid Reflection
Discovery Process Worksheet

Find out how you truly see yourself
and how others see you.

You have had a personal brand this entire time. You just didn't know what it was. This activity will help you better understand how others see you and how to use that to make your brand more powerful. After you complete this worksheet, you will be able to start to take control of your narrative.

Step 1. Identify your characteristic traits (and a few things you want to be known for).
Write down an exhaustive list of single or multiple words.

Example

Positive characteristic traits:
speaker, strategist, xyz expert, loyal, trustworthy, happy, fun, loving, kind, compassionate, sailor, equestrian, high energy, passionate, detail-oriented, inventive, organized, creative, bold, funny, nature lover, artist, social, loves to be on stage, giving, caring, professional, outdoors, loves clouds, inventor, innovator, athletic, community builder, inclusive

Now write down a few characteristic traits that you can work on.

Example

A few characteristic traits to work on:
cocky, talks too much, arrogant, timid, shy, lazy, possessive, sarcastic, bully, vindictive, gossiper, unmotivated, whiny, stubborn, elitist, chauvinistic, racist, sexist, ageist

WORKSHEET

Now it's your turn. Write your answers in the spaces provided:

Positive characteristic traits:

A few characteristic traits to work on:

Step 2. Ask others to describe you in one word.
Ask 10 other people (these can be people you work with, colleagues you know outside your work, family, friends, and others whom you know) to list a single word (or a few if need be) that describes you as they know you. If you are a manager, do not ask people who report to you, as results will be skewed.

Also avoid using one central group—like only family members or friends from high school. Diversify for the most accurate results.

It is key that all the people you ask know that their answers are completely anonymous. You can have a designated friend collect the answers, or have a central location at your office where people can drop their responses off, or have people mail their answers to your home in anonymous envelopes. Make sure to tell the people who are writing these notes to be completely honest! You can do this by saying, "I need your help. I'm looking to build my personal brand. I want to know what words you feel describe me—good and bad. The more honest you are, the more it will help me. If someone were to ask you about me, how would you describe me to that person? Can you please write down some words that say exactly what you feel about me, then put them in this box?"

Ask each person for three to five good qualities and one to two traits that you can work on.

Example

Traits I am known for:
speaker, energetic, outgoing, caring, innovative, creative, funny, sailor, likes to sail, loves the ocean, entrepreneur, communicator, educator, teacher, friendly, leader, podcast host, radio host, social media, supportive, loving, empathetic, world traveler, keynote speaker, personal branding expert, marketer, stick figure artist, artist, mentor, actor

Example

Traits others think I can work on:
chicken with head cut off, poor listener, talks over people, too energetic, not calm, too many things going on, unorganized

WORKSHEET

Ask others to list single or multiple words that describe you. Write down the traits that others said you can work on. Transcribe these in a **different color**.

Step 3. Collect all the answers.
Gather your own answers and the answers from the others. Group similar traits and qualities in the chart boxes below.

Example

1. Community builder	2. Innovative, innovator	3. Athletic, equestrian
4. Supportive, loving, empathetic, caring, loyal, trustworthy, social, inclusive	5. Energetic, outgoing, funny, friendly, happy, fun, high energy, passionate, loving, kind, caring	6. Podcast host, radio host, bold, funny
7. Sailor, likes to sail, loves the ocean, sailor, nature guy, outdoors, loves clouds, nature lover	8. Stick figure artist, artist, artist, stick figure drawer, compassionate	9. Creative, entrepreneur, leader, strategist, inventive, creative, inventive, xyz expert
10. Athletic	11. Mentor	12. Actor
13. Educator, teacher, professional, detail-oriented, organized	14. Keynote speaker, speaker, world traveler, loves to be on stage, keynote speaker	15. Social media, communicator, personal branding expert, Twitter person, marketer, branding expert, communications strategist, likes to tweet

Optional: Transcribe the traits onto two different colors of sticky notes. Choose one color for your answers and another color for the answers of others. (E.g., if you have 30 items, write them on 30 sticky notes.) Do the same for the words and phrases that others see you as, but write them on a different color of sticky note. Then find a wall, mirror, or large whiteboard, and start to cluster your Post-it Notes that are similar into groups.

It's your turn now. Gather your own answers and the answers from the others. Group similar traits and qualities in the chart boxes below.

WORKSHEET

Step 4. Take a look at the traits you said you can work on, and compare them with what others say.

Don't be discouraged. Instead use the information to improve yourself. Work on forming better habits: take courses; read books; enroll in personal development workshops; learn about privilege, diversity, and inclusion; take specialized college courses; and make other efforts to minimize the negative effects that these traits could cause to your brand.

Step 5. Step back and look at the assortment of traits.

In the example answers above, you will notice three things:

- Some boxes have similar traits that you and others identified (boxes 2, 4, 5, 6, 7, 8, 9, 13, 14, and 15). These are traits congruent with your personal brand.
- Some boxes only have traits that others mentioned about you (boxes 11 and 12). These are traits that others see in you but you don't see in yourself. If a few people are identifying traits about you, for example, being funny, then you probably are funny but can't see it yourself. However, if you only have one person saying you are funny, that isn't enough data to incorporate into your brand.
- Some boxes only have traits that you identified and others didn't mention (boxes 1, 3, and 10). These are traits that you see in yourself but others don't see. These may not really be your strengths.

Step 6. Remove all the boxes that only have one color (unless five friends are saying you are something that you do not see in yourself).

Remove the boxes that are outliers. Look at the clusters that have traits that both you and others see in you. Name these groups as one trait that best summarizes the words within it. If one group says "funny," "humorous," "lighthearted," or other variations of these traits, then choose a word or set of words that best captures them all.

Step 7. Categorize your responses.

If you asked enough people to participate, you should have three or more cluster categories that you are now looking at. They should fit into:

1. Career
2. Life
3. Personality

Pick one cluster from each of these three categories. Choose ONLY three of the clusters. These three overall traits or qualities will be the foundation for your brand. Add them in the spaces here:

Brand Trait 1 (Career)	Brand Trait 2 (Life)	Brand Trait 3 (Personality)

These three "pillars" will set the foundation for your brand. These three elements are the intersection between what people think about you and how you see yourself.

Once you have selected the three groups, look back at the name you gave each group (Step 7) and make sure you like it. These three elements are the intersection between what people think about you and what you want to be known for.

That is the sweet spot. It is easier to convince people of what they already know, as opposed to convincing them about something new. You have had a brand this whole time, and this activity helps you to *take control of the narrative*. You will need this foundation to build on, and it may change over time. But at least now you can focus on these groups as a starting point.

If someone asks you what you are all about, you could answer by specifying all three clusters that you choose, and it should capture the essence of who you are. Sure you are other things, but you don't want to overwhelm people. Have you ever met someone and minutes into the conversation they are telling you about this and that and that and this, and you lose interest before you even get to know them?

There is power and magic in the number three. And now you have three solid elements to build on.

At UCI, Ryan often tells his colleagues to take charge of their personal brands—and walks them through exactly how to do it. One person at UCI who ended up going through the Rapid Reflection Discovery Process with Ryan was Kevin Huie, the director of student success initiatives. When originally going through the process, Kevin believed that there would be so many different answers he would receive, that he wouldn't be able to fit them under three categories. As he collected his responses, he found that even though the answers differed, they fell into three key categories: student success (which related to his role at his job), supportive (which related to his personality), and storyteller (which related to who he is as a person). When Kevin was able to identify that his core traits fell into three different succinct categories, not only did he have a better understanding of who he was, but he knew how he could go forward and relate to others better.

Once you finish the Rapid Reflection Discovery Process, you will get a clear picture of how you see yourself, and you will be able to get a better picture of how the world sees you, even if unintentionally. By understanding the difference between the brand you have and the one you want, you can learn how to expose elements of your story to fill in the gaps and create more connections. Ultimately, by the end of this book, you will be able to intentionally expose your whole story to create a lasting and legitimate impression on the people you come across in your life—and the people who come across you.

CHAPTER 6

YOUR BRAND PRECEDES YOU

When brands and products try to hide their shortcomings—a flaw in their product, lack of ethical standards, tumultuous financial stability, or other challenges—it never works long term. If the company is already established, spinning the story might work for a while. That is, until someone calls the brand out on what it is doing, or they face a lawsuit—or worse, they are dragged through the news and their reputations are castrated by consumers who stand up against and boycott them. When the company isn't established, consumers usually see right through the deceit. That is because either they can see how bold the claims are that are made by a company that does not have the history to back those claims, or they can see through the founder's inability to be vulnerable and authentic when wearing a mask, pretending that everything in the company is going perfectly. And instead of working with the brand or using the product, consumers will avoid it outright.

MORE FROM LEONARD

CUSTOMERS DON'T WANT PERFECTION

Why doesn't putting on a mask and portraying a facade of success work? Why do so many people outright avoid or condemn the brands and products that act as if everything is perfect? It's simple. The marketplace isn't looking for perfection, and brands are beginning to understand this. That is why smart companies are doing everything in their power to try to showcase their brands as being real. Brands are creating messaging that's honest and vulnerable and really connects with consumers. Rhett Power, author of *The Entrepreneur's Book of Actions: Essential Daily Exercises and Habits for Becoming Wealthier, Smarter, and More Successful*, wrote an article in *Inc.* magazine titled "Trust Is as Important as Price for Todays [sic] Consumer." In the article, Rhett discusses how more than 73 percent of consumers consider transparency more important than price. He states that what consumers are looking for most are brands that they feel they can trust. They are looking for brands that are creating educational content for them to consume, setting up listening networks to make sure their voice is heard, and are owning up to their mistakes when they make them.

Cheryl Snapp Conner, who specializes in crisis PR at Snapp Conner PR, shared a story of one of her friends who runs one of the most successful technology companies in the United States. The CEO of the company had been stricken with a huge personal tragedy; he lost his son to suicide. Normally he discussed business on his outlets. But instead of crawling into a hole (which he probably felt like doing), he made a brave decision to open up about what had happened. When he posted the story that shared his heart's deepest feelings, along with what was in his mind, people began responding in droves. Their hearts went out to him. That was probably the most vulnerable moment of his life, but speaking from his heart and sharing that moment was truly the right thing to do. It wasn't just right for his business; it was right for his mental health because he had the love and support from his peers in a time when he needed it the most. If he hadn't shared, who knows what the trajectory of his life or business) would have been like from that point forward, as the pain of losing his son slowly ate away at his soul.

Who is bigger, Warren Buffett or Geico? Who can you relate to more? Chances are, you may potentially find some affinity when you are thinking about Warren Buffett eating at McDonald's and drinking Cherry Coca-Cola. But when is the last time you thought, "I can totally relate to Geico. It completely gets who I am as a consumer, and it knows exactly what I'm looking for!" Geico isn't doing anything wrong per se, but it isn't maximizing what it could do to create a deep level of camaraderie with its audience. If you're like us and the people we talk to on a regular basis, that thought has never crossed your mind.

It's not just Warren Buffett who stands out though. It's people like Tony Robbins, Oprah, your favorite YouTube star, the industry expert you follow for insights on Twitter, and the salesperson at your favorite store that you have built a bond with. These are the people whose personal brands you resonate with and whom you ultimately decide to trust or work with.

This philosophy doesn't just involve the CEO of a company and public figures. Think about why so many brands like Netflix and Spotify want you to log in to their platforms using your name. They want you to have a personalized experience when you are using their services. They do this by giving you your own custom username, allowing you to attach your own picture to your avatar, customizing their recommendations based on other content you have already consumed, and making each individual's profile unique to that singular user's experience.

CREATING A RELATABLE BRAND

The goal is to create a brand that people can trust, can relate to, and want to go back to. That starts with vulnerability. Think about it; we don't trust people who look perfect and act as if they have everything together. They put on an aura of unachievable success, and it makes it that much harder to connect at a deep emotional level to the people who wear these masks.

Instead, look at the person who is walking up to the podium to receive an award. On their way up, they trip over themselves. The people watching laugh. But that trip and the laughs that come with it do something phenomenal; they humanize the award winner to no longer be superior to us, but to be just like us. Research reported in an article from the *Annual Review of Neuroscience* titled "The Neural Basis of Empathy" says that our brains are wired to grow a deeper affinity and liking for this person because they aren't seen as better than us any longer; instead, they become another human that we can connect with. The study states that empathy is based on the shared representations of painful or embarrassing moments of others, which allows people to see themselves in others. In other words, it drives human connection to a deeper level. It works so well that people have speculated whether or not Jennifer Lawrence has been faking her falls at award shows, since they become the most talked-about incidents of the events.

This means that in order to build a personal brand that people can trust, we can't keep wearing our masks of success or happiness or having everything together. Instead, the only way we can succeed is by taking the mask off, ditching the act, and exposing ourselves—our whole selves. We need to expose our stories, even the hardest ones, to help cultivate connection, compassion, and empathy.

Chances are, if you are anything like us, you have had secrets that you kept, whether they are legal issues like Ryan had, or financial failures like I faced, or even problems in your relationships with loved ones. When you hide your secrets, people can use them against you. If you were paying attention when Meg Whitman ran for governor of California, you can probably recall the outrage that was cast by the media and the public when we discovered that she did not disclose that she had employed an illegal immigrant, her housekeeper, who had worked for her for 10 years and whom she just happened to fire before running for governor. Because she stood against illegal immigrants, when this news came out, she seemed heartless and mean. She tried to go on the defensive, but that skeleton in her closet cost her the election. If she had been forthcoming about the incident, her $140 million investment in her campaign could have had an entirely different result.

The truth is that when you expose your secrets and your weakest vulnerabilities, something magical happens: you become untouchable. You develop an armor where the shortcomings in your life no longer become a hindrance that holds you back from achieving your dreams— but a foundation that you can stand on to hold your ground and become immune to attacks. Much like how Ryan was able to maintain his spot on the television show *Break Through the Crowd*, you will also be able to show that you have owned up and grown from the events that once prohibited you from moving forward.

THE SECRET OF SUCCESS

To get a better understanding of how powerful the act of exposing ourselves is, we want to share an example of a colleague by the name of Dan Raaf. We met Dan digitally when he first wanted to start a growth hacking agency. He was a humble and hungry entrepreneur who was fresh out of prison for robbing a bank (which was not a successful robbery, because he used a very poorly handwritten note), but he was too embarrassed to be forthcoming about that. We had many conversations over the course of months, and in those conversations I insisted that he should be forthcoming about what he did, instead of trying to hide the robbery. Once he did open up about his past, his content started to resonate with others and was read over a million times. This in turn gave him an opportunity to work with other big market movers who enlisted him to work on their accounts, and he was able to move out of a shack into the apartment he wanted in Hollywood. Ditching the act and exposing himself was an essential component in Dan's ability to turn his life around and build the growing business he wanted.

In order to do this the correct way, you can't just write or share a post here and there. Ditching the act is a *lifestyle* that encompasses all areas of your life, both digitally and in person. It's the biggest secret that is shared among the top leaders in the world who are cultivating change and getting everything they want in life. It's what Keith Ferrazzi learned in the secret society he was a part of at Yale, which wasn't really a society of secrets, but more a group of people who opened up and shared their vulnerabilities, struggles, and shortcomings with each other.

Ditching the act means something different to many people, and it may mean something different to you.

- When Michael Simmons first started ditching the act, he wondered how he would be perceived after sharing his short-comings. He didn't get mocked or ridiculed the way I thought I would have. Instead, he ended up getting better results than Ryan and I got combined. He now has over 1,000 people enrolled in his courses. Plus, when Michael ditched the act, he created deep bonds with his community and met his best friend.

- For Aaron Orendorff, ditching the act means overcoming the insecurity that comes with near constant rejection from outbound marketing, and has been the driving force for creating strong bonds with his audience while boosting his credibility. When he ditched the act, he went from being exiled from the ministry, to becoming a budding writer, and ultimately to being the editor in chief at Shopify Plus.

- For Winnie Sun, it means breaking the mold of her upbringing (in an Asian household) and expressing who she truly is. Doing this helped her to become one of the most influential financial advisors in all of America and secure multiple accounts with high-net-worth individuals.

- For Rahfeal Gordon, it means sharing his story of growing up poor and the struggles he faced during childhood, which drives deep connections with his audience and turns spectators into friends. When Rahfeal ditched the act, it helped him launch his series of books and speaking engagements across the world.

- To Iman Oubou, whether you've faced a mental health issue, sexual harassment, or struggles in entrepreneurship or your job, ditching the act means to be transparent with what you have gone through. Transparency is especially helpful if you come from a minority background, because so many more people will reach out to you and thank you for sharing your struggle than you realize, even from demographics you don't even expect. Ditching the act is a huge part of what helped her go from being Miss New York US to successfully launching and building SWAAY, a large media company for business-minded females.

- To Cheryl Snapp Conner, ditching the act means tying in your personal elements, including your hobbies and your vulnerabilities and even your wins, to humanize yourself. This helped her become a *Forbes* contributor and one of the world's top crisis public relations experts.

- To Dana Shalit, it means taking the mask off and being truthful about her own struggles with being overworked and overweight.

It's what she did to quit her event planning business and start social marketing to replace her income, then launch her own charity.

- For Hai Truong, it means unlearning what he thought he was supposed to do and how he was supposed to be, and it helped him overcome his fear of being different from what he observed others were like. It's what he did to go from hopping careers he was not aligned with and burnt out on to finding a career that he felt most in harmony with.
- For Pansy Lee, it means standing up for what she believes in at the office and holding onto her values, ethics, and commitment to her customers. It's what she did to get buy-in from her team to change the company culture, earn internal promotions, build the trust of a team that had her back, and earn external promotions as she became a director of product and design.
- For Mark Metry, it means facing his social anxiety and gathering up the courage to want to become the best version of himself possible. It's what he did to go from being shy, depressed, and overweight, to running an iTunes top 100 podcast and being in the best shape of his life.
- For Sara Bliss, it means getting out from underneath the shadows of ghostwritten books to putting herself in front of the work she has spent her entire life doing. By ditching the act, she went from being a ghostwriter to authoring the book she was told was nothing more than a magazine article, getting into a bidding war with publishers, and landing national media coverage on television and in major publications.

You'll be learning more about these people in the chapters that follow. And just to finish off the list:

- For Ryan, it means owning his whole story, FTC and all. Ditching the act is what Ryan did to jump-start his speaking career and get paid to speak across the world.
- And for me, it's what I did to turn my life around, create lifelong bonds with people across the world, and get married to my wife.

"Being authentic is simply being honest with yourself and everybody else about who you are, where you are, and where you are going. If you're being your authentic self, you have no competition."

—Social marketer David A. Braun

None of us knew that what we were doing had a name, and we called it different things, like being vulnerable, authentic, open, and truthful. Yet those words are more often tossed around without any real substance behind them. The truth is that we were taking our masks off, tossing them on the ground, and living as whole selves. And in return, our relationships, personal lives, and careers changed into exactly what we had once hoped for them to become. In an interview with *Forbes*, when Brené Brown was asked if society supports people who are viewed as vulnerable or if we come across as weak, she said, "The difficult thing is that vulnerability is the first thing I look for in you and the last thing I'm willing to show you. In you, it's courage and daring. In me, it's weakness." Even though you may see vulnerability as something that you are embarrassed or ashamed of, others will see it as your true courage shining through. No matter who you are, taking off the mask, ditching the act, and exposing yourself is the exact thing you need to do to achieve exactly what you are looking for within your life, career, and business.

BEING HONEST WITH EVERYONE (NOT JUST YOUR FRIENDS)

Chances are, you may already be ditching the act in your personal friendships without even realizing it. It's when you call your best friend and tell them about the problems that you are facing in your relationships and at work, and they either lend you their ear or provide you with advice and support to help you overcome the situation you are in. It is what is constructed within the strongest relationships that you currently have right now with your best friends and family. But ditching the act is not just limited to your best friends and family. The benefits also quickly become clear both in the office and in newfound relationships. As you have read earlier, Ryan and I both shared our extremely personal stories with our bosses to create an unbreakable bond. We created relationships that we can rely on and that we can call upon to get help and offer help in return. It has helped both of us re-create our careers beyond what we could have ever fabricated in our imaginations.

You have also probably seen what happens when you don't ditch the act. When Ryan didn't open up about things that were going wrong at work and when everything was crashing down on him, it took Cyn by surprise and almost cost them their relationship. When I didn't open up about the struggles my wife and I were facing as a newlywed couple, it ate me alive and took me to a few moments where I almost lost all hope in our marriage. When you tell your loved one how your day was, do you tell the truth, or do you just say that it was busy at work and that you are tired, but things are fine and you are on track to hit your bonus? When you lie by omission, you get disconnected with the people who matter to you because you can't share how you really feel. In fact, you face the same potential consequences that the brands and companies that hide their flaws do; you set yourself up for potential self-destruction.

A real relationship does not have judgment. Our relationships are designed to provide support and to listen to each other. This can also translate in the digital world. There you will be able to find communities that will not judge you, but instead support you. However, it only happens if you are real. Exposing our stories, even the hardest ones, helps cultivate connection, compassion, and empathy, much like it did for the people that you have just read about. Exposing yourself will even help you foster a committed audience, potentially one with a cult-like loyalty.

I had an opportunity to witness just how powerful a cult-like loyalty is, not just in my digital relationships, but also when I went to speak and share my experiences at the Cult Gathering in Banff, Canada, an annual gathering of the most cult-like brands across North America.

One person that I became digital friends with created a cult-like following with her makeup brand. Megan Martinez, the founder of Chaos Makeup, reached out to me one day when she was asking for advice on what to do in a particular situation. As we talked, I learned more about her story of how she was sexually abused at a young age, spoke up about it, and got out of the situation, because she truly believes that no one should stay silent. Because she stayed true to her values, she temporarily became homeless, living in her car. She worked three jobs for two years and saved up money to get her own place. She then became a makeup artist, ended up getting celebrity clients, and started her own makeup line. While growing her brand, she emphasized her support of animal activism, the rescuing of animals, and her love for science.

Megan grew the brand's cult-like following to the hundreds of thousands, but then one day she began losing thousands of followers by the day. She assumed this happened because of all the personal content she was posting, but it could have been due to a social media network purging its bots and deleting accounts, or due to someone talking about her brand negatively in a community, or because of a provocative post. None of us are 100 percent certain about why she lost followers, but Megan became scared and thought that posting her personal beliefs was what was causing her to lose so many of the fans she worked so hard to generate. She made a decision to play it safe. That decision involved removing all the references that originally resulted in her cult-like following. She removed photos that reflected her belief in animal activism and deleted her bio and any other mention of herself, both on social media and on her website. She no longer had a voice, and her makeup brand looked like any other company's brand.

When Chaos Makeup became just like any other company, someone with a YouTube channel of 500,000 subscribers made up lies stating that she didn't deliver her product to customers. Since her brand's website no longer had a personal presence because she played it safe, she was no longer in control of the brand's narrative. She became victim to having others control her brand's narrative—and that's exactly what they did. When she tried to defend herself, they cut up the video and made her look less authentic.

After I learned of this situation, I told her that she needed to go back to her roots and what built her cult-like following to begin with. She needed to add back in all the personal elements that made her brand what it is. And that is what she decided to do to reclaim what she almost lost, all due to a decision based on her belief that she needed to stop being herself.

YOU WILL BE UNCOMFORTABLE

Human nature will do everything in its power to resist change. The more successful you are, the harder you will find it to reveal your flaws. The same goes for many of the clients we sign on; we tell them up front about the mixed emotions they will face before we even engage into a contract with them. The problem is that they are usually professionals who have climbed their way up the career ladder by making everything look perfect. In the past, characteristic traits like being bold, being sure of yourself, and having a strong reputation were the traits required to move up in your career. But today, authenticity, vulnerability, and a sense of curiosity are the traits that fuel one's visibility and credibility in the market. This shift is what makes it so difficult for people who want to build a personal brand in this new world to do what they need to do, because they have been so set in doing things the old way.

But the old way doesn't work anymore.

One client we worked with was a successful entrepreneur who had a few inventions that saved lives. We hopped on a few phone calls with him and documented his entire life story, and then we created a strategy to get his name into the market. However, he hated how much authenticity was in the bio we created. He loathed how the story of how he got to where he is today was portrayed, and he didn't like the fact that we included his dog in his bio. He couldn't get over the fact that we wanted him to ditch the act and expose himself for who he truly is. On top of that, we told him to go on a photoshoot with Evan Duning, a photographer who specializes in editorial and who regularly has work featured in high-end fashion magazines and on billboards. Once our client received the images from Evan, he didn't like a single one. He said that the person who cut his hair made him look bad. It was obvious that he had a specific way that he wanted to be seen.

This client blamed everyone else for not portraying him a certain way. *That's because he wanted to be seen as someone who he simply wasn't.* Some people just don't get it. Ultimately, he was so dissatisfied with how he truly looked in the mirror, that he walked away from the opportunity to have a world-renowned personal brand that showed who he truly is, before even getting started or testing his pictures and content to see how he would be perceived by others.

Another set of clients we worked with contracted us for the launch of their book. When they saw the initial assets we created for them—their bios and other written content—they told us that this is not the direction that they wanted to go in. Instead, they wanted us to build their brand the way they believed would work best: by showcasing success, having a perfect image, and looking like they have everything put together. We strongly advised against their actions and told them it wouldn't work. They didn't want to listen. Instead of taking our advice, which they were paying top dollar for, they pushed forward with promoting their personal brand the old-school way. The results? They ended up missing their goal and didn't get onto the bestseller list they wanted. That's because they were more invested in stroking their own egos and using old-school tactics that no longer work, as opposed to having a grasp on what the market wants, providing value, and building connections with the people who would be reading their message.

On the other hand, some of our clients believe we do have the magic formula, but still they are reluctant to change because of their personal brand they have worked so hard to create. For example, prior to engaging with us, one of our clients, Joseph M. Bradley, worked his way to become a vice president of a Fortune 50 technology company through working hard, putting his best foot forward, and becoming his best version of himself. He had previously done it in other positions, like CEO and president of smaller start-ups.

In our process of helping clients create bios, we do long interviews that cover the entire span of our clients' lives. Oftentimes, bios are highlight reels, especially for successful executives. But how relatable are these stories? They aren't that relatable at all. In fact, they often create more of a disconnect with the reader than they do a connection. This is why we look for moments in people's lives that showcase just how human they truly are. The good stories—the ones that create camaraderie—are those random or obscure elements that are relatable. After hearing all the amazing ups and downs in Joseph's life, one thing caught our attention. When he was young, his goal was to be a paper boy. Why? Because he wanted to buy video games. Because Ryan and I played video games, suddenly Joseph was no longer an unapproachable technology goliath. We learned he was just like us, and that was the moment we bonded.

Since Joseph had earned his executive positions in the tech world, it was not easy for us to convince him that his public persona required authenticity and transparency. It took many months of prodding and pushing him to expose his vulnerabilities, while his instincts pushed him to share a perfect image of himself with the world. After a year of working together, we came to a point where we all felt comfortable with his brand. Ultimately, we helped Joseph share his experiences as an authentic leader. Now he has more traction than ever as he shares his views around the globe about the impact of digital humanism in a world that is now immersed in artificial intelligence and robots.

Why did ditching the act work for Joseph? Why didn't it work for the two other clients we mentioned?

Just take a moment to think about the last time you went on your favorite social media platform. What did you see?

You probably saw the exact same thing I saw. The exact same thing Ryan saw. The exact same things that Iman, Aaron, Winnie, Michael, Hai, Pansy, Dana, Cheryl, Mark, and Rahfeal saw: People touting their successes and accolades. People who put on masks and pretend to be living their dream life by talking about how great work is going, how their relationships are phenomenal, and how they can travel the world to do whatever they want whenever they want.

This culture of sharing victories makes people like us feel inadequate and unable to relate to what others are experiencing. And sometimes it goes as far as where we begin to despise others for their success. What's worse is that many of the people who are sharing their wins aren't even as happy or as successful as they portray. They are wearing a mask that we feel we need to wear as well. But the truth is, we need to take that mask off.

Mark Metry spent the first 18 years of his life not wanting people to know who he was. His friends and everyone else he knew were out there chasing their version of the American Dream to reach their personal goals of earning a six- to seven-figure income. Mark, on the other hand, had already accomplished that by the age of 15.

Mark's financial success didn't make him feel any better about himself. He hated everything about who he was. He was insecure, shy, overweight, depressed, and anxious; he felt untalented, and he hated the person he saw in the mirror. Mark was imprisoned by his own fears, but it was a prison in which he felt most comfortable. On top of that, Mark felt he didn't have the mental tools to cope with life, so he pretended to be somebody else in order to protect himself from the outside world.

After so many years of putting on an act to conform to the world's definition of success, there came a time when he was 19 where he hit a crisis point and wanted to end it all. Instead of following through with that decision, Mark decided to radically change who he was by first imagining who he could become.

One day, Mark came across a random challenge on LinkedIn called #LetsGetHonest that urged users to share something that they wanted to get off their chest. Mark gathered up the courage and took a shot at doing this by recording a two-minute video about the problems he faced with social anxiety. That initial video garnered some traction, and people reached out to Mark, telling him that he was very brave, while others told him that they had the same problem as he did.

Because Mark found initial traction with ditching the act and exposing his truth, he made a decision to converse with highly intelligent people from all walks of life. He did so through a podcast. By being his inquisitive, curious, and authentic self, people took notice, and doors began opening for Mark in both his personal and business life, as decision makers of projects began reaching out to include Mark in what they were doing.

Mark didn't think much about the situation after he first uploaded the video, but when he looks back, he realizes that the reason he was powerless in the early years of his life was because he was trying to hide everything, not just from himself, but from the outside world as well. That first video was one of the beginnings of a psychological cognitive shift where his brain started to form thoughts around not being shameful or guilted about his social anxiety. And by changing his own life, Mark was giving mental permission to others who felt just like him to do the same for themselves.

By continually documenting his journey to find himself through experiences, by journaling to a public audience, his family, and friends, and by using social media, he shot out a radio frequency about who he is so others across the world could connect to him. Today, not only has he lost a lot of weight and could be considered healthy, but millions of people listen to his podcast, *Humans 2.0*, and he speaks on stages around the world.

Our culture shaped us to share all our wins, but not our losses. But you, my friend, are in charge of changing that culture. By refraining from holding back your shortcomings and by sharing your whole self, you won't only propel yourself toward success; you will help rebuild the landscape for creating true human connections with others.

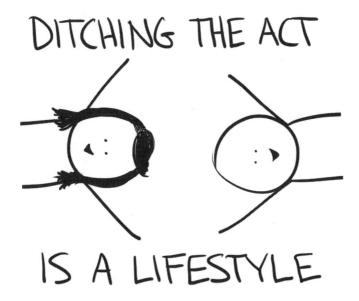

CHAPTER 7

PUT YOURSELF OUT THERE

The highlight reel. It seems like a good approach to take when greeting your coworkers or when sharing to the public on a digital property, but not only is it the worst approach; it will limit your ability to create a brand that matters and that builds authentic connections. Look on countless Instagram accounts and you will see feeds featuring only the best moments, or worse, staged moments. The most important thing

LEONARD TALKING

to understand is that people who are portraying perfect lives filled with superficial successes aren't taken seriously, except by the wannabes who want to also live a lavish life. Everybody else will be turned off, either feeling inadequate or simply not able to feel a connection to the people on those feeds. It is an approach that pushes away people rather than drawing them in.

BEING RELATABLE

Brené Brown spent over a decade studying vulnerability and empathy. In her book *Dare to Lead*, Brené discusses human psychology and how being vulnerable allows us to relate to others. She states that the reason we relate to others is because we are emotional beings who thrive on human connection, and the reason we connect to flawed people is because vulnerability is the cradle of emotions that we crave—the birthplace of love, belonging, and joy.

According to her research, what the people you want to interact with are looking for most is someone they feel like they know and understand. A person who is relatable to them, not just in their hobbies and interests, but also in their struggles, vulnerabilities, and failures. In this chapter we will go over the various levels of exposure, along with the rankings that go with them. We rank levels of exposure from Level 1, which consists of exposures that should be easy for you to share, to Level 4, which consists of your darkest secrets. We also cover Level 5 exposures, which include topics such as sex, religion, and politics—Level 5 is when sharing goes too far.

There's a reason why Bill Gates and Warren Buffett dress like average people. They understand that there is judgment toward wealthy people who show off what they have, so in order to maintain relevance, Bill and Warren portray themselves as similar to you and me—starting by dressing down. It's the same reason that the most successful people in the world do not talk about religion, politics, and sex. These polarizing topics will quickly push away an audience of your colleagues, clients, customers, and followers, and they may never want to do business with you. There is one caveat, however. If you run a business that caters to a specific religious group, like jewelry for Christians, or you work for a political party or candidate, or you are the conductor of a sexual harassment training program, then talking about Level 5 exposures is an essential component of your brand.

THE EXPOSURE LEVELS

There's good news. It doesn't matter whether you have been homeless or struggled with poverty, or if you have been extremely lucky and fortunate, or if you are somewhere in between. Regardless of who you are, you have experienced life firsthand, and that life experience gives you the ability to share your struggles, vulnerabilities, and failures, to drive connection with others. All you have to do is learn how to identify what portions of your life to share (which we will walk you through), and success will be waiting for you on the other side.

As long as you can uncover your vulnerabilities, then share your firsthand experience, you will be able to connect to others at a much deeper level. If you're sitting here and thinking that you have had a cushy life up to this point and haven't faced any struggles, we will even show you how to uncover the struggles you've faced, too.

In this chapter, we will help you identify *what* to expose. Then in the next chapter, we will show you *how* to expose these areas of your life.

Exposures fall into five different levels, as you'll see in the Exposures Ranked by Level Worksheet. Our focus is mainly on Levels 1 to 4.

Level 1 exposures are minute things that happen on a daily basis and yet are often never shared with peers. An example of a Level 1 exposure is when you trip over yourself, spill coffee on your shirt, or forget to pack an essential in your luggage, like a belt or a pair of shoes, on a flight out of town.

Examples of Level 4 exposures are failing in business, failing at a relationship, mishandling a difficult family situation, falling short on a project, losing what was valuable, being hurt by others, and so much more. Most of these exposures are what we consider to be things that could leave us fear ridden if they were ever made public by others. Yet Level 4 exposures are the same things you have gone through that will drive deep connections with others.

We will push you to work your way up to sharing Level 4 exposures by beginning with Level 1 and working your way through the different levels in numerical order. Level 5 exposures are things that you should never share, unless they are directly correlated to your business or are essential in disclosing and/or sharing for your career.

Exposures Ranked by Level Worksheet

*It is important to understand
the various levels of exposing yourself.*

Level 1 Exposures

Level 1 includes things that you are thinking or things that happen to you that you might not think to share.

These are ranked at the lowest level of exposure and show people that you are human.

Examples

> The silly things you do (or don't do):
>
> Spilling a beverage on yourself, misplacing your keys, making a spelling typo in a social post or important email, forgetting to water your plants and having them die, washing your car after six months, missing a workout

> Things that impact your mood:
>
> Having a pimple, having a bad hair day, getting inadequate sleep, feeling exhausted, feeling sick, being sick, having a poor Wi-Fi signal, making time for date night, going to a large store like Costco, having your flight be delayed, going to the DMV, buying a book but not having the time to read it, misplacing or losing your water bottle, being late due to traffic

Level 2 Exposures

Level 2 includes interactions you have with others and things you notice about how you feel.

Examples

Interactions with people:

Getting in a fight with a coworker, missing someone's birthday

Things that are causing you stress:

Having too many things on your plate, getting too many emails, missing a deadline, having difficulty keeping in touch with your friends, not having friends, dealing with a lovely but annoying dog that keeps barking, having to clean your home, not understanding how a specific new online platform works, telling friends you can't hang out because you have to do your homework, being the designated driver, being broke, not being able to afford a headset, studying for finals

Accidents:

Forgetting your wallet, losing your ID or passport, sweating through your shirt when giving a talk

Things that make you feel nervous and anxious:

Attending a significant event, dealing with online dating, having your car break down, having a slow computer but not being able to afford a new one, going to a high school reunion

What you observe:

Watching your relatives get special treatment, seeing yourself gain weight over the holidays, noticing your parents age, noting interactions with customer service

WORKSHEET

Level 3 Exposures

These will start to feel more serious.

Examples

> Challenges you face:
>
> Having a problem at work, losing a friendship, getting in a fight with another person, having to work when your friends have the night off, having to discipline your children, being yelled at by your boss, getting writer's block, having your life fall apart, having unsupportive friends or family members, experiencing medical problems, feeling guilt, wanting to change professions

> Sexual preferences:
>
> Revealing your sexual identity, coming out of the closet

> Things that you did or that happened that you are not proud of:
>
> Doing drugs (see Level 5), doing something embarrassing, dealing with lying in bed for two weeks straight because of low self-esteem, getting into a fight with a coworker, spending five years on a speaking reel but not be anywhere near finished, not being able to go have fun because of marital issues, being bullied, being caught for a DUI or other related crimes, gossiping

> Financial challenges:
>
> Not having money for gas, not having enough money for your kids to play sports, feeling overworked and underpaid, having too many expenses, having too high a car payment, losing your home

Level 4 Exposures

These are things you are extremely scared to share.

Examples

Business failures:

Having a failed business, being involved in litigation over a business you are involved with, losing what was valuable

Personal setbacks:

Being divorced, infidelity, being a single parent, losing a family member, robbing a bank or committing another similar or worse crime, being or formerly being homeless

Emotions and feelings you are having:

Having a failed marriage or long-term relationship, breaking up before a planned wedding, experiencing heartbreak, being hurt by others, feeling like nobody loves you, feeling like a failure, having depression or anxiety or another clinical diagnosis, not being able to quit a habit like smoking, betraying a friend, dealing with disability

Abuse:

Being abused or sexually assaulted, being taken advantage of as a child

Financial challenges:

Being so broke that you are considering filing bankruptcy, filing bankruptcy, having funding drop out, getting fired, struggling with poverty

Level 5 Exposures

This is when sharing goes too far.

DO NOT share these exposures.

Examples

> Ego:
>
> Talking about how successful you are, the kind of fancy car you drive, the exotic toys you own

> Politics:
>
> Giving your views on politics, candidates, policies, international trade

> Religion:
>
> Talking about religion in general, promoting your religion to others, joining a satanic cult (or any cult really)

> Sex:
>
> Describing sexual or lewd acts you have either done, want to do, heard others doing, or fantasized about, sharing pictures or videos of body parts or pornographic content, making unwanted sexual advances

> Policies prohibited by your employer:
>
> Revealing trade secrets, disclosures, private data, things that could violate your employment agreement and get you fired (like doing drugs), mishandling intellectual property

GETTING OVER FEAR

If it feels crazy or unbelievable to even consider sharing a Level 4 exposure, that's your human instinct. It's natural to feel that way. Level 4 exposures are things that your parents probably told you that you shouldn't share with people—and probably with good reason. Even more so if your culture tells you to not share certain things. For example, many Asian Americans are raised not to share. But when you learn the power of connectivity of showing that you are a real human, the way you view exposures will completely change. We will help you work your way up to sharing Level 4 exposures by walking you through how to share Level 1 to Level 3 exposures first.

Even though Ryan had to share a Level 4 exposure due to his experience with the Federal Trade Commission back when he was first building his personal brand, he often went dark when it came to ditching the act and exposing himself. That's because it was just so uncomfortable for him to do it, so he decided not to ditch the act and instead just shared advice and his positive experiences with his friends and followers. Yet I continued to push him to open up and share his whole self. When Ryan unwillingly began sharing his exposures regularly, he was so uncomfortable with how it felt to be so open and vulnerable that he needed to start at Level 1. One of the first things he shared to open up and start ditching the act was how he felt stressed after taking three flights in a row. He couldn't figure out how to relax from the overwhelming schedule of flying back to back for speaking engagements. When he reached out to his followers on Twitter and asked for tips on how to relax after such intensive trips, Ryan ended up with a response that he hadn't seen for a long time. Instead of there being a few likes here and there, he ended up with droves of comments from engaged followers who were interested in his well-being.

Ryan soon opened up about how he needed to hide a pimple before speaking on another stage. That tweet became the most engaged post of the entire conference. On top of that, the videographer saw the tweet and changed the filter on the camera to hide the pimple. Now Ryan is opening up about his Level 4 exposures and creating relationships that move the needle in his career and life.

REAL-LIFE SUCCESS STORIES

Ryan isn't the only example of the benefits of removing the mask and really opening up. Here are eight exposure success stories:

1. **Hai:** In his previous job as a senior writer and content producer, Hai felt he needed to project the perfect version of himself, and it felt as if he were walking on eggshells. This impacted his health and his energy, as he was constantly trying to be someone who he wasn't each day. When he made the decision to share his lower-level exposures with his peers and his colleagues, and decided to document how much he had done in his job whether it was recognized or not (which definitely wasn't easy for him), it helped him get a promotion to a new job, and the exercise continues to empower who he is in the workforce. The dynamics between him and his boss also evolved into a different, and much better, experience than before, a relationship characterized by mutual respect, empowerment, and autonomy.

2. **Michael:** Michael used to run a company that held over 600 events with some of the most well-respected public figures, and he won many awards and accolades for what he did, including being named one of the Top 25 Entrepreneurs Under 25 by *Businessweek* and one of the Top 30 Entrepreneurs Under 30 by *Inc.* magazine. When he first ditched the act, he felt as if he put out a homing beacon that attracted others to him who resonated with how he felt about the truths he experienced in his life. In 2013, after spending two years reading through content related to Brené Brown and vulnerability, Michael made a commitment to write a post every weekday that scared him at some level. Aside from attracting others who felt the same way as he did (including his best friend whom he talks to for hours on the phone once a week) and accelerating the pace of relationships, he felt it was therapeutic, and he became more aware of who he is. Another side benefit is the massive success he attained with his writing, which has been published in nearly every major media publication and has been read tens of millions of times. It also led to a significant increase in sales of his courses.

3. **Winnie:** After Winnie, a financial advisor, got real, she felt invincible because she truly became comfortable in her own skin without worrying what others thought about her. This led to a whole slew of experiences that a financial advisor does not usually have the chance to luck into, including being invited to the fanciest parties, texting Randy Jackson from *American Idol* at any given time, and being able to tweet at Kathy Ireland and receiving a response. Businesswise, Winnie has signed multiple eight-figure accounts (some as high as $40 million) based on her digital relationships. She was also named the #1 Female Financial Advisor by *US News & World Report*.

4. **Iman:** Iman majored in biochemistry and molecular biology, was crowned Miss New York US in 2015, and launched a successful media business. As someone to whom success seems to come easily, she made it her mission to be vulnerable and transparent both about the misogynic behind-the-scenes struggles she faced being a female entrepreneur when raising capital and about the detrimental hardships that come from building a business from scratch. The result is that others who look to her story don't feel bad about where they are today, knowing that success is within reach, unlike the stories that gloss over the details of just how hard it is to truly reach success.

5. **Aaron:** Aaron started writing and speaking publicly as a teenager. Through his experience, he found that people do not respond well when you cast yourself as *the hero* and say things like, "I'm great; look at me! Why can't you be like me?" Rather than bring them closer, stories that center on personal success push audiences and readers away. "When I began getting honest," says Aaron, "I began leading with, 'Listen, I'm going through it too. Here's what I've struggled with, failed at, and found ways to overcome.' That became the starting point of connecting with others on a deeper level. Rejection and failure unite us as humans, not individual success."

6. **Cheryl:** As a publicist who works closely with public figures, Cheryl believes that people focus too heavily on the negatives that come with sharing, like being bullied or laughed at. She

feels people should consider themselves as one cohesive brand. A CEO she knows loved to knit but felt she couldn't post about it because it was un-CEO-like and would hurt her brand, and Cheryl believed that was a bad decision. On the other hand, another public speaker and makeup artist she knows openly told a group of people that one set of photos was her professional set, but this other set was what she looks like in the mornings when she first wakes up. Cheryl said that reality check gave people a lot of encouragement and was well received.

7. **Pansy:** As the manager of teams that work on products, when Pansy shared her own struggles at the company as she met with her employees, she opened up the door for her teams to be vulnerable with her and share their struggles too. When they expressed their personal goals with her that weren't work related, she encouraged them and helped them to actualize their dreams. This sparked so much loyalty that some of her employees stuck with the company for over five years. They also felt more motivated and so worked harder to achieve great results. This is also what drove Pansy to rise to the rank of director, both internally at companies and through external positions she applied for.

8. **Leonard:** On the other hand, when I started sharing, I went straight for the Level 4 exposures. That could partially be the reason why I was able to end up with 2 million reads on my content within the first six months of writing. Yet not many people are like me and can share experiences like failure and heartbreak immediately.

THE POWER OF EXPOSURE

One of the members who was enrolled in our course, Chris Varvaro, EDM producer and pioneer of the #pursoundmovement, had over 10,000 followers on his social media platforms, but very few people were engaging with his content. He was frustrated because he felt like he was trying everything but wasn't getting the results that he wanted. He was so sick of spinning his wheels, that he sent me an email stating that he wanted to take some time away from social media to work on himself. I asked Ryan to share the results he was receiving when he started to share his Level 1 exposures with Chris. Ryan then told Chris to try sharing that he wanted to walk away from social media on his social media channels and gave him the exact text of what to say. Within 10 minutes of posting, we received an email back from Chris saying how he couldn't believe that it worked, and how this post had more engagement than anything else he had created prior.

Before Ryan shared his Level 1 exposures with a wide audience, he would send me texts complaining about the situations he was in. Whenever he sent me a text, I would tell him that he shouldn't just be telling me these things; he should be sharing them openly. That frustrated him even more, because he didn't know how to position what he had to say, and he thought that sharing things like this would make him seem weak. So we went back and forth, and I ultimately gave him something to copy and paste that he could put onto his social outlets. This led to hundreds of comments per post and led to his audience actually engaging with his content.

WHAT WORKS DIGITALLY WILL WORK IN REAL LIFE TOO

Dana Shalit comes from a family of entrepreneurs. She used to run an events planning company and always felt that she needed to trade hours for dollars. This left her completely overwhelmed to the point where she couldn't see herself getting out of her scenario. Was she going to have to work hard and be left exhausted for the rest of her life?

Much like looking through the Instagram feeds of today, when looking at Dana's life through the lens of social media in 2012, it seemed like she had it all. The exciting parties, the glamor of being around a certain crowd of people, and an active lifestyle. The truth was, she was barely holding it together, due to the stress and health issues that come with working day and night, like tacking on 20 extra pounds, facing extreme exhaustion, suffering from panic attacks, and having no time for herself.

Dana was introduced to an opportunity by someone she respected to try something called social marketing and become an ambassador for a health-based product, which could potentially help her get out of her event planning business. Social marketing would require Dana to meet people in person and get them to try the product. She decided to fully embrace the lifestyle, by exercising, meditating, and treating her body like a temple. She ended up getting results that helped her shave those extra pounds and set herself free from the panic attacks, but that wasn't the driving factor in what helped her get out of her event planning business.

In the first year, she struggled with facing rejection on a daily basis, not just from strangers, but also from her friends and family. She was regularly being told that what she was doing wouldn't work, which left her feeling discouraged. So she sat down and had a conversation with her mentor, opening up about her vulnerabilities. That act allowed their relationship to evolve into one that moved the needle. That in-person conversation was the source of the driving force that enabled her to quit her event planning business that she had started two years earlier. Yet that wasn't the only thing that triggered her motivation; she took the same candor, and when she met with new prospects, she explained to them the true struggles she faced while working so hard to get out of her event planning business, like the exhaustion she faced and her panic attacks.

As others started to appreciate her vulnerability and began to join her, her business grew. Seven years later, Dana has been able to live a truly healthy life. She has founded a charity called Artbound that funds arts programs in countries such as Nicaragua, Guatemala, Kenya, and India, and is a Canadian who spends her winters in Venice Beach, California. The one simple act of ditching the act and being vulnerable became Dana's secret weapon for freeing herself of the tiresome lifestyle that once consumed her life.

Understanding what to expose is only part of the battle. The other side of it is positioning. You don't want to sound like you're rambling and complaining about the experiences that you are facing in life. If you do, you will look like someone who isn't appreciative of what he or she has and potentially is a serial complainer. Instead, you need to pull from these experiences and share the bigger story around them.

If you feel like you may have as much difficulty sharing a Level 1 exposure as Ryan, then don't worry. We will provide you with the Overcoming Fear and Sharing Worksheet in Chapter 11 that you can use to copy from and paste examples to your social outlets to see what kind of response you end up with.

Now you should have a thorough understanding of why you should share low-level exposures and what the different levels of exposure are. In the next chapter, we will introduce you to the most essential component of this entire book, the Exposure Résumé.

CHAPTER 8

DITCH THE ACT AND BE YOURSELF

You understand the clear importance of *why* you need to ditch the act and be yourself. Now it is time to move deeper into *what* to do and what order to do it in. We will teach you how to develop your own Exposure Résumé. The Exposure Résumé will be your foundation for truly being yourself. It will give you the tools you need to take off the mask and start driving true

IT'S

LEONARD

connection with others. Whether your goal is to get a promotion, find a better job, have a deeper relationship with your employees, or build a personal brand where you create lifelong success like the well-known personalities Gabrielle Bernstein and Ryan Seacrest, the first step to the entire process is the Exposure Résumé.

The Exposure Résumé will provide you with a simple tool for compiling your list of failures and weaknesses that will give you a true connection with others. You will answer three questions for each skeleton in your closet that you want to expose. Once you answer these three questions, you will have what you need to expose your true self, not just to others, but to yourself as well. You won't be starting from scratch, however. Our stories as well as the stories of the other successful people who have taken off the mask and ditched the act have equipped you with an understanding of how beneficial opening yourself up can be.

The Exposure Résumé is what will help you shape your message to deliver content that impacts others. Now let's get started. The best way to begin is to fill out the following Exposure Résumé Worksheet.

Exposure Résumé Worksheet

Your Exposure Résumé is your résumé for success.

An Exposure Résumé can relate to both your personal life and your career. Take a look at the chart below:

Date	What You Did	Result	Still Alive?
2014	Worked at Pepsi	Quit	Yes
2016	Made start-up	Failed	Yes
2017	Met love of life	Broke up	Yes
2018	Went back to school	Got degree	Yes
2020	Director of Human Resources	Promoted	Yes

As you can see, it doesn't matter what challenges you face. At the end of each situation, you come out alive. That means that your personal brand follows you around until the day that you die.

To maximize the strength of your personal brand, you can't rely on your career or your business. You may not still have it a year from now. The only thing you can rely on is your personal brand. The Exposure Résumé gives you exactly what you need to uncover in order to stand on your personal brand for the rest of your life.

You can build your Exposure Résumé in six steps.

WORKSHEET

Step 1. Answer the following three questions for each of the "skeletons in your closet" that you want to expose in order to ditch the act to reveal your whole self and drive differentiation, growth, and loyalty.

1. What is a secret that you've been hiding from everyone because you're fearful of what others may think of you?
2. Why are you so scared of telling others about that event, and what makes you feel so ashamed about it?
3. How do you feel people would react and think of you if you told them the truth?

Here are Leonard's answers:

What is a secret that you've been hiding from everyone because you're fearful of what others may think of you?

LEONARD: I was scared to tell people that my electricity was shut off. I got an eviction notice and was about to lose everything, so when people asked me how I was doing, I said that I was fine and that business was great.

Why are you so scared of telling others about that event, and what makes you feel so ashamed about it?

LEONARD: I thought others would think that I was a loser and that I wasn't good enough. Because of that, I thought they would judge me for being so broke and wouldn't want to be my friend anymore and that they would abandon me.

How do you feel that people would react and think of you if you told them the truth?

LEONARD: I was scared that others would look down on me and that I wouldn't be good enough to be their friend or peer if they learned the truth. I thought they would have kicked me out of their life and that I would lose respect and dignity.

Now it's your turn to answer the questions.
(Print multiple sheets as necessary.)

What is a secret that you've been hiding from everyone because you're fearful of what others may think of you?

Why are you so scared of telling others about that event, and what makes you feel so ashamed about it?

How do you feel that people would react and think of you if you told them the truth?

Step 2. Realize that your perceived truth about this particular "skeleton" has some fictional elements that you made up in your own head.

You're thinking of what-ifs, not what is happening.

In the list below, check the boxes of what you think will happen when you share your secret. Don't worry if you find it difficult to check any but the last box; we thought the exact same thing, but then all of the following happened (except the last box) when we shared our stories.

WORKSHEET

- ❏ I will able to control my own narrative.
- ❏ I will be able to be truthful and honest with not just others, but myself as well.
- ❏ By being honest with myself, I will be able to gain confidence and like myself more.
- ❏ By being open and honest, others will be open and honest with me.
- ❏ I will be able to attract genuine and honest people into my life who can become friends, mentors, business partners, and clients.
- ❏ I will be able to create deeper relationships with others and build a network of trust.
- ❏ I will be able to build genuine connections with others because they will trust me for being so honest and open.
- ❏ I will be able to be in an environment where we work together to lift each other up instead of tearing each other down.
- ❏ I will be able to start to inspire the lives of others because they will see how open and honest I am with my own shortcomings, and they will know they don't have to be perfect either.
- ❏ People will begin to pay attention to what I'm doing.
- ❏ People will begin to respect me.
- ❏ People will begin to follow me on social media.
- ❏ I will become an authority in my space, and others will cite me in their blogs, articles, videos, conversations, speeches, and so forth.

- ❏ People will be able to connect with me because they have gone through similar events themselves.
- ❏ People can't use the things in my past against me because I got ahead of them by already making my past problems known.
- ❏ People will call me brave and stand behind me because I am sharing what others are afraid to share.
- ❏ No one will expect me to be perfect, nor will I expect others to be perfect either, because we are all flawed creatures who are fighting our own battles, no matter how successful we look on the outside.
- ❏ People will invite me onto their podcasts to share my story.
- ❏ People will want to interview me about my story.
- ❏ People will want to do business with me because they can connect to me at a deeper level.
- ❏ I will have more opportunities to move up and progress in my life.
- ❏ I will have better relationships with people that I am close with.
- ❏ It will give me confidence to take on new challenges and opportunities.
- ❏ I don't believe any of the above will happen because I'm a Debbie Downer and I hate everything in life, but I will give this exercise a try anyway because I have nothing better to do with my life. (If this is you, that's okay. This used to be us too, and look where we are now.)

WORKSHEET

Step 3. Design your story behind this "skeleton," and don't leave out any details.

If you had the opportunity to share your whole story behind this "skeleton" now, what would you say? (Write it here.)

Step 4. Repeat Steps 1-3 for as many "skeletons" as you can.

Try to identify at least five initially, and allocate time later to go back later and really think about the things that you are fearful to share. Store these additional answers in a folder called your Exposure Bank. These "skeletons from your closet," could be embarrassing moments, stories from your past, hardships you went through, and so forth. You can write them down fully expressed, or write them as a list to expand upon them later. Use the prompts in steps 1–3 to start building out the story behind these events. The Exposure Bank of stories will inspire the content you create that will connect you with others.

Step 5. Build your new Exposure Résumé to funnel the skeletons into line items.

It is time to reference your Exposure Bank that you have now built in the above steps, and retrofit your failures, missteps, and pains. Instead of touting all your accolades, let's use the identification of these failures to discover and highlight the skills, strengths, and experience that you now have as a result.

Looking at your Exposure Bank, list your skills after having learned from these failures, missteps, pains, etc.

Skills

_____   _____

_____   _____

List your strengths after having learned from your failures, missteps, pains, etc.

Strengths

_____   _____

_____   _____

WORKSHEET

Show how your skeletons translate into an updated experience section that includes what you've learned through pain, failures, etc. Add dates, your job title, and the name and location of the company. Then describe your responsibilities and achievements in terms of impact and results. Use examples, but keep them short.

Experience

Dates from–to: _____

Job title: _____

Company, location: _____

Dates from–to: _____

Job title: _____

Company, location: _____

Dates from–to: _____

Job title: _____

Company, location: _____

Use the next section to highlight any new relevant passions and activities, and describe how you like to give back to help others avoid the mistakes you have made. It's good to include how your experiences have made you a better leader. Highlight any volunteer experiences that were a result of learning from your mistakes.

Activities

_____

_____

_____

Step 6. Use this new Exposure Résumé to establish and build your brand/following/readership by sharing the stories that you have established in your Exposure Bank.

If you fear that you will look weak to others, the truth is that you won't. Remember if they are Level 3 or Level 4, you can build up to sharing by continuing to share Level 1 and Level 2 Exposures, until you find the courage to start sharing your bigger "skeletons." It will be scary. But learn to let your fears guide you, because people will be able to relate to your pain, insufficiencies, and failures.

Refer to step 5 and think of the lessons you have learned, and the new skills that you have acquired as a result of what has gone wrong. Share your stories in your Exposure Bank that you have identified through the process of building out your Exposure Résumé. Share them on Quora, Medium, LinkedIn, your blog, and your other social media platforms.

For more details on how to specifically share these stories, refer to Chapters 9–12 to understand the steps you need to take.

Here is an overview:

- Write your Exposed and Authentic Bio and incorporate your whole story, including what went wrong.
- Build content around lessons learned.
- Develop a brand that owns your authentic journey.
- Use digital platforms and become a resource to others who face similar challenges.

WORKSHEET

YOU HAVE ALL THE TOOLS

Now that you have created your Exposure Résumé, your foundation is set. Everything you need to authentically be yourself lies within the Exposure Résumé. It will serve as your source when you prepare your Exposed and Authentic Bio that will make an instant connection. What's uncovered from the Exposure Résumé is what will help you spark conversations at work to build deeper relationships with your employees and colleagues. The stories that spring from here are what you need to create either written or visual content and build your authority and trust in the market.

When you start sharing these stories, you will grow a social media following. You will be doing everything that you need to do in order to build a successful personal brand, which will lead you to success in any career or business of your choosing. Now that you have a solid foundation, all you need to do is follow the Expose Yourself Process to turn each action item into a reality. If this makes you feel overwhelmed, don't worry. We have broken down this entire process to an exact science with the minimal number of steps possible to achieve your desired results in the quickest amount of time. And this process works for everyone, no matter what a person's background is. It will work for you. That's because the end result of the entire process humanizes who you already are.

When you share at work, don't go all out with a Level 4 exposure immediately. Start with Level 1 to build toward the Level 4 exposures you plan to share later. Since you already have an established relationship with your coworkers, if you go straight out the gate with a Level 4 exposure, they may think you are having a breakdown. So start small and gradually work your way up toward sharing your more vulnerable moments. This will help you connect with others in the office. It will help you find common ground to relate to them. They might start to open themselves up to you, and you will find that you can form deeper, more authentic relationships.

PUTTING YOUR WORK INTO ACTION

How deep were the moments you shared in your Exposure Résumé? Were they Levels 1–3 exposures or Level 4 exposures? If they were just Levels 1–3 exposures that touched the surface of fear, we want to challenge you to go at the exercise again. Share the most painful, vulnerable moments you can. If you're too scared to share these moments publicly, that's okay. The Exposure Bank allows you to store these stories for a future date, when you build up the bravery to share these critical, life-changing moments with others. Not many people can blaze into the world sharing their most painful moments. However, if you work your way up through Level 1 to Level 4 exposures slowly and surely, you will be able to get to that point where you share these connecting moments with others, much like how Ryan gradually built up the courage to share both his DUI and his encounter with the Federal Trade Commission.

Whom will you be sharing these Exposure Résumé moments with? How will you be sharing these moments with the world? If you have a job, start there. Talk over what you plan to share digitally with your boss. Get your boss's buy-in and support to help you launch your personal brand. Don't just go out there and start sharing without checking with your manager. There may be social media policies and other guidelines that your company wants you to follow. Do your best to locate these policies and make sure you stay within those guidelines so you don't put your career at risk.

THE 10 COMMANDMENTS OF SHARING DIGITALLY AND AT WORK

There is a right way and a wrong way to share your stories and what you have experienced. Follow these simple rules to make sure you create content that will not work against you.

- **Rule 1.** Do not share anything related to politics, religion, or sex.
- **Rule 2.** Do not share anything illegal.
- **Rule 3.** Do not share anything that can be hurtful to another

person, regardless of age, gender, ethnicity, work ethic, disabilities, and so forth.

- **Rule 4.** Do not defame anyone.
- **Rule 5.** Do not shame anyone.
- **Rule 6.** Do not make it sound like you are better than anyone else.
- **Rule 7.** Do not share anything that you have not vetted to be true.
- **Rule 8.** Use the pause test to think over anything that you may want to share in the heat of the moment. After 24 hours, does this still seem like something you want to share? If it isn't, don't share it.
- **Rule 9.** Taking a stance against a popular opinion is okay and is highly recommended in many situations, as long as it does not relate to items identified above.
- **Rule 10.** Do not share pictures of your genitalia or topless photos if you are female (even if you are asked), and don't ask if you can share them with others.

Aside from protecting yourself, you need to really consider how ditching the act and being yourself will help you in your career at your current company or at companies where you plan to work. When you are sharing your plans with your boss, make sure that you do not come across as only looking out for yourself. Remember, the entire goal of this exercise is connectivity. When you share, make sure to indicate how this will be a win-win situation for both you and your employer, by explaining how you plan to showcase your employer's brand and help elevate the company as well.

If you are the boss and have a team that reports to you, the moments within your Exposure Résumé can be your ticket to earning surprising loyalty and camaraderie from your team. Earlier in this book, you learned about the deep connections both Ryan and I have with our employers. That didn't just happen because we were vulnerable and open with our bosses. They were open and vulnerable with us too, so we were able to reciprocate with each other. Ryan's boss

Iain shared some very personal and sad challenges that his family had experienced. When Iain opened up to Ryan, it made Ryan see his boss not just as a boss, but as someone who is a real person that he cares for. When Christopher opened up to me and shared the struggles he had in his personal life, our relationship evolved way past just that of an employer and employee, to that of loyal friends who have each other's back.

When you share the moments within your Exposure Résumé with your direct reports and colleagues, you will create deeper personal connections with a team that will have your back and support you as the true leader you are. As the director of her team, Pansy practices this regularly to show the individual members of the team that they are all in it together (including herself), and she has seen the loyalty and drive within her team continually excel through higher employee retention, better communication throughout teams, and a higher sense of trust between teammates.

WHEN SHARING GOES TOO FAR

Sharing has its limits. When you share too much information with someone in the wrong way, you can end up pushing people away as opposed to bringing them closer. Chances are, you have gone through a crisis in the past. And if you haven't, you have probably witnessed someone going through one. If the person wasn't an extremely close friend, however, your natural reaction might be to avoid that person. In the same way that a crisis can scare people away, sharing a Level 4 crisis that you are going through could lead to others avoiding you as well. So if you are struggling and gasping for air due to a particularly troublesome moment, it may be best to share those moments with a professional, such as a therapist, and overcome those moments in private before you share them publicly. The worst thing you can do is to push people away instead of bringing them closer to you and your overall vision.

There is an invisible line when it comes to sharing. When you share your own personal stories, if you push too far (especially if you haven't shared a lot previously), people may think you are having a breakdown or a midlife crisis. That occurs when you add in the excruciating pain you are encountering from a current event. To prevent this from happening, work on sharing stories *after* you have worked your way through the obstacles, as opposed to while you are experiencing them firsthand.

If you work at a job, you may be limited to what you can share, as opposed to owning your own business, where you have much more freedom. If your company has a strict no-tolerance drug policy, you may not be able to share your ayahuasca journey from Peru or dive into all the details of what happened at Burning Man. If you did, you may be called into the human resources office and have an uncomfortable conversation that could lead to your termination.

This invisible line isn't just limited to your employer. It also relates to your relationships. If you are in a relationship with or are married to an extremely private person, you should do your best to respect that person's privacy. You may also have a friend who may have a stalker, be involved in a sketchy business, or for any other reason want to fly under the radar and have no digital footprint. If you are sharing a story that relates to a person like this, make sure you are anonymizing who the person is, so you do not break the person's trust.

HOW SHARING WORKS

Sharing works in two ways. There's that relationship you have with a close friend, and you share your struggles in a car at night, over a drink at a bar, or on the phone via long text message chains or voice calls. Then there is what you share with the public. For myself, on certain platforms, I have over 500,000 people who follow me. On the other hand, my personal Facebook profile only has my friends whom I have known for years who do not judge me (for the most part). On my Facebook profile, I share some of the biggest struggles I face on a daily basis, because I have a network of people whom I can trust. However, on my public profiles, I usually share my struggles after I have overcome them. What's the difference? The narrative of what I'm sharing.

If I were to share my struggles publicly as I go through them, then I could be mocked or ridiculed for what I share. But when I share my struggles after I have overcome them, then instead of being mocked or ridiculed, I have, time and time again, been met with a reaction where people were empathetic to what I went through, called me an inspiration, and found hope in the words I shared. Why? Because they related to my struggles. You don't want to make the same mistakes I did when I first started ditching the act and being myself. You want your vulnerability to connect with others instead.

WHOM TO INITIALLY START SHARING WITH

Now that you know what not to do, and you know the two different types of people whom you can share with, you need to make a choice. Do you have friends whom you trust, or are they jerks who put you down every chance you get? If you have friends you trust, you want to start sharing your moments with your friend network. However, if your friends are jerks and have always put you down and belittled you, if you share your vulnerabilities with them, you may not get the reaction you are hoping for. Instead, move to share with a public network. Some public networks include Quora, Medium, and LinkedIn, and there are many others online. Quora may be a great place to start, as it has a "Be Nice, Be Respectful" policy, to reinforce a positive environment.

Before you share your stories with others, draft them privately in either a journal or a document on your computer. If you never feel brave enough to post these moments, you will still benefit by getting a better understanding of who you are and becoming a much braver, more resilient person. In fact, a study from *Frontiers in Behavioral Neuroscience* titled "Writing About Past Failures Attenuates Cortisol Responses and Sustained Attention Deficits Following Psychosocial Stress" found that writing about past failures improves the body's response to new setbacks that may arise, by lowering cortisol levels (which are responsible for stress) and making one think more strategically about how to deal with new stressors in life.

AVOIDING NEGATIVITY

It may seem like you are taking a risk or betting on chance, but you won't be. You will be following a proven formula that is designed to get results. So instead of running from your fears, run toward them and let them guide you. Get your content online, and watch it work its magic.

Remember when you did the Rapid Reflection Discovery Process Worksheet? There is only one way that would cause people to react poorly to the message that you are communicating. And that is if you have not worked on improving or eliminating the traits that you identified in that process, such as having a sense of cockiness, being arrogant, not listening, being a know-it-all, being a one-upper, and so forth. If you experience negative responses, you need to take a close and critical look at how the message was delivered, because chances are, these traits are being carried over into what you are either saying or writing. You will need to refine how you are presenting your vulnerabilities, without sounding like you are being critical, condescending, or arrogant or are doing it for pity or sympathy. You will need to work to restructure the stories and share them again.

If you have worked to eliminate these negative traits, then you have absolutely nothing to worry about when sharing your content. However, if people are still being negative and critical of you, it's not you; it's them. These aren't the friends you want in your life. You need to take a close hard look at these friendships and really decide if you want to continue on with these relationships. It may not be healthy for either you or your negative friends to continue down the same path if this type of behavior continues.

PUTTING IT OUT THERE

Once you start sharing with your friends, you will gain more confidence to share with others. Take that confidence from your personal life and bring it to work. Then take that confidence to the public. Try it in various aspects of your life and watch the results compound.

There are many things you don't want to share, and we want you to start small. The small stuff is good, but what about the medium stuff and the really scary stuff?

Try sharing some minimally embarrassing moments from your Exposure Bank. When Ryan went to speak at the Influencer Inc. Summit, he wore a maroon suit that matched the exact color of the chairs and tablecloths at the event. He didn't want to share that moment, but he ended up receiving a lot of positive feedback and a few good laughs. Try thinking of a minimally invasive moment that you can make fun of and share that with others. It's not easy, and Ryan still struggles with this daily, but when I kept pushing him forward, it has helped him become braver too. If Ryan and I and all the countless people in this book can share our vulnerable moments, you can start taking off the mask, ditching the act, and being yourself too. We implore you to give it a try and report back with your results.

Next, we will take a deeper dive into the Expose Yourself Process so you can build the personal brand you have always dreamed of.

PART 3

REVEAL YOUR WHOLE SELF

CHAPTER 9

STEP ONE: POSITIONING IS AN ART FORM

One of the most common mistakes beginners make when it comes to creating a compelling personal brand is to look at people who are 5 to 15 years into building their brand and try to replicate how these people position themselves. It almost always fails. Why? Because it took years upon years to achieve name brand recognition, gain trust from the community, and command respect from just their name. To position yourself as a guru or influencer, you have to earn that authority, and it is something that takes positioning, relationship building, and most importantly time; it doesn't happen overnight.

It's essential to know where you want to go and what you want your brand to look like in the future; however, you can't start at the finish line. You have to go through the steps necessary to get to your future goal—and there is an order. The key is not skipping steps, but starting at the beginning and working your way up. Even if you do the right things in the wrong order, it won't work. For example, when I first met Ryan, he was creat-

LEONARD

ing blog posts everywhere on a variety of topics, by the dozens. He was reaching out to event planners, doing everything he could to get them to consider him to speak at their events—even for free. He would pitch his ideas at every single pitch event he could. He would bring speakers to the UCI ANTrepreneur Center and interview them to try to leverage their reputations into his own. He volunteered at conferences like the Lean Startup Conference and pretended to be part of the media to get in front of speakers like Eric Ries and Steve Blank to write articles about them, but then he tweeted out Eric's name wrong. He went to festivals of all sorts and networked with every person he could. He would take any chance he could to speak, even if it required him to drive up to Los Angeles multiple times a week. He also told anyone and everyone that he wanted to speak at any event possible.

Now Ryan wasn't doing anything wrong, technically. He was doing a lot of things that do fall within the Expose Yourself Process. Yet he was running around as if he were a chicken with its head cut off. Or what Ryan would consider to be a ginger chicken with its head cut off.

Ryan was doing many things right but was missing the core component that was holding him back from the resounding success he has now. And he wasn't doing any of the subsequent steps in the right order either. Ryan was so far into the weeds that he couldn't see what that missing core component was, because he was so busy doing what he believed would work for him. As many people who go out to build their own personal brand do, we often find it difficult to see what we are missing because we are trying to hit milestone after milestone. Sometimes it just takes an outside perspective to really figure out what that missing component is.

When Ryan and I were able to sit together and structure out all the components of what he was doing, it became evident to me what he was missing. And when I shared with him what he was missing, it was like a lightbulb went off in his head and that eureka moment came to him. Once it was presented to him, he knew just how important that component was. He understood how that missing piece could help him get his brand in order and start to see the fruits of his labor.

What was that missing component?

The missing component is what will bridge the gap between you and the people you wish to interact with that will help you achieve your goal, whether your goal is to get a promotion, to find a better job, or to land new clients for your business. It's what will help you establish instantaneous trust with anyone you meet, digitally and in person. It's what will help you create new relationships where others you encounter will feel as if they have known you their entire life. It's what will help you position yourself in the right way to get exactly what you want out of life. That missing component is Step One of our Expose Yourself Process: crafting your unique bio and your personal brand position and strategy.

The missing component is your Exposed and Authentic Bio, which we will return to a little later in the chapter.

A big part of this missing component lives within the Exposure Résumé you have already created. And it encompasses many of the stories of your life that brought you to where you are today. You will be able to harness the lessons of the Exposure Résumé to help create a clearer, more compelling personal brand.

Your unique bio is what will ultimately be what people see to build an instantaneous connection to you, allow them to get a full understanding of what you stand for, and drive people to want to do business with you. In order to create a compelling bio, you will need to present your exposed and authentic life. This will help you cultivate credibility within the market and drive brand growth without relying on outbound pitching, much like Ryan was doing at the beginning of his personal branding journey. The authentically exposed life is attractive and draws in the type of people you are looking to attract, creating a stream of inbound leads. The art of positioning, then, relates to the art of exposure.

So how do you express your exposed and authentic life?

The Exposed and Authentic Bio Worksheet will walk you through the steps to make the most compelling bio with what you have today.

The Exposed and Authentic Bio Worksheet

Develop your bio so people feel as if they have known you their entire life.

Your bio is the most important part of your entire online presence. When people consume your content, when they connect with it, they will look you up. When they read your bio, they will make a determination of whether or not they like you, want to follow you, start a conversation with you, interview you, invite you to speak at an event, offer you a unique opportunity, or do business with you (by either offering you a position at their company or buying your product or service).

In order to gather stories that will build your long-form bio, you must take a deep dive into your past. There are two ways you can go about that:

Option 1. Find a friend to help interview you (best option).
Option 2. Interview yourself.

Step 1. Fill out the Pre-Interview Questionnaire.

Because each person has a unique life experience, it is important to develop questions that are relevant to you. Think about the times in your life identified in the left column, and match them with a single word from the right column that best represents that time period.

Pre-Interview Questionnaire

Times in your life (write in word from right column)	Feelings/emotions/memories (only use words once in left column)
1. Early childhood (first memories until elementary school): _____ (A1) 2. Youth (elementary school to high school): _____ (A2) 3. First job/first entrepreneurial experience: _____ (A3) 4. College years (whether or not you went to college): _____ (A4) 5. Early career (first few full-time jobs, or start-ups you began): _____ (A5)	Angry · Joyful · Trusting · Fearful · Surprised · Sadness · Disgusted · Loved · Loss · Interesting · Optimism · Serenity · Acceptance · Submissive · Apprehensive · Awestruck · Distracted · Disapproval · Pensiveness · Remorseful · Bored · Contemptuous · Annoyed · Aggressiveness · Ecstatic · Admiration · Terrified · Amazement · Grief · Loathing · Rage · Resilience · Authentic · Faith · Grace · Beauty · Loyal · Wealthy · Abundance · Familial · Hopeful · Truthful · Complicity · Humorous · Introspective · Secretive

Here are some other direct questions. Please write specific examples that come to mind in the right column.

Question prompts	Provide specific examples
6. What people made a significant impact on your life (significant other, mentor, family, business partner, etc.)?	A6:
7. What are some of the most challenging moments you have experienced in your life (refer to your Exposure Résumé for ideas)?	A7:

WORKSHEET

8. What do you currently do for work? List your skills, responsibilities, talents, specialties, expertise, etc.	A8:
9. What do you do for fun (hobbies, activities, sports, etc.)?	A9:

Step 2. Build your Custom Interview Questionnaire.

Using your answers from Step 1 (A1–A9), fill in the following blanks for each of the nine questions (Q1–Q9) below. This will form the interview questions for someone else to ask you (if you are doing this alone, ask yourself these questions).

Note that the story and emotional ranking boxes below each question are to be filled in by the interviewer when he or she interviews you and should remain blank during this step.

Also note that it is very important that the interviewer say the words "question one," "question two," "question three," . . . *before each question*. You will be using a search function in later steps to find certain areas in the document. If your interviewer does not say these exact words, you will not be able to easily search for your specific answers.

Custom Interview Questionnaire

Q1. Question one. Can you share three stories from early childhood that make you remember this time as feeling (A1)_____? Title your stories.

Rank the stories according to which you (the interviewer) felt was the most interesting or compelling.	Circle the emotion that you (the interviewer) felt the most when you heard the story.
Story 1: _____ _____ (Circle rank) 1st 2nd 3rd	empathy · compassion · support · happy · rooting for them · love · excitement · surprise · anticipation · fear · sadness · disgust · offended · off-putting
Story 2: _____ _____ (Circle rank) 1st 2nd 3rd	empathy · compassion · support · happy · rooting for them · love · excitement · surprise · anticipation · fear · sadness · disgust · offended · off-putting
Story 3: _____ _____ (Circle rank) 1st 2nd 3rd	empathy · compassion · support · happy · rooting for them · love · excitement · surprise · anticipation · fear · sadness · disgust · offended · off-putting

Q2. Question two. Can you share three stories from your youth that make you remember this time as feeling (A2)_____? Title your stories.

Rank the stories according to which you (the interviewer) felt was the most interesting or compelling.	Circle the emotion that you (the interviewer) felt the most when you heard the story.
Story 1: _____ _____ (Circle rank) 1st 2nd 3rd	empathy · compassion · support · happy · rooting for them · love · excitement · surprise · anticipation · fear · sadness · disgust · offended · off-putting
Story 2: _____ _____ (Circle rank) 1st 2nd 3rd	empathy · compassion · support · happy · rooting for them · love · excitement · surprise · anticipation · fear · sadness · disgust · offended · off-putting
Story 3: _____ _____ (Circle rank) 1st 2nd 3rd	empathy · compassion · support · happy · rooting for them · love · excitement · surprise · anticipation · fear · sadness · disgust · offended · off-putting

WORKSHEET

Q3. Question three. Can you share three stories from your first job, early entrepreneurial experiences, or work that you did but weren't paid for, that make you remember this time as feeling (A3)_____? Title your stories.

Rank the stories according to which you (the interviewer) felt was the most interesting or compelling.	Circle the emotion that you (the interviewer) felt the most when you heard the story.
Story I: _____ _____ (Circle rank) 1st 2nd 3rd	empathy · compassion · support · happy · rooting for them · love · excitement · surprise · anticipation · fear · sadness · disgust · offended · off-putting
Story 2: _____ _____ (Circle rank) 1st 2nd 3rd	empathy · compassion · support · happy · rooting for them · love · excitement · surprise · anticipation · fear · sadness · disgust · offended · off-putting
Story 3: _____ _____ (Circle rank) 1st 2nd 3rd	empathy · compassion · support · happy · rooting for them · love · excitement · surprise · anticipation · fear · sadness · disgust · offended · off-putting

Q4. Question four. Can you share three stories from your college years (or when you were around 18–25) that make you remember this time as feeling (A4)_____? Title your stories.

Rank the stories according to which you (the interviewer) felt was the most interesting or compelling.	Circle the emotion that you (the interviewer) felt the most when you heard the story.
Story I: _____ _____ (Circle rank) 1st 2nd 3rd	empathy · compassion · support · happy · rooting for them · love · excitement · surprise · anticipation · fear · sadness · disgust · offended · off-putting
Story 2: _____ _____ (Circle rank) 1st 2nd 3rd	empathy · compassion · support · happy · rooting for them · love · excitement · surprise · anticipation · fear · sadness · disgust · offended · off-putting
Story 3: _____ _____ (Circle rank) 1st 2nd 3rd	empathy · compassion · support · happy · rooting for them · love · excitement · surprise · anticipation · fear · sadness · disgust · offended · off-putting

Q5. Question five. Can you share three stories from some of your first experiences working full-time, or from early start-up experiences, that make you remember this time as feeling (A5)_____? Title your stories.

Rank the stories according to which you (the interviewer) felt was the most interesting or compelling.	Circle the emotion that you (the interviewer) felt the most when you heard the story.
Story 1: _____ _____ (Circle rank) 1st 2nd 3rd	empathy · compassion · support · happy · rooting for them · love · excitement · surprise · anticipation · fear · sadness · disgust · offended · off-putting
Story 2: _____ _____ (Circle rank) 1st 2nd 3rd	empathy · compassion · support · happy · rooting for them · love · excitement · surprise · anticipation · fear · sadness · disgust · offended · off-putting
Story 3: _____ _____ (Circle rank) 1st 2nd 3rd	empathy · compassion · support · happy · rooting for them · love · excitement · surprise · anticipation · fear · sadness · disgust · offended · off-putting

Q6. Question six. Out of these people (A6) _____, which three people had the most significant impact on your life? Please share a story for each that showcases the real-world impact on who you have become today. Go into detail, making sure to explain your feelings, emotions, thoughts, challenges, successes, and long-lasting lessons learned. Title your stories.

Rank the stories according to which you (the interviewer) felt was the most interesting or compelling.	Circle the emotion that you (the interviewer) felt the most when you heard the story.
Story 1: _____ _____ (Circle rank) 1st 2nd 3rd	empathy · compassion · support · happy · rooting for them · love · excitement · surprise · anticipation · fear · sadness · disgust · offended · off-putting
Story 2: _____ _____ (Circle rank) 1st 2nd 3rd	empathy · compassion · support · happy · rooting for them · love · excitement · surprise · anticipation · fear · sadness · disgust · offended · off-putting

WORKSHEET

	empathy · compassion · support · happy · rooting for them · love · excitement · surprise · anticipation · fear · sadness · disgust · offended · off-putting
Story 3: _____ _____ (Circle rank) 1st 2nd 3rd	

Q7. Question seven. Life throws curveballs, like when (A7) _____ happened. Of these challenging moments, which three events had the most significant impact on your life? For each one, please share a separate, more in-depth story of what actually happened, how you felt, how you worked through it, what lessons you learned, and how you are stronger because of going through those events. Remember to be candid, and don't hold back. You can always edit later, and you can trust that I will hold all that you share in strict confidence. Title your stories.

Rank the stories according to which you (the interviewer) felt was the most interesting or compelling.	Circle the emotion that you (the interviewer) felt the most when you heard the story.
Story 1: _____ _____ (Circle rank) 1st 2nd 3rd	empathy · compassion · support · happy · rooting for them · love · excitement · surprise · anticipation · fear · sadness · disgust · offended · off-putting
Story 2: _____ _____ (Circle rank) 1st 2nd 3rd	empathy · compassion · support · happy · rooting for them · love · excitement · surprise · anticipation · fear · sadness · disgust · offended · off-putting
Story 3: _____ _____ (Circle rank) 1st 2nd 3rd	empathy · compassion · support · happy · rooting for them · love · excitement · surprise · anticipation · fear · sadness · disgust · offended · off-putting

Q8. Question eight. So, for work, I see that you do a lot and have many skills, including (A8) _____. Of all these, what are the three things about work that you love the most, that give you the most fulfillment, and that you are best at doing? Give some stories of how you help people, how you solve problems, or how your expertise manifests itself in real life. Paint the picture of how you work with people and what your passions are in your current career path. Title your stories.

Rank the stories according to which you (the interviewer) felt was the most interesting or compelling.	Circle the emotion that you (the interviewer) felt the most when you heard the story.
Story I: _____ _____ (Circle rank) 1st 2nd 3rd	empathy · compassion · support · happy · rooting for them · love · excitement · surprise · anticipation · fear · sadness · disgust · offended · off-putting
Story 2: _____ _____ (Circle rank) 1st 2nd 3rd	empathy · compassion · support · happy · rooting for them · love · excitement · surprise · anticipation · fear · sadness · disgust · offended · off-putting
Story 3: _____ _____ (Circle rank) 1st 2nd 3rd	empathy · compassion · support · happy · rooting for them · love · excitement · surprise · anticipation · fear · sadness · disgust · offended · off-putting

Q9. Question nine. Of these things (A9) _____, which three are your most favorite hobbies or activities? Share a specific story for each, making sure to explain why you love it so much. Give details on how you were exposed to it, how it makes you feel when you do it, and how it has impacted you to become the person you are today. Title your stories.

Rank the stories according to which you (the interviewer) felt was the most interesting or compelling.	Circle the emotion that you (the interviewer) felt the most when you heard the story.
Story I: _____ _____ (Circle rank) 1st 2nd 3rd	empathy · compassion · support · happy · rooting for them · love · excitement · surprise · anticipation · fear · sadness · disgust · offended · off-putting
Story 2: _____ _____ (Circle rank) 1st 2nd 3rd	empathy · compassion · support · happy · rooting for them · love · excitement · surprise · anticipation · fear · sadness · disgust · offended · off-putting
Story 3: _____ _____ (Circle rank) 1st 2nd 3rd	empathy · compassion · support · happy · rooting for them · love · excitement · surprise · anticipation · fear · sadness · disgust · offended · off-putting

WORKSHEET

Step 3. Conduct your Life Story Interview.

Best option: Find a friend to interview you and record the conversation. When we onboard new clients, we talk on the phone with them over a recorded line and ask them specific questions to tease out the best stories from childhood, youth, and their college years. In addition, we have them tell us about their jobs, their love life, and their values and struggles, and about how they got to where they are today.

Ask a friend to interview you by using the exact questions presented in Step 2. Instruct your friend to rank your three stories from 1st (being best) to 3rd in the space provided below each question, in regard to how interesting the stories are to them. Then ask your friend to circle the emotion that represents how he or she felt for each story you shared. You will use these rankings to determine which stories to include in your bio.

Tips to make the most of your interview:

If you have a friend interview you:

- Print out the questions and evaluation boxes or get a digital copy (**ditchtheact.com/resources**) for the interviewer. Your friend will need this in order to rank your stories and identify which emotion relates to which story during your interview.
- Find a quiet and private place to talk, and record the answers on your phone or an audio-recording device.
- If doing the interview over a web-based platform (e.g., Skype, Zoom, Google Hangouts), make sure both you and your interviewer are in a private and quiet location, and remember to record the conversation.

If you are interviewing yourself:

- Find a private and quiet location, and answer the questions presented in Step 2; then rank the stories and identify emotions for each.
- Don't forget to record your answers on your phone or a recording device.

And to repeat this point because it is so important. The interviewer must say the words "question one," "question two," "question three," . . . *before each question*. You will be using a search function in later steps to find certain areas in the document, and you will need these exact words to search for your specific answers.

Step 4. Transcribe the conversation.

Now that you have your interview recorded, you can submit it to a transcription service to turn what you talked about into a text document.

We do not encourage you to read the transcription from beginning to end. As noted later in the chapter, in Step 6, you will be using the search function in the transcription document to jump to specific sections.

Step 5. Organize your stories

You should now have a transcription of your interview. It will be a very long document. Don't read it; just have it open and available. Now open a new document, title it "First Name Last Name Long-Form Bio," and save it. In this new document, write the following with spaces in between so you can fill in responses:

- **Question 1:** Early Life
- **Question 2:** Youth
- **Question 3:** First Job/Entrepreneurial Experience
- **Question 4:** College Years
- **Question 5:** Early Career
- **Question 6:** People Who Inspired Me
- **Question 7:** Challenges
- **Question 8:** Career Now
- **Question 9:** What I Do for Fun

WORKSHEET

Step 6. Pull the best stories together.

Get the filled-out Custom Interview Questionnaire. This should have both story rankings and identified emotions relevant to each story.

Starting with the first question, see which of the three stories you talked about was ranked as 1st by the interviewer. Then go to the transcription document and use the search function in the document.

In the search bar, type "Question one." (***Note:*** Depending on the transcription, the wording may have transcribed as "Question one" or "Question 1," so if one search term doesn't work, try the other.)

The search will take you to where the first question was asked. Scroll down until you find the section where you talked about the story that was identified as the most interesting of your three stories.

Copy the specific story and paste it into your new bio document under the section that corresponds to the question.

Repeat this process for each of the nine questions:

- Review the Custom Interview Questionnaire to determine the most interesting story (according to the ranking) for each question.
- Use the search function to find that section in the transcript and copy it.
- Paste the entire section into your bio document under the section that matches the question.

Step 7. Clean up the text.

You should now have all your top stories pasted into your new bio document. It is time to go through and clean up the text. When your recording is transcribed, there is a good chance that some of the words transcribed will be incorrect. Also, when you talk, you don't always talk in proper sentence structure. Go through each of the stories and edit them so that they are clear, are cohesive, and have a good flow, and remove any unnecessary words so that each story reads well.

Step 8. Make headlines for each section.

Now it is time to go back through the document and rename the headers for each of the sections with something creative that ties into the story for that section.

What your headlines look like now	Examples of personalized headers
Question 1: Early Life	Watching WWF with Grandma
Question 2: Youth	How Hockey Changed My Life
Question 3: First Job/First Entrepreneurial Experience	Picking up Trash at Knott's Berry Farm
Question 4: College Years	Discovering the Value of Real Friends
Question 5: Early Career	From Taking Calls to Selling Cars
Question 6: People Who Supported Me	The Mentor Who Set Me Straight
Question 7: Challenges	Overcoming My Biggest Fear
Question 8: Career Now	Developing an Attitude of Gratitude
Question 9: What I Do for Fun	Smooth Sailing

Step 9. Make (emotional) transitions at the end of each story.

You are doing great, and you are almost there! You have your best stories laid out in chronological order. But you don't want your bio to just be a list of stories. The real magic comes in the lessons learned, the emotions, and the transitions between the stories and how each shaped you to be your unique and awesome self.

In this step, you will go back to each of the sections and write a transitional paragraph at the end of each section, which will be the emotional glue between your stories.

Refer to the filled-out Custom Interview Questionnaire. Look at each story that was identified. What emotion did the interviewer select? Use that as your indicator for what to write for your transition.

Note: Readers of your bio may feel disconnected if the story creates the emotions that lead to disgust, being offended, or a topic that is off-putting. If your top ranked story evoked these emotions from the interviewer, consider talk therapy so a mental health professional can help you reframe how you perceive your story, or move to the second ranked story to include in your bio.

Now go back into your bio document, and at the end of each story (before the headline in the next section), write a paragraph that shares the insights, lessons, feelings, and emotions that you had or others had about each story.

> Based on the emotions that your stories evoke with the interviewer, here are some other words to consider using in your transition paragraphs
>
> Joy · Ecstatic · Familial · Relieved · Introspective · Humorous · Submissive · Bored · Complicit · Apprehensive · Trusting · Truthful · Loyal · Secretive · Serene · Resilient · Loved · Surprised · Beauty · Pensive · Distracted · Fearful · Terrified · Wealthy · Abundant · Optimistic · Faithful · Hopeful · Amazed · Authentic · Accepting · Sadness · Grief · Loathing · Remorseful · Loss · Interested · Angry · Disapproving · Annoyed · Contemptuous · Awestruck · Admiration · Grace

Step 10. Include your call to action.

At the end of your bio, you want to capitalize on the fact that people who have read the whole thing are invested in you. Make it easy for them to get in touch with you. You can do this by putting your email address or phone number at the end of your bio.

You put a lot of hard work into creating this bio, and it is time to help your readers take the next step to connect with you. Decide where and how they should connect, and write it in a direct manner that is clear.

Step 11. Build your intro to showcase your accolades.

Did you notice that during this entire Exposed and Authentic Bio Worksheet, we didn't talk about your accolades? In Q8, you told stories about your talents and passions and why you do what you do, but that is different from your accolades.

It is time to build an intro that will sit at the top of your bio, and you are going to write it in the third person. This will act as if a third party were to introduce you.

The first sentence starts with your name, your job, and your top three accolades.

Examples

(Your Name) _____ is a (what you do for work) _____ that is recognized by _____ (if possible, add links), _____, and the _____.

If you don't have any accolades, it isn't necessary to complete this part of the bio yet. You can include them as you earn them (as explained in Chapter 16), when you are success-stacking.

The next sentence would add to this if you have other accomplishments. If you don't have any other achievements, you can skip this until Chapter 16.

His/her _____ work in (the field of) _____ has been featured in publications ranging from _____ to _____.

The rest of your bio will be written in the first person.

Step 12. Let your personality shine through.

It is time to make your first-person intro that will be below the third-person intro and above your early years story.

Your readers have already gotten what they expect to hear right out of the gate, since you listed what you do and your accolades, but this is where you show them that you are a lot more interesting than your job and accomplishments. It's time to let your personality shine.

First, introduce yourself in a warm, friendly manner. Describe who you are as a person, tell where you live, and give some fun facts about you and those things that matter most to you.

Include something about you that is unique. Some kind of introspection that you have. Consider including a little about your family so people can relate to you. If you have a pet or a passion, or there is something quirky about you, share it here.

Hello! My name is _____, and I'm a(n) _____ at _____. I live in_____ with my wonderful wife/husband, _____, our daughters/sons, and my best friend in the entire world, _____, our golden retriever.

Step 13. Include what you do.

This is the final step! You are almost there! Add in what you do for work and what your responsibilities are or your business is about. Consider adding your findings from the Rapid Reflection Discovery Process Worksheet in Chapter 5. Later you can add your three words from the 3-1-3 Challenge (which you will learn about in the next chapter)!

Once this final piece is in place, your bio should be ready to rock and roll!

The overall structure of your new long-form bio should be as follows:

- Third-person top-level overview of accolades
- First-person introduction sharing your uniqueness and your energy
- Your 3-1-3 Challenge words (to be added after you work through Chapter 10)
- What you do for a living
- Headline for Story 1
- Top Story from Question 1: Early Life
- Transition
- Headline for Story 2
- Top Story from Question 2: Adolescence
- Transition
- Headline for Story 3
- Top Story from Question 3: First Job
- Transition
- Headline for Story 4
- Top Story from Question 4: College Years
- Transition
- Headline for Story 5
- Top Story from Question 5: Early Career
- Transition

- Headline for Story 6
- Top Story from Question 6: People Who Inspired Me
- Transition
- Headline for Story 7
- Top Story from Question 7: Challenges
- Transition
- Headline for Story 8
- Top Story from Question 8: Career Now
- Transition
- Headline for Story 9
- Top Story from Question 9: What I Do for Fun
- Transition
- Call to Action

To see what a successful bio should look like, visit **leonardkim.com/about-leonard-kim** and **ryanfoland.com/about**.

Congratulations! You now have an Exposed and Authentic Bio that makes you uniquely yourself!

Congratulations. In completing the Exposed and Authentic Bio Work-sheet, you have made huge strides in building your intentional personal brand. This is a step that so many people fail to accomplish, and yet you have done it. And this is one of the crucial factors that will separate you from others who are out on the path to greater success in both business and life.

One key thing to remember when you have your Exposed and Authentic Bio is that much like how you are a living, breathing being, your bio is a living, breathing document that continues to evolve and grow. As you progress in your career and attain more success, develop new philos-ophies, and go through new experiences, you will need to have your bio evolve with you. It may be a final document today, but in six months to a year from now, you will need to go back in and refresh your bio to keep it up to date with who you will evolve into becoming.

WHERE DO YOU WANT TO GO?

Now that you have your Exposed and Authentic Bio, you will need to fig-ure out where you want to go with your personal brand. What is the ulti-mate end result? Do you want to get a better job? Create a better relation-ship with your employees? Break into a brand-new industry? Be seen as an expert in your space? Take your business to the seven- or eight-figure mark? You don't have to be crystal clear about exactly where it is that you want to go, but you need a general idea of where you are heading. And as time progresses, that ultimate result can pivot or evolve.

When I first started writing, I only had one intention: to share my experiences with others so they wouldn't make the same mistakes I did. As I started to gain traction, I pivoted and wanted to be seen as a mar-keter in the start-up space. As my brand further progressed, I wanted to be seen as a great writer. Then I pivoted again to become a personal brand-ing expert, as the market kept saying that is what I did best.

Ryan, on the other hand, had a clear idea of what he wanted to do from the get-go. He wanted to get paid to speak around the world. That was his top goal, and to this day, it is still his biggest priority. Because his vision of what he wants is clear, he is able to progress much further than if he didn't have a strategy laid out. The pivots within his goal of speaking changed just minimally, to make them more congruent with our business. To align our goals together, Ryan went from being seen as a master communicator, to us holding personal branding and professional recognition workshops at large companies across the world.

Other examples of people ditching the act and landing in their dream roles include:

1. **Hai:** Hai started his career hopping around to various industries, with a job doing fund-raising for nonprofits, roles in recruiting, desk jobs in the real estate industry, his own company, and eventually a transition that included a year in construction—a job that he landed through an introduction from his girlfriend. He worked under the table, then progressed to freelance writing, and bounced around into a few other careers. When Hai decided to figure out what he wanted to do with his career, he stopped himself from taking the first opportunity that came his way, then eventually landed a job at UCI and began working with start-ups. Hai was happy with that career choice for a while, until he became stagnant in his role. After two years of self-reflection and hitting the breaking point of being overworked, underpaid, and underappreciated, he came to the realization that he needed to switch roles, and he is much happier with the position he is in now at UCI as a marketing strategist.

2. **Michael:** Michael has taken his company through a few transitions. He went from holding events with famous speakers, to ghostwriting for successful executives, to running courses on learning how to learn. Throughout each transition, Michael kept his personal brand intact as a well-respected writer who thoroughly researches each concept he shares. By focusing on a blockbuster content model of spending around 40 to 50 hours on each piece of content he creates, Michael has been able to attract the attention of the masses in whatever project he plans to do, while sifting through the noise.

3. **Winnie:** Winnie's pivots were more internal, relating to the way she shared. Coming from an Asian household, she found it dif-

ficult to open up and share her true personality, as it is frowned upon in the Asian American culture. Yet she pushed herself to be open about her personal life, even though her parents couldn't understand what she was doing. Winnie slowly opened up more and more, until the members of her community started to treat her like she was their best friend. And even though her parents didn't understand what she was doing, it was okay, because she felt good, proud, and comfortable with what she was doing.

4. **Iman:** With degrees in biochemistry and biomedical engineering, Iman thought she would spend her entire career in the world of sciences. Yet after spending five years in the industry, she felt she needed a change. Iman spent a lot of time going to pageants while at school and during her career in the sciences, and as a result, she was named Miss New York US in 2015. She also launched a podcast called *Entrepreneurs En Vogue*, and in November 2016, she founded SWAAY Media. The pivots in her life didn't stop when she became an entrepreneur; as her company has changed directions for growth, she has pivoted a few more times. Through all the pivots, she stayed true to who she is, and not what the market wanted from her.

5. **Aaron:** Aaron graduated from university, earned his master of divinity degree, and—after two years in full-time ministry—he transitioned into academics as a communications instructor and college faculty member. At the same time, he opened up his content marketing business (IconiContent) and began pitching his writing to major publications. After landing features in multiple places and building strong relationships, in late 2017 Aaron became editor in chief at Shopify Plus—a multibillion dollar e-commerce technology company.

6. **Pansy:** Pansy made a few career shifts, from working in sales, to working in marketing, to becoming a product manager. Through her career in corporate America, she worked at companies such as Microsoft, IBM, Deloitte, RL Solutions, Intuit, and Maple Leaf Sports and Entertainment Partnership. As Pansy was working through her career, she got tired of marketing

because she had no control over what went into the product, so she shifted roles and went into the product side of the business. As she pushed to change the culture of a company she worked for to transform its reactive culture into a proactive one, she began being promoted, and she was scouted by other companies offering higher promotions, which she took advantage of. Most recently, she holds a position of director of product and design.

How do you figure out where you want to go? You will want to complete the Personal Brand Positioning and Strategy Worksheet below. The more detailed and comprehensive you can be when filling it out, the better your overall results will be once you jump-start your personal branding efforts.

Personal Branding Positioning and Strategy Worksheet

This worksheet will help you flesh out your goals to create your positioning and overall brand strategy. Do your best to fill out the information, and keep the worksheet as a reference guide for later.

WHERE YOU ARE TODAY

Where do you stand now?

What do you currently do for a living, and how much experience do you have?

I am a(n) _____ (a writer, a graphic designer, a technology executive, a chef, etc.) with _____ years of experience in my field of _____ (industry). Through my work experience, I learned _____ (skill 1), _____ (skill 2), and _____ (skill 3).

How many promotions have you received?

In my career, I have been promoted _____ (number of times).

What is your degree (if you have one), and where did you earn it?

I have earned a(n) _____ (degree) from _____ (school).

In what ways does your degree relate to your work experience, or is what you do irrelevant to what you learned in college?

_____ (school, work, growing up in the ghetto) has taught me invaluable skills I use on a regular basis at work, which include _____ (skill 1), _____ (skill 2), _____ (skill 3).

What are your biggest accomplishments?

My biggest accomplishments in life include _____, _____, and _____.

How many social media followers do you have?

I have _____ (5,000, 10,000, 50,000, 100,000, etc.) social media followers.

WHERE YOU WANT TO GO

Once you know where you stand, clarify where you want to go.

With my _____ years of experience in _____ (industry: technology and leadership, etc.), my goal is to position myself as a leader in the following three categories (IoT, education, travel writing, website design, orthopedic surgery, digital leadership, pizza sales, etc.):

1. _____

2. _____

3. _____

My career goals include the following:

- I want to earn _____ more than I do now.
- I want to break into the _____ industry.
- I want to be known as a(n) _____ (a writer, a graphic designer, a technology executive, a great operations manager, a chef, etc.).
- I want to gain significant social proof and following, reaching an aggregate of _____ (1,000, 5,000, 10,000, 25,000, etc.) social media followers.
- I want to achieve a milestone like _____ (publishing a book, doing a TEDx Talk, being featured in a prominent publication, landing more clients, etc.).
- I want to become a _____ (well-paid speaker, writer for a large media outlet like the *New York Times*, operations manager, executive at my company, CEO of a company like the one I work for, a founder of a $100 million company, etc.).
- I want to surround myself with _____ (type of people).

WORKSHEET

- I want to engage with customers and clients to help create the following (outcomes/deliverables): _____

  _____

  _____

- I want to help consult _____ (ideal customer type).
- I want to get hired as a(n) _____.
- I want to be promoted to _____ (position).
- I want people in my company to know me as _____.
- I want people in my industry to know me as _____.
- I want to be known as _____ (type of expert) of _____ (niche).

COMPETITION

Understanding who the leaders are in your industry is important in figuring out what makes you different and how you can stand out. Who are the leaders in your industry that are doing what you want to do?

The leaders in the market include:

_____

_____

_____

_____

_____

Of the above list, whom do you feel most similar to?

_____

_____

_____

What makes you different from these leaders (characteristic traits, values, ethics, humor, personality, etc.)?

_____

_____

_____

_____

_____

What makes you unique (different levels of experience, special approaches, different mindset, your strategy for solving problems, etc.)?

_____

_____

_____

_____

Why would someone want to follow you or see you as a leader (background as a parent, compassionate team builder, friendly and kind, likes golf, etc.)?

_____

_____

_____

_____

_____

WORKSHEET

SELF-EVALUATION

SWOT ANALYSIS

Instead of thinking how your company compares with other companies, think of yourself and how you compare with other people in your field. What differentiates you from the rest?

Strengths (better communicator, fresh ideas, more compassionate, etc.)

Great _____

Driven _____

Bridging the gaps between _____ and _____

Experienced _____ leader

Strong _____ background

Core values _____

_____

_____

Core ethics _____

_____

_____

Weaknesses (less experience, less visibility, mediocre PowerPoint design skills, etc.)

_____

_____

_____

_____

WORKSHEET

Opportunities (different niche, could build strong community, friendlier and more responsive, speak multiple languages, etc.)

_____

_____

_____

_____

Threats (changes to your industry, negative colleagues at work, being intimidated by others, etc.)

Internal _____

_____

_____

External _____

_____

_____

PRIMARY PLATFORMS

What are the top three platforms you plan to use (Quora, Medium, LinkedIn, Facebook, Twitter, Instagram, etc.)?

l. _____

2. _____

3. _____

WORKSHEET

DEFINING YOUR CORE MESSAGING

These answers will help you define your core messaging.

Where you see yourself in 5 years?

_____

_____

_____

_____

Where you see yourself in 10 years?

_____

_____

_____

_____

In order to get there, you will need to be able to define the topics you can talk about.

Work-related topics you can discuss confidently

_____

_____

_____

_____

Three selected traits from your Rapid Reflection Discovery Process Worksheet

1. _____

2. _____

3. _____

WORKSHEET

WHERE YOU WANT TO BE FEATURED

Part of your success involves sharing your story and/or expertise on different platforms. Which ones do you feel would best propel your career or business?

Targeting outreach

Think of podcasts, radio shows, conferences, trade shows, speaking engagements, and TEDx events related to your industry that you could participate in, etc.

_____

_____

_____

_____

_____

_____

Publications and other media that cover the topics you can discuss

Vogue, Cosmopolitan, Forbes, New York Times, Washington Post, Popular Science, Wired, TechCrunch, VIBE, ReadWrite, Newsweek, Better Homes & Gardens, GQ, Influencive, Reader's Digest, CMO, BBC, _Wall Street Journal, Black Enterprise_ magazine, _Inc._ magazine, _Interesting Engineering, Fast Company, SWAAY, Business Insider, USA Today, Bloomberg,_ Reuters, CNET, NPR, _Los Angeles Times,_ PopSugar, _The Atlantic,_ CNBC, etc.

_____

_____

_____

_____

_____

_____

WORKSHEET

Congratulations on completing the Personal Brand Positioning and Strategy Worksheet! You now have another essential tool in your arsenal that will give you clarity to ensure you stay on the right track when building your personal brand. You might not be able to see the end result yet, nor how you will get there, but you will refer to this worksheet through the rest of the book and beyond to get to your desired result. Much like how your bio is a living, breathing document, your Personal Brand Positioning and Strategy Worksheet is a living, breathing document that will also continue to grow.

If you haven't filled out the Personal Brand Positioning and Strategy Worksheet yet, we implore you to go back and fill it out, as the most successful people in the world create business plans for success. The only way you will achieve success is if you have completed your business plan, or Personal Brand Positioning and Strategy Worksheet, for your own career or business success.

DO WHAT IS...

IMPORTANT (TO YOU)

CHAPTER 10

STEP TWO: DISCOVER WHAT MAKES YOU STAND OUT

In sixth grade, I was standing on the top of a ladder with a staple gun in one hand and a string of Christmas lights in the other when something happened that changed my life forever.

No, I didn't fall off the ladder, nor did I staple myself, or electrocute myself either. What did happen was that I was asked a question by my neighbor, Mrs. Kowaguchi. She said in her elderly voice, "Ryan, I have a problem that I need help solving."

RYAN SPEAKING

"Sure, Mrs. Kawaguchi," I replied, from the top of the ladder, eager to help.

"The problem is that I can't put up my Christmas lights," she answered.

Without much thought, I responded by saying, "Yes, of course I'll help you solve that problem," Then quickly added, "But it will cost $20 an hour."

She looked at me with a big smile and said, "Deal, you can start tomorrow."

For me, that was my eureka moment that started my holiday light-hanging business, and it was the beginning of my ongoing journey as an entrepreneur. A journey where, over any other business model or philosophy, I focused on being a great problem solver first.

Do you know why people want to hire or support you? There is usually a clear reason why they want to become your client, lead their organization, work for you, or see you make a mark in your industry. Aside from their needing to know, like, and trust you, they also want to know that you can solve a problem that they have.

Enter the 3-1-3® Method, a process of discovery with a specific formula that you can follow. It is Step Two of the Expose Yourself Process, and it will help you figure out the problem you are best suited to solve.

I have spoken across the world, teaching thousands upon thousands of people how to harness the power of the 3-1-3 Method, which you are about to learn. Once people go through the 3-1-3 Method, they usually are able to see their business life through a whole new lens. When they implement the 3-1-3 Method in their life, they begin seeing that they are increasing conversions, landing more clients, and building relationships with more people who are vested in helping their business.

An example of someone whose business was transformed after he discovered the 3-1-3 Method is Dan Bennett, formerly a professional videographer who really struggled with how to show what made him unique and differentiate himself from other digital agency owners, who could have essentially said that they did the same thing as he did. Before Dan and I worked together, he was under the impression that it was best to outline all the different things he was great at doing, like video production, digital design, media creation, and web development. After working through the 3-1-3 Method, Dan realized the power of communicating the core problem that he was solving, which was that organizations don't do well when it comes to storytelling. Once Dan was able to incorporate this component into how he communicated what he did, he began landing more clients and with less effort, and he saved a lot of time by painting a clear picture of what he did for the exact market he catered to.

What the 3-1-3 Method does is to outline the problem you are best suited to solve, your solution to the problem, and your target market who has that problem. You will be able to explain what you do in as little as three sentences, one sentence, or even three words. Hence the name, 3-1-3. The 3-1-3 Challenge Worksheet next will take you through the process. To help you with this challenge, refer to the worksheets you have already completed.

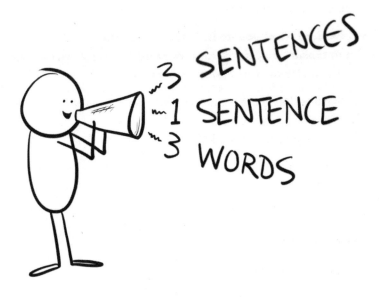

The 3-1-3 Challenge Worksheet

Use the 3-1-3® Method to explain who you are
in three sentences, one sentence,
or even as few as three words.

Most people struggle with answering the question "What do you do?" The 3-1-3 Challenge can help. Give it a try!

Step 1. Explain what you do in three sentences.

In order to explain what you do in three sentences, see if you can come up with a sentence for each of these questions:

1. What is the problem you solve (without saying what you do)?
2. What is your solution?
3. Who is your target market?

Before you jump right into it, look through these Mad Libs–esque examples of how different types of people might approach this first step of the 3-1-3.

Employee Example

A middle manager at a bank who has direct reports

1. **The problem that you solve (P).** Define the exact problem. ***Example:*** The problem is that when people don't have _____ (systems to follow, motivation, clear direction, effective leaders to look up to, etc.) at work, they end up _____ (miserable, unproductive, quitting, wasting time, burning through revenue, etc.).

2. **The solution to the problem (S).** Define the exact solution. ***Example:*** I create small-group workshops in _____ (developing systems, inspirational leadership, change management, improving processes, etc.), keeping my direct reports _____ (happy, productive, excited, career driven, etc.).

WORKSHEET

3. **The market that you cater to (M).** Define the exact market. *Example:* The target market consists of the direct reports in my department who find themselves _____ (unsatisfied, unhappy, unproductive, wanting to leave, etc.) and in need of strong _____ (leadership, systems, training, etc.) to help them achieve their highest potential.

Executive Example

CEO of an international shipping company

1. **The problem that you solve (P).** Define the exact problem. *Example:* The biggest problem faced by people who ship internationally is _____ (poor tracking, no accountability, markups by middlemen, etc.) causing _____ (millions in lost revenue, lack of visibility, etc.).

2. **The solution to the problem (S).** Define the exact solution. *Example:* We have built _____ (end-to-end tracking, incentivized reporting, full visibility, blockchain technology, etc.) keeping our clients _____ (happy, growing, scaling, informed, trusting us as their preferred provider, etc.).

3. **The market that you cater to (M).** Define the exact market. *Example:* The target market is medium-sized businesses that depend on international shipping for _____ (parts, inventory, documents, etc.) that rely on us for the best _____ (rates, reliability, speed, etc.).

Educator Example

Faculty member at a university

1. **The problem that you solve (P).** Define the exact problem. *Example:* The problem is that _____ (students, graduate students, first-gen students, underrepresented students, etc.) who don't feel a personal connection to the subjects they study will _____ (lose interest, drop out, waste their time, waste money, waste their parents' money, etc.).

WORKSHEET

2. **The solution to the problem (S).** Define the exact solution.
   Example: I specialize in _____ (active learning, creative, motivational, AI tech, immersive tech, personalization, strength-finding, etc.) strategies in the classroom to keep the learning _____ (fun, exciting, enjoyable, connected with student goals, etc.).

3. **The market that you cater to (M).** Define the exact market.
   Example: The target market is concerned _____ (students, undergrads, postdocs, graduate students, faculty, administration, stakeholders, etc.) located in _____ (specific location), who want to improve _____ (graduation rates, real learning, student success, enjoyment, etc.) and have a _____ (vested interest, ability, funding, passion, etc.) for modernization of education so that more _____ (underserved, low-income, talented, first-gen, etc.) students can find passion and success in their educational experiences.

Now you try. Identify and explain the problem you solve in one sentence:

The problem is:

_____

_____

_____

_____

WORKSHEET

Not so easy, right? Many people simply cannot state the problem that they solve when put on the spot. We challenge you to try again by answering the following questions:

I. What is the problem that you solve (without saying what you do)? Define the exact problem in one sentence.

   Employee Example: The problem is that when people don't have clear direction at work, they end up hurting the bottom line, due to unproductivity and wasted time.

   Executive Example: The biggest problem faced by people who ship internationally is incorrect tracking that causes millions in lost revenue and lost products.

   Educator Example: The problem is that undergraduate students who don't feel a personal connection to the subjects they study can become easily disengaged, ultimately increasing their chances of ending up on academic probation or dropping out.

Tips

- Only highlight one problem.
- Explain the pain in the problem.
- Don't mention your solution (seriously).
- Use specific language and get to the point.

The problem is:

_____

_____

_____

_____

Now read over what you wrote. Does your problem sound like one that is so severe, it needs to be solved immediately?
No? Try again!

WORKSHEET

The problem is:

_____

_____

_____

_____

Does it now? If not, share your problem statement with others, see what they think, and keep trying until you have something you're happy with.

2. What is your solution? Identify and explain your solution in one sentence.

Employee example: I specialize in developing and improving upon workflows that ensure my direct reports are increasing their productivity by 10 percent each quarter.

Executive example: We have built an open source network that provides transparency, specifically for international shipping, that keeps fees low and our clients informed through the entire process.

Educator example: I bring real-world experiences into the classroom through artificial intelligence technology, specifically to improve graduation rates among students on academic probation.

Tips

- It's okay to not explain your entire solution; think "tip of the iceberg."
- Be sure to just explain the "what," not the "how."
- Does your solution solve the problem you identified earlier?
- Is it a clear solution that is easy to understand?

Now you try!
    Define the exact solution.

The solution is:

_____

_____

_____

_____

    Having a hard time trying to fit it all into one sentence?
    Notice how the solution statements above are focused on the "what" and not the "how"? It leaves just enough information for creating a bit of curiosity within the listener. Your sentence should do the same. It should be packaged in a concise way that gives a clear idea of what you do, while creating a bit of mystery.
    Try again!

The solution is:

_____

_____

_____

_____

    Not happy with it? Keep trying until you find something you're happy with. Share with your friends and see what they think, or try it out and see what kind of reactions you get; then continue to tweak it.

WORKSHEET

3. Who or what is your target market? Identify and explain your target market in one sentence.

Employee example: The target market consists of underperforming direct reports in my sales department who need help in learning how to achieve their target quarterly productivity measures.

Executive example: The target market is medium-sized businesses that specialize in manufacturing in the United States that depend on international shipping for parts and that rely on us for the best rates and detailed tracking of packages.

Educator example: The target market is made up of first-generation freshman students at the University of California, Irvine, who have been put on academic probation and are in threat of being expelled for low performance in coursework.

Now you try!

Tips

- Don't use the words "anyone" or "everyone."
- Get granular with who your target is.
- Include details like location, psychographics, income, and other key identifiers.

The target market is:

_____

_____

_____

_____

WORKSHEET

Now go back to your sentence. Can you get any more specific? Can you add more elements that narrow it down?

If you are still having a hard time with this, look at your existing employers, customers, or the people who regularly read and like or comment on your content.

Try it again!

The target market is:

_____

_____

_____

_____

Congratulations, you have your three sentences, which consist of your problem, solution, and market: 1, 2, 3! Now it is time for Step 2, where we condense the three sentences to one sentence!

Step 2. Explain what you do in one sentence.
Now that you have your three sentences down, can you combine them into one sentence that incorporates all the elements together?

Here is an example of three elements in one sentence in the order of solution, market, problem (SMP) using the analogy of a manager.

(S) I create the strong training systems for (M) employees in my department who have low productivity and strong resistance to change (P) so that they don't get fired.

Now it is your turn to take your three sentences, extract the core elements (problem, solution, market), and try to write them out in all the six variations.

PSM: (P) The problem is this, and (S) I solve it by doing this for (M) these people.

_____

_____

_____

_____

PMS: (P) I solve this problem for (M) these people, and (S) here is how I do it.

_____

_____

_____

_____

MPS: (M) These people (P) have this problem, and (S) this is how I solve it.

_____

_____

_____

_____

MSP: (M) These people need (S) my solution of this to solve (P) this problem.

_____

_____

_____

_____

SMP: (S) My solution is this for (M) these people who (P) have this problem.

_____

_____

_____

_____

SPM: (S) My solution is this, which solves (P) this problem that (M) these people have.

_____

_____

_____

_____

We're happy you completed the second step of the 3-1-3 Challenge. Good job!

Now you have six different one-sentence explanations of what you do, all in one sentence! When people ask you what you do, you can have an intriguing response for them.

Step 3. Explain what you do in three words.

The final step of the 3-1-3 Challenge is to take two things that nearly everyone could relate to and combine them together, creating an analogy or metaphor that people can quickly grasp. One element relates to you and the other element to what you do.

This is _not_ a tagline.

It's designed so people can easily picture what you do in terms of other things that they understand using their own imagination.

WORKSHEET

Here are some examples of the first element, which should relate to you, your personality, how you work, etc.:

Professions
- Blacksmith
- Carpenter
- Craftsworker
- Sensei

Famous people
- Jimmy Kimmel
- Oprah
- Constance Wu

Cartoon characters
- Charlie Brown
- Curious George
- Fairy Godmother

Fictional characters
- Superwoman
- Lara Croft
- Ted Mosby from *How I Met Your Mother*

The second element will relate to your type of profession, industry, or expertise.

By taking the two familiar elements and combining them, people will naturally try to figure out the relationship in their head, and they will get insights about who you really are as a person in addition to what you do.

Next are examples of descriptions using this metaphor method. Can you guess which one goes with which industry?

a. Jimmy Kimmel of Podcasting	_____ Mortgage lender
b. Blacksmith of Branding	_____ Machinist
c. Mei Lin of Vegans	_____ Accountant
d. The Charlie Brown of Blogging	_____ Banker
e. Energizer Bunny of Bookkeeping	_____ Customer service
f. Queen of Home Finance	_____ Paralegal
g. Robin Hood of Hollywood	_____ Teacher
h. Wonder Woman of Depositions	_____ Web designer
i. Ted Mosby of Finance	_____ Podcast host
j. Cardiologist of Websites	_____ Veterinarian
k. Rachel Zane of Law	_____ Sous chef
l. Han Solo of Filing Paperwork	_____ Office administrator
m. MacGyver of Coding	_____ Marketing manager
n. Banksy of Photoshop	_____ Writer
o. Lara Croft of Lab Experiments	_____ Recruiter
p. Composer of Strategy	_____ Lawyer
q. Air Traffic Controller of Complaints	_____ Independent film maker
r. Head Coach of Student Success	_____ Videographer
s. Broker of Talent	_____ Risk manager
t. Pianist of Metals	_____ Programmer
u. Referee of Risk	_____ Director of operations
v. Doctor meets Pet Lover	_____ Scientist
w. Sensei of Storytelling	_____ Graphic designer

WORKSHEET

The minimum number of words to accomplish this is three: one element (that portrays you), a relational term, and the second element (that portrays what you do). If the elements you are using are multiple words, then the three words could become five or six words total. Don't get stuck on the number of words. The idea is to create a metaphor for what you do, leveraging what people already know.

How do you come up with the elements to *relate* to each other? Here are some tips to come up with the first element:

Think of a famous person that you are like: _____

Think of a cartoon character that you are like: _____

If you were a car, what type of car would you be? _____

If you were a hotel, what type of hotel would you be? _____

If you were a fictional movie character, who would you be? _____

Now think about *what you do*—your answers will be the second element of your metaphor/analogy that represents what you do.

What can describe what you do in one word?_____

What is the one thing you do best? _____

What business are you in? _____

What is your specific expertise? _____

What is your best talent? _____

What is your industry? _____

Now combine the first and second elements together. Mix and match, have fun, and get creative with it.

(thing/person/car/cartoon, etc.) + (relational term) +
(thing you do/business/expertise/talent/industry, etc.)

I am the _____ of _____.

I am the _____ of _____.

I am the _____ of _____.

I am like _____ meets _____.

I am like _____ meets _____.

I am like _____ meets _____.

Think of me as the _____ of _____.

Think of me as the _____ of _____.

Think of me as the _____ of _____.

Do any of them jump out at you? If so, share them with friends and see if your analogy or metaphor describes the essence of you and what you do. Remember, it does not have to be an exact match. It should be enough information for people to get an idea of what you do without your telling them exactly what it is. The fun for them is piecing together the two elements and coming up with their own insight. It's like a puzzle or a game, and our brains love games.

WORKSHEET

APPLYING THE 3-1-3 IN REAL LIFE

Great job completing the 3-1-3 Challenge!

Now you can incorporate your three words into your Exposed and Authentic Bio in Chapter 9, and when people ask you what you do, refer to your three sentences, or your one sentence, or even your three words. You're on your way to success!

Crafting Your Social Media Headlines

Aside from your profile and cover photo, your social media headline is the first thing that people see when they land on your page. Headlines should be short, and they take a bit of creativity to craft in order to entice people to want to get to know you.

It's hard to fit your accolades, what you do, your education, and your personality all into one tiny message, but it's possible.

To create your social media headline:

1. Start with your three-word analogy or metaphor.
2. List the biggest place you have been featured. (If you haven't been featured anywhere, don't worry about it. You can add a hobby or what you do for work.)
3. Use emojis to highlight your interests.
4. Provide a call to action.
5. Make yourself easily accessible by listing your email address.

People care about what you do and your accolades and want you to be humanized.

Tips

- Use "|" instead of "," to separate items because it is easier to read.
- Use emojis to give you a sense of personality.

Here are two examples:

The Geek of Greek cuisine | Top Chef finalist | Featured in Los Angeles Magazine & Zagat | I feed you like family (insert emojis here) Available for catering cook@chef.com

Matchmaker of Homes | LA Realtor serving newlyweds | Featured in The Knot & The Spruce (insert emojis here) I find where you'll spend your lives together ilove@weddings.com

WORKSHEET

Congratulations! You have completed the 3-1-3 Challenge! Now you will be able to use what you came up with in the last section of your bio to ensure that your positioning and your story are compiled together. With your newly made bio, your Personal Brand Positioning and Strategy Worksheet completed, and the three words from the 3-1-3 Challenge incorporated into your bio, you will be able to have a full understanding of the direction you are going.

NAILING DOWN THE STAKES

Now you are ready to get your message out in the world. The question is, how? To begin, add to your digital platforms, like your website, your social media profiles, and the other channels you use to network and create content. It is a good idea to make sure you are getting your message out on multiple platforms. We know people who have built their entire brands on a single platform that no longer exists. Once the platform went out of business, a handful of our friends had to start over from scratch. That is why when you take a look at either my content, Leonard's, or that of many of the other experts featured in this book, you will notice that we don't rely on just one platform, as we have no control over whether algorithms will change, if platforms will evolve into pay-to-play models, or if a platform will unfortunately shut down.

We have learned that the only thing any of us will ever own on the web is our own websites. Your site should be the center of everything. If you are unsure of what domain name to buy, name your website after yourself. If your name isn't available, add in your middle initial or your middle name. If that isn't available, add a prefix or suffix. You need to own your own website and direct people there. On your website, you will be able to include your Exposed and Authentic Bio, design your website to accomplish your goals that were identified on the Personal Brand Positioning and Strategy Worksheet, and add in the findings from the 3-1-3 Challenge.

What if you have a job? You should still build a website, because you might not be in the same position forever. Your website may help you get an internal promotion or find a better position at another company.

What if you have a company? You should still have a website for your personal brand, because people aren't going to care what your business does until they know who you are first. People will need to buy into you and feel as if they have known you their entire life before they ever consider doing business with your company.

Once you have your website set up, work to create your social media accounts on multiple platforms if you haven't already. If you need help with naming, work on making sure the names are as consistent as possible. There are multiple sites that will allow you to check to see if a domain name and a username are available. Pick ones that are consistent through as many platforms as possible.

After you pick a consistent username, you will want to start working on creating content for your primary platform you identified in the Personal Brand Positioning and Strategy Worksheet. We will walk you through the steps to create the content for these platforms in the next chapter.

Understand this: not building your brand is like not backing up your computer or your phone. When it comes time to look for a new job, pivot your business, or start over from scratch, you will have nothing to stand on. On top of that, people may not believe you actually accomplished what you did. When Leonard went from bankrupt start-up to bankrupt start-up over and over, he had one recurring theme in his life. He had to constantly reinvent himself because his entire reputation went up in smoke each time. When I followed down the same path at UCI and thought I was about to lose my job, I had nothing to show for my entire experience either, because nothing I had done was documented.

But if anything were to happen to our careers now, we wouldn't have to start over from scratch. We'd have a leg up on the competition. How does that work? You may have heard someone make outrageous claims that sound untrue. A case in point is when Soulja Boy was interviewed on *The Breakfast Club* and stated that he was the first YouTube rapper, that he started the digital streaming movement, and that he discovered Migos. Humans have been conditioned to question the truth of what they hear, so Soulja Boy told them to look it up and to Google or YouTube it. Whether or not what Soulja Boy said was true, the takeaway is that when you make claims, naturally, people will look up what you say to be true, and if you don't have the proof documented, then you could be called out for your claims as being false. If you don't have documented proof that can back your claims, others may not believe you, just like how many people did not believe Soulja Boy's claims. And if you don't build your digital footprint now, you may not be able to put your foot down and stand on your own accomplishments either.

Once your foundation is firmly established, you will be able to work toward creating a stream of inbound leads and career opportunities. The more authentic you make your bio, the more people will want to reach out to you to become your clients and offer you leadership roles. Often direct messages and emails will lead to your strongest connections, the ones that will move the needle in your life. Whether through a new friendship or a client relationship, your engagement with the world will attract engagement back to yourself. The money and success you are looking for will come in different shapes, in different sizes, and at different times. More often than not, they will start in your inbox. The important thing is to have your foundation set, so you can own your story.

Take a look at how others have reaped the benefits of having a place for people to get to know them without ever meeting them:

- Winnie took herself outside the box of a typical financial advisor and put the true essence of who she is back into her personality.
- Even though Iman is scared to be vulnerable, and has had breakdowns in her room crying by herself, feeling that no one cares whether or not she succeeds, she braves forward and does things how she wants to do them and isn't controlled by the opinions of others.
- Michael shares to bridge the gap between him and the people he shares with, then dives deep into those connections.
- Rahfeal went from sharing his origin story in person, to writing multiple books, being on TV, being in documentaries, and speaking across the world.
- Aaron has positioned himself right in the center of e-commerce and marketing circles and has become an influential voice in the space.

- Dana went from being an overworked event planner, to building schools overseas.
- Mark went from being anxious, feeling depressed, and wanting to end his life, to having a top 100 podcast on iTunes and speaking across the world.

And with the results of the 3-1-3 Challenge giving you a clear idea of the problem you solve, you are one step closer to discovering what makes you stand out. What you're looking for now is well within reach, so let's move onto the next step, where Leonard will discuss how to overcome your fear and start sharing the various parts that make you your whole self!

CHAPTER II

STEP THREE: OVERCOME FEAR AND SHARE

Every Thursday at 1 p.m. PST, I host a radio show on the VoiceAmerica Influencers channel. When I first started my show, I invited guests to come on and share their stories of how they became the absolute best at what they do and achieved success as an influencer in their space. With one particular guest, I asked leading questions to push him to open up about his most vulnerable moments. He mentioned that he got in a lot of trouble as a kid, so I asked him to share what kind of trouble he went through. Instead of diving deep into details, he just scratched the surface and said he had trouble with authority. I asked him to expand upon the topic, but he didn't really provide that great an example and was holding back, so I shared an example from my childhood. After that, I reworded the question so I could dig up more information, but he still resisted. So I continued to push, hoping that he would open up.

LEONARD

Needless to say, it didn't happen. The more I pushed, the more he resisted. It ended up being the boringest radio show I have ever had to host. He didn't overcome his fear and share his true story with me, so I couldn't connect with him at all. And because of that, I wish that I could turn back time to get that hour of my life back. Quite frankly, I wish I had had another guest lined up, so I could have pushed the original guest off the line and spoken to someone else who could have been more intriguing.

After our show was over, he told me that he hadn't relived those moments of his past, growing up, for such a long time. He told me how he was scared to reveal his whole truth and asked if he should've shared those details with me on air. I said, "*Absolutely!* Those details are the foundation of who you are and are what distinguishes you from others, as *your story is what drives true connections.*"

FIGHTING THROUGH FEAR

Fear is a dangerous thing. Much like how this radio show guest resisted opening up, fear has held me back in the past. When I was scared to open up and share the pain and turmoil I went through in my life, it only sent me further and further into a hole—until I ended up getting evicted from my home.

On the contrary, when you share your fears, people connect with you at a much deeper level. Why is that? Lady Gaga said, "Pain is such an equalizer and in a time of catastrophe, we all put our differences aside and we come together because we need each other or we can't survive." Our pain is not our weakness. What we consider our flaws is what makes us unique and relatable. In fact, it truly is the equalizer that allows us to connect at the deepest level possible.

When you pretend that everything in life is okay, you become less relatable—oftentimes not relatable at all. Building a personal brand is not just about differentiating yourself from others—it is about being yourself, your whole self, and knowing who you are.

It's one thing to be scared of sharing. It's another thing to not be sure about what to share. If you have a problem identifying what you should and shouldn't share, we will walk you through Level 1 through Level 4 exposures again in this chapter, through the Overcoming Fear and Sharing Worksheet (presented later in the chapter), which is Step Three of the Expose Yourself Process, that will help you get started.

THE POWER OF YOUR NETWORK

You picked up this book because you want to achieve success. Maybe a goal of yours is to build a massive following in the tens of thousands or even hundreds of thousands of followers. As two people who have substantial followings on multiple platforms throughout social media, Ryan and I can tell you for certain that simply having a following does nothing. Well, it can add to credibility and make you look more reputable on the surface, but it isn't what will help you pay your bills or truly move the needle in life. What will help you pay the bills, move that needle, and achieve the success that you are looking for—whether it is finding a new job, getting a promotion, getting your employees on board with your idea, landing in the C-suite, or building an eight-figure business—is building a network of the right people.

Coincidentally, when you build a network of the right people, you will also grow your social media following at the same time. By building a network of the right people, I was able to take massive leaps in my career to double my income, time and time again (which is probably not as hard as it sounds, since I started at American Honda earning less than $30,000 a year) and then become one of the leading personal branding experts in my space. Ryan's network actively looks out for him and refers him to paid speaking engagements across the country, which propels him even further as a renowned speaker. But we're not the only ones who have been able to reinvent our careers and achieve massive success by having the right network of people. It worked for Winnie, Aaron, Iman, Hai, Michael, Pansy, and the others who have been highlighted through the book as well:

- Being able to connect with people at a human level is what drove Hai to his position as a marketing specialist and is what will lead him into managerial roles in the future.
- Pansy leaped into director positions by exposing her truths to the members of her team and by supporting them when they shared their truths with her.
- Aaron's strong professional and personal relationship with the former editor in chief of Shopify Plus, Tommy Walker, grew into a full-time position there and then led to the opportunity to take over his friend's role when Tommy left. Plus, his willing-

ness to give to others has allowed him to call out for help, and receive it, when he needs it for certain projects.

- Rahfeal's desire to constantly improve the lives of others has helped him create a network that always has his back as he speaks across the globe.
- Even though Michael knew the most successful people in the business world, when he opened up, his network evolved into meeting people like me, his best friend, and many others he can have open and vulnerable conversations with.
- Iman feels that being yourself is the shortcut to make growing a business a little easier, as she has been able to have better connections, fundraise better, create better articles, get more users, and have a more supportive network to help accomplish those goals. She does this by making sure that she responds to all the people who message her and lets them know that their message means something to her.
- Winnie has been able to break through the vanity content that others produce, and drive true relationships that have turned into really good friendships.

STANDING OUT

Building your network digitally allows you to find people all across the world. But if you're too scared to show your whole self, you will end up with a profile that looks like everyone else's, shares the same things everyone else is sharing, and makes you blend in with everyone else too. You won't stick out.

Not sticking out is one thing. But there's an even bigger problem that arises when we try to avoid exposure by spinning or hiding the truth. Most of us avoid revealing these truths with the world because of fear or embarrassment. These could be things that are more serious, such as being in significant trouble or behaving poorly in a past relationship, or they could even be doing dumb things in high school like cheating on a test. They could also be times that you made mistakes in college, like getting too drunk at a party.

If you don't expose these truths, they will eat away at you. And that pain will continue to eat away at you until you can take off the mask, ditch the act, and expose yourself. How deep can that pain be?

In 2018, Ryan received an email from Tom, his biggest bully in school. Tom had a four-year-old daughter who was constantly being bullied, so he looked up solutions for bullying online. He came across some material that Ryan had posted about antibullying; then after reading it, he became remorseful and sent Ryan an email apologizing for all the bullying that he did as a child. That guilt stuck with Tom from his childhood, all the way to his daughter's childhood, until he was able to release it through his apology.

If you are scared of coming clean and exposing your whole truths, you need to understand just how much more damaging it is to have your skeletons be dragged out by others, and we will get further into that later in this chapter. Don't worry. We won't ask you to start sharing your most embarrassing moments out the gate. There are four levels of sharing that you will eventually grow to feel comfortable with. These range from Level 1 to Level 4 exposures.

It's highly recommended to start small. The lower-level exposures allow you the opportunity to get your feet wet at being real and begin to share not only moments of the past, but current vulnerable moments too. We will go over what these moments look like—and when to look out for them—in the Overcoming Fear and Sharing Worksheet below. The *true power* of ditching the act will reveal itself to you when you learn to expose who you are as you experience life in real time. Once you do this, you won't have anything to hide from, and you will drive deep connections with others because you will become more human like them. And as you become better and better at it, you can work your way up to sharing your most vulnerable moments, or Level 4 exposures. Sharing these moments is what will make you stand out to create loyalty, showcasing you as a real human being that is uniquely you. That is the heart and the essence of this book. Over the rest of the Expose Yourself Process, we will lay out exactly how to get to this level where you are truly ditching the act.

Now, take a moment to work through the Overcoming Fear and Sharing Worksheet.

Overcoming Fear and Sharing Worksheet

Before sharing an entire article or full-length video about a huge struggle you faced, start small. Share a Level 1 or Level 2 exposure that is the size of a tweet. As you get in the habit of sharing small things that scare you, you will build the confidence to share bigger, more vulnerable stories that rank higher in the levels of exposure. Simple, everyday mishaps, thoughts, feelings, funny things you see, and dumb things you do can be the start of your journey to overcoming fear and sharing.

DAILY LEVEL 1 EXAMPLES

Consider sharing things like . . .

- A random thought that comes to mind
- The agony of getting up early
- Your thoughts about traffic
- Losing or misplacing something simple
- Issues you are having with your pets
- Drama with small things around the house
- The cleanliness of your car
- Realizing your shirt is on inside out
- A bad hair day
- Technology hiccups that are frustrating
- The annoying parts about going out
- Being lazy and calling yourself out
- Customer service gone wrong—what happened and why you are upset

Here are some examples to get you started:

- Wow, I can't believe I just walked into my shower with my head-phones on!

- I need an apron . . . tired of side pant stains.
- Don't you just hate it when you type in a long password wrong and have to do it again?
- I wanna pop this pimple so bad, but I'm trying to have nice skin.
- I hate when I paint my toenails and then I can't wear my fuzzy socks around the house for hours.
- Do you know that moment when you want to text someone but you don't want to be annoying so you post about it, or is it just me? I guess it's just me.
- Out of butter. Had to make my omelet with margarine.
- Waking up 15 minutes before your alarm goes off on a Monday morning is a cruel form of torture.
- Am I the only one who when traveling feels like the gate is always at the end of the terminal?
- Moved some apps about on my phone and now I can't find anything . . .
- It's a cruel lesson to learn when you've only had three hours sleep and you think you have coffee, but you don't.
- OMG, I can't believe I spilled coffee on myself, again. I'm a total klutz! When's the last time you spilled coffee on yourself?
- Some people think that they can be perfect all the time. But every time I walk out of the house, I bump into my wall. If I'm not perfect and bumping into everything, why do I need to keep living up to society's standards of perfection?
- Have you ever gone to work and realized that you forgot your keyboard that you borrowed from the office at home? I did! And now I have to turn around and go back home to get it. Darn!
- Forgot I had a meeting with a client today and accidentally wore tennis shoes. What should I do?
- Oh my. I was walking and a bug just flew into my eye!
- I need to watch a tutorial on "how to successfully get into a car when carrying a big umbrella."
- So lame. Bought a new iMac, finally set up my desk to use it this last week to hash out the rest of the book, and the keyboard already stopped working.

WORKSHEET

- I am exhausted. What do you do when you are in a desperate need of a recharge?
- Oops! I was at the gym for over an hour before I realized that my shirt was on backward.

DAILY LEVEL 2 EXAMPLES

Level 2 includes interactions you have with others and things you notice about how you feel.

Consider sharing . . .

- An argument you had with someone and how it made you feel
- Embarrassment about missing something important
- Feeling stressed out to where you feel like stopping on a project you need to do
- Your feelings about how you have a looming deadline and you can't seem to get motivated to start
- Your feelings about how you are lonely and have not hung out with close friends in too long
- How you are so annoyed with online dating, highlighting a date gone wrong
- Your frustrations with technology and your outdated phone
- Your feelings about midterms, finals, or other tests that you had to study for, and whether you did well or poorly on them
- The guilt you feel for not finding the time to spend with your kids
- Financial difficulties, and how they are impacting your life and lifestyle
- Mistakes that you made that are costly
- Working relationships gone bad, like someone scamming you
- Losing things that are expensive to replace
- Being nervous about a talk or presentation you have to give
- Your anxiety about a special event of yours or someone close to you

- Disputes or fights with your relatives
- The sadness that comes with watching your parents age

Here are some examples ready to go:

- Just had an argument, and I think we both think we won. But in reality I think we both lost.
- I am so frustrated with my progress, I feel like stopping. What should I do?
- Does anyone else avoid what needs to get done, until the deadline is tomorrow?
- Good friends are hard to find. I keep telling myself that on days like these when I have no one to hang out with.
- I am not sure if I feel more guilty for not being able to spend time with my kids or for posting about it online.
- Budgeting my "eating-out" funds is great in theory, until it is Sunday night and the last thing you want to do is cook.
- Not going to lie. Considering taking a break from social media for a while.
- You pay people to do specific work for you, and they don't do the work. Then they try to disappear on you. What do you do?
- Is it normal to be nervous about attending your own birthday celebration?
- There is nothing more draining than fighting with a sibling (as an adult).
- Am I a bad person for not wanting to go out with my friend on her birthday because I don't feel connected to her right now? Friendships are a struggle for me right now.
- Who else feels like you sometimes just don't have any drive or motivation?
- It is always difficult to forgive people who have done harm to me. Is that normal?
- You never know how a person's absence will affect you until the person has passed. You don't have to be close to people in order to feel their powerful presence or the connection they have with you and others. Life is short, so cherish those close to you.

WORKSHEET

- What do you do when a client doesn't respond to *any* form of communication with you during a project that is ongoing and on a tight deadline as it is . . . Oh, and did I mention that the client is in another country?
- Spent the day going over and over my presentation for Wednesday, and I'm still not sure it's up to standard.

Now you try:

Step 1
Think of something that you are scared of sharing.

Step 2
Write it down in one to three sentences.

Step 3
Share your writing with someone in person and on your digital networks.

Awesome! You made it through the Overcoming Fear and Sharing Worksheet. Now go and share some low-level exposures on your digital accounts with friends, and try to ease into sharing these in the office. Make sure to start small, so you can gather up the courage to get deeper into your more vulnerable moments. You may not be able to jump straight to the deep end immediately, so slowly work your way up to this level.

If you feel that you are too scared to ever share your Level 4 exposures, you may not be the only one. However, not sharing these moments will open you up to be at the whim of the narrative of others. And that narrative can turn quite brutal, if not destructive of your career. See how this played out with Ryan and his Level 4 situation with the Federal Trade Commission.

When I first spoke with Leonard, I never disclosed my encounter with the FTC with him. It wasn't until someone commented on a post of a media feature highlighting me that this information came out. That comment was someone else's narrative of how they interpreted the situation, and the comment was so bad that it almost caused my media feature to be removed by the publication. This wasn't the first time that the FTC issue came to catch me off guard either. When it was brought up at my job, I had to have a heart-to-heart with my boss and my boss's boss, and share my side of the story to plead my case about why I should keep my position. Luckily, my character and actions at the university built a case for why I should stay employed.

These incidents where others were controlling my narrative could have cost me my career. They could have prevented me from keeping my job, let alone becoming a renowned speaker. I got lucky to have employers who listened to my side of the story and saw that the FTC situation was not what defined me. When I fully disclosed what had happened, including the negative impacts it had on my life and how hard the situation was for me, they better understood my passion for helping others avoid making bad decisions that had real consequences. They did not fire me. Instead, they let things play out. I was close to seeing everything I had worked for fall apart because of this skeleton in my closet.

I was lucky in this situation. In most cases like this, I would have lost my job. Yet I was beyond fortunate. Not disclosing and keeping Level 4 exposures private could end up doing the same thing to you, and you may not have the same luck I did. However, if you are in front of the situation before anything even arises, you have the opportunity to control the narrative, instead of letting others control that narrative for you. Hiding your truths is just as bad as lying. And technically, it is lying by omission. You can't truly take off the mask, ditch the act, and expose yourself, until you no longer have any truths that are hidden.

My disclosure gives me demonstrable expertise unique to my personal brand. Even despite the FTC investigation, when I brought light to the issue, I was able to leverage the Level 4 exposure not just for my own benefit, but for the benefit of our company, InfluenceTree, too. When people heard about what I did for a living and researched me further, the FTC issue no longer was a problem in working with others. Instead, it became a part of who I am.

Many people who watch my videos, read my articles, and listen to my podcasts reach out to me. Some ask me for advice and spark up conversations, while others ask to work with me. One of my listeners and also a guest on my podcast, Hadari Oshri, did some research on me after our show. She was intrigued by my story, including the challenges with confidence I faced when being bullied. Hadari opened up about how she was bullied too, and that was a part of the reason she founded her company, to inspire other women like herself to be more confident.

Hadari wanted help in owning her own story and learning to be more honest with the community of women she was helping. And she felt that I could help her accomplish that goal. But she would've never reached out to connect further, had I not been afraid to be my true, authentic self. Hadari became a client of ours at InfluenceTree, and I helped her share the struggles she faced on her path to success, to really connect with her customers. Now she addresses the real issues women face around confidence and positive body image, revealing her own experiences in order to instill confidence in women like herself.

Our relationship didn't stop at the client stage either. We've evolved into becoming good friends. And as our relationship grew, so did Hadari's success. She has increased her reach to a worldwide audience, helping her company expand overseas. She has created the opportunity to work with bigger leaders in the fashion space, and she is invited to speak at industry conferences. By getting real and finding the confidence to share her skeletons, Hadari was able to amplify her own personal brand to a much higher level than she would've if she'd continued to wear her mask.

EXPOSING YOURSELF
BEFORE SOMEONE ELSE DOES

Ryan already took ownership of what happened with the Federal Trade Commission and even included the incident in his bio. When clients came up to us to discuss working together, instead of being appalled by the FTC ordeal, they saw how honest and open Ryan was, and it brought us closer together instead.

How far back can things go that come back to bite you? In 1974, George W. Bush was arrested for driving under the influence of alcohol. In the year 2000, when he was running for president, this information was leaked to the press. Something George Bush did 26 years ago was coming back to haunt him—and the DUI was going straight for his goal to become president and earn his seat in the Oval Office.

In his book *Decision Points*, President Bush (G. W.) looked back at the situation and discussed how much stress this caused not only him and his family, but all the campaigners that supported him throughout his run for president. He also talked about how he almost lost everything just because he didn't get in front of his skeletons in the closet. In hindsight, President Bush wished he had just been forthcoming with this information so it would have been hard to use against him, in the same way that Barack Obama had been forthcoming about his prior use of cocaine.

When Barack Obama admitted to using cocaine in the past, it didn't cause the media people to attack him in a frenzy during his election, like they did President Bush. Instead, people accepted his actions because he was up front about them.

These are two of the most high-profile public figures in the twenty-first century. They both had skeletons in the closet. One got out ahead of it and didn't have to deal with the repercussions. The other almost had his decades of sacrifice for public service, along with his legacy, ruined by one tiny drunk skeleton, driving a car when he shouldn't have—something that many of us may have done when we were younger, whether or not we were caught.

Think about other situations where people weren't forthcoming about their skeletons. What ended up happening to them? And don't just think about public figures either. You could probably picture people who are your friends, family members, or colleagues, who faced blowback by not being forthcoming about something.

Now think of others who have made their skeletons an essential part of who they are. There are many speakers, actors, musicians, business executives, and maybe even colleagues who have taken ownership of all their skeletons and have come out ahead of them. You may have read a story of a convict who reshaped their life after they were released from prison, or a speaker who shares their darkest moments of drug abuse and thoughts of suicide with their audience, and sparks authentic inspiration. One of the greatest examples is Chuck Palahniuk, the author of *Fight Club*, *Choke*, *Survivor*, and other *New York Times* bestselling books that were turned into movies. Chuck was a complete train wreck and still may hold onto a lot of what made him the amazing author he is to this day. After a fight over a sewing machine, his grandmother was murdered by his grandfather, who killed himself soon after. His dad was murdered by his girlfriend's ex-boyfriend. He lost his mother to cancer. He grew up in a trailer home for most of his life, and when he wanted to do drugs and party, he would bring out his alter ego, "Nick." He put all his pent-up anger and rage into *Fight Club*, and it was picked up by a publisher, then turned into a movie, but Chuck still held most of that darkness. That was translated later into more of the books he wrote, more fact than fiction, based on his own experiences. Chuck was so much worse than I was when

I was going through my downward spiral, but he is an international success that is well respected for his craft. That's because he owns his truth—the good, the bad, and the reality of his ugly.

Bad timing is an unlucky factor that can cause a small incident to get out of hand. Cheryl had a client whose past included an incident that would normally not be seen as a big deal, but because of the timing of when the Harvey Weinstein ordeal came to light, it caused a local outrage. Even though it seemed like nothing could be done to give Cheryl's client a chance to survive the situation, the client did. Sometimes, when situations get out of hand, the best tactic is to retreat and not say anything for a while. When the client went dark for a while, the company was able to continue business as usual, and the market forgave the client for the incident.

TAKE CONTROL OF YOUR NARRATIVE

When you expose your failures and your weaknesses, you control your own narrative both now and in the future. But it does so much more than that. In your mess is your message. And that message is what will allow you to connect deeply with the people who read your content; who watch your videos; who meet you in person, follow you on social media, or hear about you from someone else who has been inspired by your true self. You can't let your fears of being judged stop you from sharing who you truly are, or you will end up on the defensive like the people in the examples prior. Instead, you need to understand that your fears are indicators that are screaming out at you, telling you that you have something that will create a deep connection with others. Much like I shared in my TEDx Talk, you need to stop running or freezing up from your fears and, instead, let your fears guide you.

Stop running and hiding from your truth. It's time for you to own it.

Your instinct is screaming out at you, telling you that you need to keep all your skeletons in the closet and take them to the grave with you. That if anyone ever learns of some of the things you did in the past, you will be forced to live with that shame for the rest of your life.

You're not alone in thinking this way. At first, I was scared too of opening up about my life of failures. Dan Raaf was also scared about opening up about his bank robbery. And Ryan had chills run down his spine when it came to opening up about the FTC issue. More than likely, all of this scares you to death too. But that's okay.

Just buy into your fears, and let them guide you—and then share them through stories, which is an essential part of Step Three of the Expose Yourself Process. You can create stories and insights using the Exposure Bank. How do you do that? We will walk you through the steps in the Story Creation Worksheet.

Story Creation Worksheet

Use the ideas and prompts in this worksheet as a template to help spark ideas for stories.

WHAT IS A STORY?

A story can be as simple as a conversation. Think about the last time you were with friends that you haven't seen in a while and they asked you what happened when you went on your last vacation, date, or work assignment. Did you share a story with them?

Stories fall into many categories. As examples, some are personal, some are scary, some are victorious, and some relate to your work. Regardless of what story you tell, stories all have the power to connect with people on an emotional level.

HOW DO YOU DEVELOP NEW STORIES?

Stories are all around us. Some of the most powerful stories are the ones that you have experienced in the past but haven't shared publicly.

If you take a look at your Exposure Bank, you will identify a few stories that may include your skeletons.

You also uncovered 27 different stories during your interview for the Exposed and Authentic Bio Worksheet, and you only shared 9 of them. That means there are 18 left, ready to be told.

You are full of stories. You just need to learn to look for them. When looking for new stories, the simple trick is to look to your past. There are plenty to choose from. Below are some questions that will get you thinking of the various stories of your life.

WORKSHEET

Questions to Spark Stories

If you can't think of any stories off the top of your head, ask yourself one of the following questions and write down the first story that comes into your head. There are a lot of questions, which will help you spark a lot of stories you might not realize you have.

- What did you see as a child that affected your life?
- What did you want to be when you grew up and why?
- What is one thing that your parents did that made you realize they truly loved you?
- Can you describe the first time you got in trouble as a child?
- What was the first embarrassing moment that you can remember?
- What was your most memorable moment in elementary school?
- What was your first day of school like?
- What is a family tradition that your family partook in that other families might think was unusual?
- What was your best memory with your pet growing up?
- Did you ever have a moment where your heart broke due to a situation your pet encountered?
- Did you have siblings, cousins, or other family members that you spent a lot of time with? Were there any heroic stories? Drag-out fights? Moments of pure joy?
- What extracurricular activities did your parents enroll you in, and what were they like?
- What was the most memorable moment you had with a teacher?
- What is the most embarrassing thing that happened to you in the classroom?
- Did you excel at any sports? Perform poorly? What was that like?
- What was the worst moment you can recollect about middle school?
- What did you and your friends begin to do as you experienced puberty?
- What was your first camping trip like?
- What was a memorable adventure with a best friend?

WORKSHEET

- What was the moment that caused you to sit in your car, blasting music as loudly as possible, while bawling your eyes out?
- What were you like in high school, and how does that compare with who you are now? If you changed, what moment defined who you've grown to become?
- What did you do the first time you ditched class?
- If you've experienced a loss of a loved one, what did you feel and how did you handle it?
- How did you get your first car? What do you remember most about your time with it?
- Have you tried any entrepreneurial adventures like setting up a lemonade stand? What was the experience like?
- Did you want to go to college? Did you go? If so, where did you go, and how did you choose your school? Was there any conflict in deciding where to go?
- Why did you pick your major in college? Did you ever feel that you should change paths or that you weren't going to make it?
- What was your best relationship like in college (or high school)?
- What was your worst relationship like in college (or high school)?
- Can you share what the process was like in landing your first job?
- As you were finding your way in life, what curveballs did you encounter that knocked you off track, and how did you deal with them?
- How did you go from graduating college to getting to where you are today?
- What was one thing that you've put all your effort into and tried with all your energy to achieve but failed at?
- How did you meet your significant other or spouse?
- How did you know that your spouse was the one for you?
- What did you learn about yourself when you went through your divorce?
- What do your children or grandchildren mean to you? What is your fondest moment of them growing up?
- What was the most unusual adventure you went on when you traveled?
- What was your worst travel experience like?

- If you could give advice to your younger self, what would it be?
- What inspires you to continually improve and become the best version of you?
- Can you walk us through what your biggest failure to date felt like?
- Can you walk us through what your biggest accomplishment to date felt like?
- When you are not working, what are you likely doing?
- What would people be surprised to learn about you?
- Why do you contribute your time and money to a certain cause? What impact has it made on your life?
- What was the biggest win of your career?
- Why did you have difficulty finding the exact career you wanted to do for the rest of your life?
- What was the most rewarding moment of your life?
- What was the most debilitating moment of your career?
- What was the most rewarding moment of your career?
- What was the most complex problem you had to solve at your job, and how did it make you feel when you achieved it?

THE ESSENTIAL COMPONENTS OF A STORY

Now that you are likely overwhelmed by the amount of stories you can call on, you need to make sure that when you create your stories, you form them in a way that connects with others.

A good story includes the following:

Core components	How it all plays out
WHO was involved?	The characters
WHERE did it take place?	The setting
WHAT happened?	The mood
WHEN did it take place?	The insights
WHY did that happen?	The motivations
HOW did you feel?	Lessons learned

WHAT KIND OF STORY SHOULD YOU START WITH?

This story template will work for any type of story you create. However, since we want you to ditch the act and reveal your true self, you will start with sharing Level 1 exposures, then work your way up to Level 4. As time progresses, you will begin to include both personal and business stories.

Step 1. Set the scene and tease out the details.

Start your story at the beginning. What was the first moment like? Did the memory start with a phone call, or did you bump into someone on the subway? Start there. Then work to re-create the environment, giving background details, like the year, day of the week, time of day, what you first noticed about the person, etc. Stories are made in the details. Laying out the who, what, when, where, why, and how creates context to the story.

Give yourself permission to think. Your memory will do the heavy lifting for you. As long as a question sparks your internal thoughts, the memory will reappear. Try to recollect what you saw, tasted, heard, felt, smelled, and thought. Start to describe the story. Use the question prompts and follow this next template to make sure that you tease out the nitty-gritty details that make your stories come to life!

WHERE I WAS: Questions to ask yourself to set the scene	Who were the key people involved?
	What did the people look like?
	What were they wearing?
	What was their mood like?
	What interactions were happening?
	What were people saying to you?
	Were you nervous, excited, anxious, or confused?

WORKSHEET

Step 2. Uncover the issues.
A good story should expose some sort of conflict or obstacle. You don't have to hit people over the head with it; let the story unfold on its own.

WHAT I SAW: Questions to ask yourself as you begin to share how the conflict starts to emerge	When did things start to go wrong?
	Who was involved?
	Did everyone know there was a conflict?
	Who said what to whom?
	When things were happening, what were you thinking?
	What was the sequential set of events that put this conflict into action?

Step 3. Lead up to the action.
Build your story to a point where a climactic action takes place. This could be a conversation or a turning point; it could be funny, exciting, or intense. This will set your story up for the action.

WHAT HAPPENED: Questions to ask yourself about when things start getting juicy	What is the particular moment that made you realize conflict started?
	Who was taking action?
	What conversation sparked this?
	Was it something that someone said?
	What did that one person do?
	What happened after that?
	How did things actually play out?
	How bad did things get?
	Who was involved, and who stayed out of it?
	What was the sequential set of events?
	What was the reason it all happened?
	Was it intentional?

Step 4. Work through the problems.

Your story is shared from your perspective. You may recall the conflict happening quickly, but it is imperative for you to draw out the details. Share how you felt in the moment, and give your reader a play-by-play of what happened.

WHAT I (AND OTHERS) DID: Questions to ask yourself to uncover how everyone is impacted by what is happening	How does the conflict pan out?
	How are the problems solved?
	How do the people in the story tie up loose ends and bring the conflict to a resolution?
	Who was involved, and how were you tied into the conflict?
	Were you watching, or were you in the middle of it?
	What time was it? Were there time constraints?
	Did you have to leave?
	Did others leave?
	Was the night almost over?
	Was there an urgency to settle the conflict?
	What was the result right after the conflict?
	Did people get angry? Did anyone cry?
	Did anyone get hurt? Did anyone fall in love?
	Was the problem not resolved? Why?

WORKSHEET

Step 5. Close it out.

The end of a story does not need to have a happy ending. It just needs to end. Sometimes, the ending comes with a lesson and an opportunity for growth. Other times, there is no lesson, or the event takes your life on a downward spiral. What matters is that you share the outcome of the conflict. Use dialogue between people and explain how different parties seemed to react in different ways.

HOW IT ENDED: Questions to ask yourself to tease out the learning lessons for you and others and to show how the story has shaped you as a person, in real ways	Was there a big insight?
	What lessons were learned, if any?
	Did it give you a new perspective?
	Did you form a new relationship?
	Did you lose a relationship?
	Do you approach similar situations in a new way?
	What were you feeling? Sad, mad, love, joy, etc. (Refer to the Exposed and Authentic Bio Worksheet for more emotions.)

Take these prompts and pretend you are sharing your story with a friend. But instead of talking to a friend, write your story down, record it on an audio device, make a video, scribble it on a piece of paper, or use a whiteboard to map it out. Share your story as a form of content, like a blog or a video.

Step 6. Name your story.

Now that you have completed your story, what does your story talk about? Take the central idea of your story and name your content accordingly. Headlines for stories should tell the readers what they will get out of the story. Does the story answer a specific question? Or does it provide insight into what to do in a particular situation? Or does it express how you felt after an incident or event? If you need help in figuring out how to title your story, use a tool that tracks how many times articles have been shared, like BuzzSumo, to see what the most popular stories are, and use those as a baseline for how to structure your headlines.

Remember: Details make a story. Your internal conversation and thoughts make your story unique and build a connection with others.

MOVING FORWARD

Congratulations! You now have the makings for your first story! Now you have something you can constantly stare at and be afraid of. But you know what? We will help you get that out into the world in the next chapter. And once you do, that fear will subside, and you will no longer be afraid. Instead, you will be one step closer to becoming who you truly are and taking away the power of anyone who wants to hold what you have done in the past against you.

Don't worry. You won't be off to the races to share Level 4 content immediately. Move slowly and share more and more openly as you grow more comfortable. Do something that scares you a little bit each day, until it no longer scares you. But don't just jump straight into the deep end, or you may end up sinking. The only way to get there is to go inch by inch. In the movie *Any Given Sunday*, Al Pacino's character says, "On this team, we fight for that inch. On this team, we tear ourselves, and everyone around us to pieces for that inch. We claw with our fingernails for that inch. Because we know when we add up all those inches that's going to make the difference between winning and losing, between living and dying." Inches are what will get you to your destination, not leaps of faith or dives into the deep end. So take each story inch by inch.

If the stories are just too hard for you to create right now, take a step back. Maybe you can start by doing a behind-the-scenes concept where everything isn't perfect. You sometimes have to expose yourself to yourself. You can expose yourself in lower ways, even for big things. The most important thing that you have to realize is that you need to just be sharing your stories, whether from the past or from the present.

When Iman first started SWAAY, she wanted to go out there and get investors to move her business forward. She knew it would be hard, but she didn't know just how difficult it would be. From not being taken seriously due to her gender (even though she had a large amount of credibility from her studies and career), to being sexually harassed, she faced frustration after frustration in trying to just get the funding to take her company to the next level. After hearing countless stories of the so-called overnight successes of other entrepreneurs, she knew firsthand that none of it was really true, that founders brushed over their stories and acted as if everything just worked out.

So even though the media has always said great, positive things about her trajectory in the business world, Iman wanted people to know that it hasn't always been easy for her, and sharing her struggles and frustrations evolved into a personal passion for her. Iman believes that before entrepreneurs set off to try to create the next billion-dollar unicorn, they need to know more about the true struggles that come with building a business. And so she pushes herself to be as transparent as possible.

As Iman shared her stories in the truest light possible, she received messages by the droves, through text messages, LinkedIn messages, Facebook, email, and so forth. People found a way to reach out to her to thank her for opening up, and it wasn't just women either. Men who had daughters reached out to thank her for sharing her story and for creating a platform that felt like a safe environment for women to come forward with their stories and share their vulnerabilities.

There were two key results that came from Iman's sharing. It educated men and boys on a lot of the personal struggles that women face, creating authentic, original, and raw conversations. It also made other women feel like they were not alone in the fight or struggle too, and that others feel the same way, which led to Iman creating a community where more women could open up and share their stories.

Iman says, "There is nothing negative that will ever come out of sharing your vulnerability and how you struggled with something. Your voice won't only be heard, but it will be listened to." Many people have reached out to share how things didn't work out the way they planned, or how they almost gave up on their dreams, or how they were so thankful that there was a support system and community that could inspire them to continue down their path toward success.

IF YOU ARE TOO SCARED . . .

Chances are, you are sitting here right now and realizing that you have truths that you do not want to share with the world. You like Ryan and me because we opened up and became vulnerable, but you still don't believe this will work for you.

Your instinct is also telling you that this is all a bunch of baloney and that you can still hide things from your past with no one knowing. In fact, we wouldn't be surprised if right now you wanted to close this book immediately. Don't!

If you're still scared, we understand. You don't need to lead with your fear. If something scares you too much to get out into the world, bury it. But not in the traditional way, in an unassuming spot down by the river. Bury it maybe 3,000 words deep into one of your story posts. Not many people will read that far into a story post anyway, but if it's there, then you're ahead of it, and that skeleton can never be used against you in the future. That's because you controlled your narrative, you told the story from your perspective, and your post is dated in the past, so anyone who tries to spin the truth won't be able to, because you can point back to the post for anyone who may attempt to attack you or your credibility in the future. In other words, you will become immune to the attacks of others.

Now that you've pushed through fear and put out the real you, you are ready for the thing that will make you visible to the people you want to pay attention to you, that will spark interest in who you are, and that will drive true connections that will lead you to ultimately achieving your goals in business and life.

CHAPTER 12

STEP FOUR: FOCUS ON FORM, NOT FORCE

We've focused so much on stories, but with branding and social media now, there is a huge uptick in the number of photos that people are sharing on their digital channels. Leonard told me a story the other day about selfies. I have nothing against them, because I take stage selfies when I'm speaking at an event, and at other times with other people, because it's

IT'S RYAN

fun and easy to do and captures the moment. I've heard of people taking a ridiculous amount of photos to capture the perfect moment, but I feel like it is hyperbole. There's no way that someone could sit around and take 200 selfies to get the perfect image, right? But Leonard's story traumatized me and made me second-guess my selfie-taking skills.

Leonard was invited to an event hosted by Toyota for the release of the Mirai, the company's mainstream fuel cell vehicle. Toyota had hired *Top Chef* winner Mei

Lin to provide a multicourse meal. Leonard invited me, but I wasn't able to go, so he asked his friend Jackie to go with him.

After Jackie called Leonard and told him she was outside to pick him up, Leonard walked up to her Audi and saw that she was taking selfies. Not just one, but multiple. They greeted each other; then when he got into the car, she continued to take more selfies as she drove. At stoplights, the selfie aggression would increase, and Leonard said he thought it was hilarious that someone would be so invested in getting the perfect lighting, angle, and look. After getting halfway to their destination, Leonard started to laugh and poke fun at her for taking so many pictures—pictures that she kept deleting and retaking in order to get the perfect image. So he did what any dork would do; he began taking photos of her taking selfies. Then he posted them on his Facebook page and tagged her.

Jackie laughed about the situation, but she still held her determination to get the perfect selfie. She kept taking pictures the entire trip, and even made Leonard wait in the car for five minutes after they were already there, until she finally got the perfect one. Leonard attests that she took over 100 photos of herself, but it could have been way more.

The scary thing is that what Jackie was doing is not an anomaly. There are people right now obsessively taking nonstop selfies.

Why do people take hundreds of selfies? It's because they want to appear perfect to the outside world. People are compelled to share their perfect image because a fundamental sense of our happiness and well-being is to feel a sense of belonging, and many people fall for the misconception that by looking their very best, they will feel accepted for who they are. But as Mel Schwartz, a licensed clinical social worker and author of *The Possibility Principle*, wrote in an article in *Psychology Today* titled "The Problem with Perfection," "if someone ever could achieve this impossible state of perfection, it's likely that very few people would tolerate him or her. For the perfect individual would be a constant reminder to all others of their shortcomings. Not to mention that they probably wouldn't be much fun to be with." This shows that people feel more disconnected to perfect people, instead of feeling closer. However, this doesn't happen just in the land of selfies. Think about how you try to appear at the office, in a business meeting, in an interview, or even on a date. You portray yourself the way you want to be seen. But does this accurately resemble who you are? It probably doesn't. And long term, playing a part never works. Not in business, not in your personal life.

So what is a better approach? The answer is an *intentional brand*, which happens when what you stand for, or who you are to the world, is who you truly are and what you believe in.

Your intentional brand includes your values and ethics. Do you speak up or stay quiet when someone is being bullied or treated poorly for their race, religion, or gender? Do you stand for equality, or do you deny it? Do you express compassion? Are you caring? How do you value friendship? Do you work toward creating camaraderie? Do you like to lift others up? Do you like encouraging people?

Your intentional brand also includes your goals, visions, passion, and desires. What do you want to accomplish with your life? Where do you see yourself in the future? What do you love doing? What have you always wanted in life? What's still on your bucket list, if you have one?

And your intentional brand also includes how you treat people. Are you humble or cocky? Do you want to spread love for the people in the world? What's your take on equality, diversity, and inclusion? Do you want to connect with others on a truly deeper level?

You may already know the answers to these questions, or you may be discovering them as you read through the chapter. It's important for you to really figure out what you plan on sharing with the world. And you may already have discovered most of this when you completed the Personal Brand Positioning and Strategy Worksheet. But how do you use your intentional brand to connect with others?

It's simple. You do it through content.

Think back to the last time when you shared a story at the bar or when you were having a really personal conversation with your parents. Or maybe it could have been a time when you were in the car crying while telling your friend about a tragedy that happened. It could even be a memory that you cherish, like how your dog first looked at you when you went to adopt her. Content is when you take those memories and translate them into stories.

What you do with this content is Step Four of the Expose Yourself Process: Speak your truth and give your stories an audience by focusing on your content strengths and spending time, effort, and marketing dollars where you see performance. The first thing you do is learn to be you.

WHY SHARING THE TRUTH MATTERS

Most people compartmentalize their life. It's a mistake. If you are at work and feel overwhelmed because of something that happened outside the office that is causing you a lot of stress, it may start to hinder your ability to perform at your best. When you don't share what is really going on, when it comes time for your review, your poor performance could potentially result in your being fired. That's because your boss will be seeing you as just another employee, and not (had you opened up) as an actual human that your boss has a deep connection with.

What if you were to talk to your superior in a different way? What if you were to share how and why you are so overwhelmed? Chances are, your boss will begin to feel empathy for you, start to get a better understanding of your situation, and might pull back some of your workload so you can handle all that's going on in your life. Your boss may even introduce options at work that could help you get back on track, like therapy sessions. If you are a manager and you share your feelings and stressors with your team, you will also be able to create the same type of results with your direct reports.

Pansy Lee supports this idea. In fact, as a leader, she takes the time and effort to go around and ask her employees if something is bothering them, long before it comes time for an annual review. As she inquires about the life of her team members, they open up to her. When they share what is truly going on, her desire is to help them with their family and relationship challenges by listening to them and by offering them support by reducing their workload until they're ready to take a full workload on again. The opposite happens as well. When Pansy finds that people have too big an ego and act as if they are entitled to the lion's share of her time, she doesn't have the same desire to help them overcome their struggles.

Leonard kept telling me that portraying the perfect image was not the right thing to do. But he married someone whose social media feed portrayed the perfect image. I wasn't sure how that happened. In fact I didn't even know it happened until Cyn texted me and asked if Leonard got married. I asked her what she was talking about, and she told me to check Facebook. So I did, and unbeknown to me, he had gotten married. So naturally I tried to figure out who it was that he just married, which turned out to be someone named Angie whom I met once in New York.

After looking through Angie's public profiles, all I could see was that she was happy, doing fun things, and taking selfies with her chihuahua. But was she really that way? According to some texts I received from Leonard, I wasn't so sure. But her social media feed didn't change. And to be frank, there wasn't much engagement on her posts either.

Fast-forward a few months. While Leonard and I have been writing this book, Angie resigned from her job due to an interaction that she had with her boss, a situation that would be classified as a Level 3 exposure. With a little support from Leonard, Angie made the decision to share this Level 3 exposure with others, both in person and digitally. Angie explained what happened to her former colleagues at work over the phone. On Twitter, Angie also wrote, "One of the most difficult things to do is to rediscover your self worth after resigning from a work environment that was filled with intimidation, bullying, and misogyny . . . Will I believe in myself again?" From what I know, this was the first time she ditched the act, and she was floored with the response. It's one thing for Angie to hear both of us talk about the power of exposing ourselves; it's a completely different experience for her to feel what it's like firsthand.

Things got real, real fast. In person, when Angie shared what was really happening, she gained support from those around her and built stronger relationships with the people she had loose connections with. Digitally, Angie's tweet led to 418 likes, 72 retweets, and 75 comments from others who shared how they experienced similar situations and came to support her (which also included help and resources to fix the issue). Her story was then featured in *Refinery29*, all due to that one singular tweet. Angie even showed me a conversation with someone whom she never met before, who was inspired because he was going through the same Level 3 exposure. Even though Leonard has been married to Angie for a while, I never really felt connected to her until I saw her true, authentic self.

These results are real, and it's hard to understand the impact unless you do it yourself. If Angie had kept this to herself and behind the facade that everything was all right, she would've been left without multiple solutions to the situation, without support from others; and worst off, it would've eaten away at her slowly until it came out in the wrong way. Now, instead of being trapped in her own mind feeling helpless, Angie has sparked up the enthusiasm to create content as tweets and as videos, and she continues to connect with others, forming deep relationships with people from across the world.

So how do you act at home? Is it the same as at work? Or when you are on one social platform versus another social platform? Or when you are talking to a close friend versus a friend you're not as close with? Or a colleague at your own work versus a consultant versus one at another company? Or a subordinate versus a superior? What are you sharing with one group that you aren't sharing with another?

Chances are, you are acting differently in every situation. The goal after reading this book should be living a more fluid, congruent life. When you stop compartmentalizing various portions of your life, you will see all your relationships begin to flourish and your career opportunities expand, and you will become attractive to the people who can eventually help you move the needle in your life. This happens both digitally and in real life.

PUTTING YOURSELF OUT INTO THE DIGITAL REALM

Once you are comfortable sharing your stories and the reality of who you are in person, you are ready for posting your stories digitally. Posting digitally will help you grow a brand where people can find you from more than just your inner circle of friends. Or if you are in business and you need to share your solution with more people, you can apply these insights to meet and build real relationships with more people. You do this by creating digital content. In the same way you shared your stories with your colleagues at work, these stories can be translated into:

- Writing
- Audio
- Images
- Live speaking
- Video

How do you pick which type of content to produce? It's simple. Focus on form, not force. What do you do best? Are you a horrible writer, but you are better at speaking in person? Video may be the best option for you. Are you artistic and love to express yourself creatively? Images may work best for you. Do you enjoy writing and sending poems to people like Leonard did when he was in high school and sent poems to girls? Writing may be your best option. You don't have to do all of them. You just need to pick and choose the primary method of delivery that you feel most comfortable with, based on your content strength.

When Leonard first started out, he felt his strongest content strength was writing. So he was then able to identify the key platforms for his personal brand growth. He started out on Quora, which helped distribute his content to a wide audience of users that were interested in the questions he was answering. Later, he moved to include Medium, because of its high ranking on search engines, and then LinkedIn, which allowed him to share his content with a more professional network. Then he made sure to include all his content on his personal blog, which he used not just as security in case another network were to disappear, but as a way to increase his credibility when people came to visit his website. He poured his energy into those platforms, and he ended up creating results that he was surprised at.

Even though I always wanted to do public speaking, I never was able to piece together the idea that I could create my own videos, until much later in my personal branding journey. Some of that was because I was intimidated by technology and because I had the misconception that public speaking is only done from the stage. Since I didn't know that video could be my primary format, I started out writing. Leonard was encouraging me to post on Instagram, but I didn't know what to post. I signed up for an account, and for months, I just watched what other people posted. It wasn't until I met Tony Robbins in Los Angeles at one of his events that he challenged me with finding something simple that I could do each day. That's when it hit me. Stick figures. It was a simple thing to do. So every day I drew a stick figure and posted it on Instagram. These days, stick figures are a big part of my personal brand and something I still do daily. In hindsight, I realize that video would have been the better route for me to start. But doing something now is better than waiting to figure out what to do. Start with something and run with it. Don't get analysis paralysis. Now I regularly do a live video on Facebook, then redistribute that to LinkedIn, Twitter, and YouTube. Once I am finished with sharing my video, I transcribe it, then share the article on LinkedIn, Quora, Medium, and my website, which includes my video as well.

And for a few more examples of others who focused on creating content that they were naturally good at:

- Michael first used Facebook to share his vulnerabilities with his friends, which evolved into running a Facebook group of over 70,000 members and writing on Medium, where his content is syndicated in major media publications like *Time*.
- Rahfeal used books to share his messages, which evolved into running his own publishing platform and opening up distribution to 40,000 locations for his book to be sold around the world.
- Hai wrote, but dreamed of podcasting, and he turned that dream into a reality.
- Winnie runs a weekly tweet chat every Wednesday at 11 a.m. PST that is constantly trending, and she shares videos on Facebook, LinkedIn, Instagram, and Twitter.
- Aaron shares content every other day on LinkedIn and Facebook, as well as multiple times a day on Twitter. Those

social platforms serve as personal connections from which
Aaron promotes his long-form articles that are business related.
- Cheryl shares her insights in Facebook groups and contributes
regularly to *Forbes*.
- Iman enjoys posting through Instagram stories and shares the
content from her site onto Facebook and Instagram.
- Mark shares his podcast and LinkedIn videos every other day.

If you're worried about how much it would cost to create content,
stop. You already have the resources to do video and writing. As long as
you own a computer and a smartphone, you have the capabilities. Creating
a video is as simple as flipping your camera forward toward yourself, and
writing can be done on any computer or smartphone. Just focus on your
strengths and stick to them.

But how do you identify the best platform to be on? We would love
to provide an extensive breakdown for each platform about their benefits
and disadvantages; yet the reality is that algorithms on each platform are
in constant flux and new social media platforms are always being created.
To be successful in sharing who you are digitally, you do not need to focus
on all platforms. You can just focus on one or two. However, to make your
decision, it is important that you take a look at factors such as:

- User base
- Distribution
- Ease of use
- Analytics and reporting systems
- The kind of people on the platform
- Integration with other technologies
- The way content gets disseminated
- The best type of content for each platform
- The time it takes to navigate through the system

For example, if you are a writer, you may want to answer questions
on Quora, because it disseminates your content to people who follow specific topics that are attached to the question that is being asked, which
will increase how many people see it. And if your writing meets a certain
criterion, it could be syndicated in a major media publication. LinkedIn

could promote your video to other executives that you are not connected with directly, through your second- and third-degree connections. And Instagram could disseminate a few of your unique images through its discovery tools: this might happen, for example, when you check into a location or include a highly viewed hashtag in your social introduction.

The most important thing is that you document your story in one of the content formats and then post it on a platform of your choice. If you spread yourself wide at the beginning, you can start to see where you should be spending your time, effort, and marketing dollars, because you will see how each platform performs based on the analytics. These data points will be essential in helping you home in on the primary platform that you want to focus on. Once you start creating content that plays to your strengths, and you select the platforms you want to create on, you can use the following Amplify What Is Working Worksheet to help you gather the information you need to boost your content to your target market.

Amplify What Is Working Worksheet

Run ads to get more exposure
(with high-performing posts).

Have content that is performing well? Make it perform even better. You can run paid ads to get your best content in front of your target audience.

Advertising your content digitally can be intimidating when you don't have the information handy. Follow this worksheet to prepare your ads before you share them.

Step 1. Pick a platform.
This is easy, and you should focus on one platform at a time. First decide which platform you want to consider amplifying your content on.

Step 2. Explore the analytics.
Without looking at the analytics, you should be able to see what content is resonating with your audience, but it is also important to look at the data. Every platform has analytics that you can go through. A quick Google search with the platform you chose in Step 1 will show you the most updated way to access the analytics on that platform. In the analytics, search to find your top post and jot down a quick reference to it.

WORKSHEET

Step 3. Promote/boost.

Different platforms have different names for promoting posts, but they function in a similar fashion. Now that you have your post from Step 2, it is time to answer the following questions to clearly describe your target audience, the audience that you want to get in front of.

How far away (in miles) do you want to target from where you are located? If you are looking for a better job, you may want to use a 15-mile radius. If you are looking for more clients, you may want to use a particular state or an entire country.

Is there a location that isn't near you that you want to target? If so, where specifically? This can be useful if you are going to be at an event or conference and want people to recognize you before you arrive.

Do you want to target males, females, or both? This matters if you run a company that targets a specific gender, for example, if you sell a beard cream.

What specific age range do you want to get your post in front of?

Name interests and hobbies of people you want to see your post. Are you interested in targeting people similar to yourself? If so, you can list your interests. If you want to target certain customers, list their interests.

What are some keywords that come to mind when you think of your ideal audience? Do you want to target people who write for publications and share with them a recent feature about yourself? Or do you want to share with human resource managers a piece of content you created, so you can get in front of new employers?

Do you want to share your ad with people who already follow you? This can help you build more trust with them. Or do you want to try to reach new people? This can help you reach a new audience.

```



```

Step 4. Choose your budget.

Many people think that running ads is expensive, but you can get started for as little as $10 on some platforms!

How much are you willing to spend on the post identified in Step 2 to share it with more people? The more money you spend, the more people will see your post.

```



```

How long do you want to run your ad? Over a couple of days, a week, a month?

```



```

Do you want to set a daily limit, or do you want to set a total limit for the campaign? On some platforms, you can set your campaign to run for as low as $1 a day, so more people constantly see your highest-performing content.

How do you want to pay for the ad? (Debit card, credit card, PayPal, bank account, etc.)

Congrats! Now you are ready to take these answers and provide the platform with all the information needed to promote your best content! If you are curious how the post performs and what type of engagement you get, know that the platform will send you a summary of the data. On the basis of how well the ad does, you can promote it again, or you can go through the steps again, pick a platform, and find another high-performing post to amplify!

As you grow your readership, think of opportunities where you can take the skills you've identified and incorporate them into your normal work. Some opportunities could include writing a blog for the company, sending out an internal email, being a part of a company video, being a guest on podcasts as a representative of your company, speaking on behalf of your company, etc.

What should the balance of your content be when it comes to sharing your personal stories? You still want to include the professional content that you have already been developing, but how much of what you are creating should include your stories?

I personally see work as a big component of my own identity, so I keep my posting ratio at 60 percent business and 40 percent personal. But Leonard keeps pushing me to change that to 60 percent personal and 40 percent business, so I'm slowly heading that way. Leonard, on the other hand, finds his relationships and personal life to be a stronger sense of his identity, so he posts 80 percent personal and 20 percent business.

As for our other friends that we refer to often:

- When looking at Winnie's content, from the surface, it looks like she is entirely business. However, if you look at her interactions with others (which accounts for over 80 percent of the content she produces), they are 100 percent personal.
- Aaron shares three personal posts for every business post.
- Michael has shifted continually between sharing personal and business content and is still looking to find the perfect mix.
- Iman's publication reaches 2 million women a month, and as her audience has grown, she has pulled back on her content production by showing, not telling.
- And Hai spent most of his time sharing the stories of others, but he is getting braver and is beginning to share his own.

Work toward a ratio of sharing personal content that is above 50 percent. I can say that this is not easy to do, but the more personal parts of my life I share, the more results I see. It doesn't matter what exact ratio you choose; just make sure that it works for you. As your intentional brand continues to grow, make sure to secure at least one place you can claim as your own personal space. My personal space lives within nature, on the ocean sailing, looking at clouds, while Leonard makes sure to keep his Facebook profile personal for just his closest friends.

Should you post and share all your stories on social media? No, not necessarily. As I was getting comfortable sharing more and more of my life on various platforms, I ran into a snag. I was so focused on the sharing part, I forgot about the importance of how sharing can be special when it is private, and not for the public eye.

I remember taking a picture of a beautiful flower that I passed by, and my first thought was to text it to Cyn. So I did. Then I thought, what a great picture; I should also tweet it. So I did. But what I didn't realize was that sharing with her, then sharing with a larger audience, took the charm out of sharing this beautiful moment. I could tell that something was bothering her, and after a bit of digging, she explained that when I send her pictures and then she sees them shared online, they feel less special. I didn't even consider that, but it makes total sense. From that point on, I made a point to share parts of my life, stories, pictures, thoughts, insights, ideas, and whatever else is on my mind with her exclusively. And it's fun.

What we share together is special, and I love sending her little messages and pictures to let her know I am thinking about her. She does the same. So make sure as you start to open up your authentic self to a bigger audience, keep some of your sharing just with your loved ones. If there are pictures that I want to share with her privately and with the public, I will ask her if it is okay. She always says it is fine, but I know she appreciates my asking first.

Your life is full of stories. Give them an audience and find the courage to start sharing. It can be as simple as going on your preferred social networks and being you. We're looking forward to hearing about your results!

In the next chapter, we will teach you how to become the camera's best friend—so your content can be seen visually across multiple platforms, and you can feel good about creating it.

CHAPTER 13

STEP FIVE: MAKE EYE CONTACT WITH THE CAMERA

If your goal is to create a real connection with people, they need to see, hear, and understand you. Video is an incredible tool to accomplish this more personal connection. If a picture is worth a thousand words, then a video is worth a million views. When it comes to engagement, video and livestreaming are crucial. People are watching more video than ever, and that is only going to increase with time. Sharing who you are through writing and pictures isn't enough anymore.

MORE FROM

RYAN

Whether you are confident at public speaking or find the idea totally terrifying, we will give you the tools to crush it on stage and in front of the camera. You will learn everything you need to know about how to use video to boost your written content.

WHY VIDEO IS KING

Step Five of our Expose Yourself Process is about learning to extract key concepts to create video content to post within already published pieces. We'll demonstrate how video content creates a personal connection and moves the viewer into a deeper sense of relationship with the creator—you. The magic behind Step Five is found in the process of learning how to publish video to add value to your written content. How many times have you searched for a video to learn more about a topic? The people you are trying to connect with are doing the same thing—which is why you need to understand how to create a personal connection through the video camera lens of your smartphone.

When you read what someone writes, you interpret it from your own perspective. You have the words that the author writes, and if you are like me, you scroll, read, and skim, looking for the good stuff. When you see someone in a video, hear their voice, and watch their mannerisms, you are adding multiple levels of input to help you really "get" what they are trying to say. For content consumers, watching video is easier than reading, and the brain is designed to process these types of visuals in a very particular way. According to a study in the Social Science Research Network titled "Reaching the Visual Learner: Teaching Property Through Art," 65 percent of the population are visual learners. Since more than half the population learn visually and need to see what they are learning, videos are more engaging.

Chris Bryant, who has been creating videos professionally with Empire Studios since 2005 and running his own YouTube channel since 2011, provides his top 10 video tips on how to create engaging video.

Film Production Veteran Chris Bryant's Top 10 Video Tips

1. **Don't get caught up in the gear.** You don't need a high production camera. Your smartphone will suffice, as the picture quality nowadays is to the point where feature films are shot on them.

2. **Natural light is your best friend.** To get the best lighting, face a big window with your camera in front of you. You might be pleasantly surprised at how great the results are.

232

3. **Audio is essential.** Many professionals argue that sound is more important than picture quality. There are many lavaliers that can be used with your phone, or a shotgun mic can be added to your smartphone with a converter.

4. **Reduce echo with moving blankets.** Locations with many hard, flat surfaces can lead to echoes. Moving blankets (or quilts) are an inexpensive way to muffle the unwanted noise.

5. **Don't forget b-roll.** Extra shots can help you tell your story and make your video even more engaging. This could be you walking in a park, another angle of yourself, the exterior location, a closeup of what you are talking about, or all of the above.

6. **Tripods are terrific.** You don't have to get anything fancy; a small desktop model will work in most applications. Stability in your shot will ensure your viewers aren't vomiting from motion sickness.

7. **Be mindful of your background (and yourself).** Make sure your background isn't distracting, and if possible, find somewhere that better tells the story you want to convey. Also take a second glance at your teeth, fuzz on clothes, and hair issues; the last thing you want is a piece of spinach in your teeth ruining your entire video.

8. **Don't overdo it with special effects.** Just because you can add them, doesn't mean you should. Transitions and titles should be simple and not call much attention to themselves.

9. **Done is better than perfect.** When filming for personal purposes, your audience isn't expecting Hollywood-quality video. Get it looking to a point you are comfortable with and get it up onto the web.

10. **Naming conventions.** Once you pick a title, stick to it; changing it later could have a huge negative impact on your search results.

11. **Bonus: Use your analytics to improve.** See what's working and what's not; then tweak future video content for maximum impact. Pay close attention to audience retention (when people end the video), demographics (who is watching), and traffic sources (how the video is found).

I don't run a video production company, and you probably don't either, but the good news is that you don't have to have prior experience to get good at making videos. Don't have any editing skills? No problem. There are software and apps for that. What you first need to do is forget about being anyone other than yourself. Seriously. You don't need to speak like anyone else. Your videos don't need to be fancy. In fact, the more real they are, the better they usually do. Many people see highly produced videos as inauthentic, and they wonder if the person is hiding something. This is why you see so many people just turning on their phone and going live, or filming random thoughts at random times of the day (or night).

WHERE TO FIND YOUR CONTENT

The problem that most people have when it comes to making videos to share is that they don't know what videos to make. This speed bump can turn into a wall, and though you are willing, you may find yourself wanting to make videos for months but never actually doing them. So what should you make videos about? The best route is to make videos based on content that you have already created.

As you start to share your stories and insights through articles, blogs, and even short-form posts on social media, you can piggyback off the work you already put in. You can simply pull out the best ideas and stories and turn them into videos, then add those videos into your posts. The trick is to focus on making the video after you have created the content, not before. Think of making videos for your content as trailers for a movie.

Once you finish writing a story, it will be fresh in your brain. This is the opportune time to create an outline that will serve as a video script. And since you are familiar with the subject matter, you don't need to memorize anything; all you need to do is create an outline that will fit on a sticky note. Then you put that sticky note on your phone, and it is there, handy to act as a guide.

The simple and powerful reality is that you should seek more opportunities to be in videos. But they need not be long videos; they could be

30 seconds, a minute, or 10 minutes. The length is up to your choosing. Videos can be summaries of your longer content, filmed in an organic way, showing your excitement and expertise on the topic covered. The easy part is inserting videos into your written posts. There is a button that you can click on in nearly every single platform, which allows you to embed your video into an article.

CRUSHING IT ON CAMERA

The hard part is getting comfortable and taking the leap to look the camera right in the eye with confidence and, ideally, with a smile. The first step toward building your confidence is to find more opportunities to be on video in general. There may be an opportunity hiding in plain sight. For people with little to no filming experience, a good place to start is at your work. When was the last time that you asked your boss for opportunities to be on camera? Many companies have increased their content marketing efforts and understand the importance of video, so they welcome the idea of making videos with their employees, such as educational entertainment videos that share insights about the trends and topics in the industry, promotional videos that discuss the product or service your company offers, and internal communications videos for training and employee engagement. But not everyone is willing to participate. Is there a project you can propose that includes elements of video? Be creative and think of how videos could help support your current job. Do you have direct reports that you can make training videos for? Could you incorporate video into your next presentation? Remember that you don't need a fancy camera; most smartphones are great for high-quality filming! The best way to get comfortable being on video is simply being on video more often.

Speaking on camera is public speaking. And remember, you are a public speaker by virtue of the fact that you speak in public. So it follows that another good way to practice for being on camera is to practice speaking in public. Oftentimes we find ourselves in groups or committees at work, church, or at our children's schools. These groups typically need leaders who run meetings, form committees, or are in charge of presenting information to the group. Offer to step up in those roles. Most of the time it is a very low pressure environment with small crowds that you can be comfortable with. Over time, you will become a better speaker and presenter, which will translate to confidence in front of the camera.

Another tip to stretch your speaking skills is to be one of the people to ask questions during Q&A. Asking a question is a quick way to stand up to your nerves. This will also help you practice asking better questions. And good question-asking skills come in handy if you end up interviewing someone in one of your videos. Think of your question as a super-quick video. Be concise, be energetic, and find your flow. And when it is all over and you realize that you are still alive, you can sit back down and feel bold.

If you work at a job, you may notice that at the beginning of the week people often ask and talk about how each other's weekends were. It makes for cordial conversation and helps us ease into our workweek. A trick I suggest for people trying to up their speaking skills is to practice what I call information regurgitation. Maybe you watched an intriguing documentary, read a book, saw a live event, or spent a part of your weekend scouring the internet getting lost in topics that interest you. Try to regurgitate interesting information that you learned with your colleagues. Repeating what experts have said, or what you read, gives you great practice of your presentation skills. And this is exactly what Step Five is all about: repackaging your own written content into a high-level video is basically a "watercooler" conversation that touches on all the good bits.

GOING FOR THE JOKE

Boring videos are, well, boring. Using humor in your videos can help to keep them lively and not too serious. I always encourage people to have a pocket joke, so that if someone tells a joke, you can be ready with one of your own to participate. Find a few that you like and be ready to tell them. And when you are outlining your videos to include in your written content, make sure to have an eye out for opportunities to add humor to make you more human. Learn to not take yourself so seriously, and you will find that you will be much more relaxed when you film.

And just as having pocket jokes helps you connect, having pocket stories helps too. You can leverage Level 1 and Level 2 exposure stories from your Exposure Résumé, and keep them handy for conversations with others. The more you practice your stories, the better you will get at telling them. And giving these stories a test drive with friends, family, or coworkers will give you a chance to see how people react to them.

FACING YOUR FEARS

Getting comfortable in creating video content means you have to learn to deal with your nerves. I speak for a living, and I still get nervous every time. It is natural and nothing to be ashamed of. A trick I use when I get nervous is one I learned from Daniel Midson-Short, who has competed at the World Championship of Public Speaking multiple years. The first thing I do is find a private area. Next I imagine my energy as a wave moving inside me, and then I wiggle it all out. Yes, I actually try to shake it out of my body. It looks ridiculous, but it works. I move my arms and legs freely and fast, flailing all around like a terrible dancer doing the worst hokey-pokey ever. I try to roll, stretch, and shake every single part of my body, and by doing so, it gets that nervous energy out! I look like a total flapping fool doing it, but I don't care. It works. Shake out those nerves.

Notice your breathing. There is a very good chance that you do not take full breaths during the day. There is even more of a chance that when you're on stage or on camera and are nervous, you are taking even shallower breaths. You need to breathe. It is very important to oxygenate your body with large, complete breaths that fill your lungs with much-needed oxygen.

BREATHING EXERCISE

Take a deep breath and see what happens with your stomach. I'm guessing that your stomach sucked in as you took the deepest breath possible. This is the incorrect way to breathe deep. When you take large breaths, your stomach needs to expand. It may seem counterintuitive at first, but with practice you can take massive breaths by utilizing your diaphragm muscle and sticking your stomach out as you breathe in deep.

Now it's your turn to try:

1. Breathe in and move your belly out.
2. Breathe out and suck your belly in.
3. Repeat steps as necessary.

CREATING A SCRIPT

Now that you know how to shake the nerves and find creative ways to get your camera skills on point, let's look at how you turn your written content into an outline script that fits on a sticky note stuck on your phone! Take the article or blog that you created and copy it into a new document. Go through it and bold the main takeaways. Then choose the three most valuable nuggets and delete everything else. Why three points? For the same reason there are three bears, three wise men, three little pigs, and three blind mice—people can easily digest three things, not four.

Now think of a real story from your life that could introduce the video. It could be what inspired you to write the article in the first place. It could be an example of the topic in real life. It could be a personal insight or lesson learned. Jot down a word or two at the top of the new document that has the three main points, choosing words that will spark your memory of the story. The power of stories is that they get and hold the audience's attention by appealing to their emotions. The compelling part of any story is how people deal with conflict, so don't be afraid to be human and share a real story.

Next, take the three bullet points you have identified, and reduce them to one or two keywords each. All you need now is a call to action to finish the outline. If this seems simple, it is. Don't overthink it. You have done the work, and now you have transformed your written content into a video outline with an intro story and three main points. There is only one piece left.

Have you ever been listening to a video, and after the person is finished, you really are not sure what they were talking about in the first place? If you've experienced this, chances are the person who was speaking was trying to fit in too many details and did not have a clear takeaway or singular focused message that they wanted to deliver. You want to have people watch your videos and "get it." The audience needs to get a specific takeaway from your video. And that should be the same takeaway in the article or blog that you are adapting into a video script.

Take the keywords to spark your memory for the intro story, three points, and main takeaway; then transfer them onto a Post-it Note. You will notice the space is limited, which is the point. You can now take that Post-it Note and put it on your phone, and you can use that as a guide when you are filming yourself or if you set your phone up with a stand.

GO FOR REAL, NOT PERFECT

The goal is not to memorize, but instead, think of it as preparing and improvising. This way, you will come across more natural. And it is normal to trip over your words, take pauses to think, and mess up a little bit here and there. Forgive your slip-ups. Understand that this will happen to you. When it comes to improving your video skills, look forward, not back. Don't allow yourself to use slip-ups as excuses to give up or stop making videos. These slip-ups make you more human anyway. Keep making videos no matter how badly you thought you did, because each time you make one, you will get better.

Slow down when you talk to the camera. If it feels awkward to you, you're speaking at the right speed. Each of us has a natural pace of speaking—some speak quickly, others more slowly. There is no right or wrong speed; however, as a general rule, you can slow your speaking rate by about 50 percent and still sound normal. The truth is that you're probably speaking a lot faster than you think. Nerves can lead to jumbles of words that make no sense to you or the viewers. With every word you speak slowly, the viewers will be thinking their own thoughts, and the spaces you provide give them time to think.

Know that you will make mistakes when you make a video, but do not apologize (especially if it is a livestream). If the mistake is really bad and you are not live, you could stop and start again. Many people watching won't even realize you made a mistake. If you stop mid-sentence and apologize or draw attention to what you did wrong, you are doing yourself a disservice. Remember that you are human and your audience is human too. It is okay if you mess up, mispronounce a word, stutter, or botch a name. Smile and continue on without drawing attention to the mistakes that you made and your audience may never know.

BODY LANGUAGE

Your body is talking even when you aren't. We don't think about what to do with our hands until we see ourselves on video and realize we are making strange, unnatural, or repetitive gestures all over the place. It's totally okay to have your hands resting at your sides. It feels weird to you, but it doesn't look weird to the viewers. One little trick to making this stance more comfortable is to pinch the middle knuckle of one hand with the index finger and thumb of the other hand. You can use your hands to emphasize a point, but make sure not to overuse gestures. This is especially true for large gestures. If you use a big hand or arm movement, use it sparingly.

I am sure you know that Americans and many others read left to right, and believe it or not, they will read you when you're on video. In fact, they will read you from their left to right, which in reality is your right to left. If you take notice, most talk show hosts are positioned on stage left, which means the left-hand side of the stage when looking toward the audience. The reason for this is calculated. If you were on stage, and had your right shoulder in front of your left when people read your body—their attention and eyes are not held because it literally slips off your left shoulder. If you put your left shoulder slightly in front of your right, your left shoulder will hold the audience's attention (almost like a speed bump). Don't believe me? Look at most actors, stand-up comedians, and television professionals. You will notice that most of them are putting their left shoulder slightly in front of their right, or are sitting at an angle where they are positioned with their right side not as far out as their left.

USE "YOU"

Have you ever listened to presentations or videos and felt like the people speaking were more interested in themselves than the audience?

Regardless of the speakers' experience level, or charisma, or lack thereof, a big reason why the speeches or videos didn't resonate with you has to do with their word choice. It is important to remember that the viewers are there to learn. When making an impactful video, it is important to use the word "you" when referring to the viewers. This makes them feel important and involved and helps them engage through active listening. Instead of saying, "Today I will be talking about . . . ," try saying, "Today you will learn about . . ."

THE POWER OF PAUSE

My fourth TEDx talk explains why great communicators use pauses for impact. Are you a pauser or a pouncer? Don't make the mistake of delivering the information in your video outline script at a blistering pace with no pauses. It is important to learn how to use pauses to create emphasis, transitions, and interest. Using pauses is also valuable when you are interviewing someone, giving a list, or sharing bullet point suggestions. Speaking of pauses, make sure that your whole video is not one big pause. Did you check the audio? Bad audio means bad video. Make sure you are in a quiet space, and it's best to use an external mic that plugs into your phone, or use a headset attached to it. If people can't hear you or the audio is bad, it does not matter how good the content is; they will swipe onward and leave your video in the dust.

HAVE FUN

Making videos can be nerve-racking, but they can also be fun. Be excited for the opportunity to share your story and ideas. And one final tip is to smile big when the video starts. Why? Not only to get you in the mood, but that way, you will have a good thumbnail to select when sharing your videos. If you don't do this, then you will have a ton of wonky mid-sentence faces to choose from.

Follow the above steps and you can be filming videos in no time.

ATTRACT THE CLICKS

Remember this. Because you put a video up, it does not mean that someone will click to watch it. On YouTube in particular, people may search for your video next to other videos on the same topic. One way to make your content more clickable is to design a compelling thumbnail.

Arun Maini, who is also known as Mrwhosetheboss on YouTube and is the United Kingdom's largest tech YouTuber with over 1.8 million subscribers, says, "You need to consider everything from the story you want to tell, to the primary colors of other thumbnails you're likely to compete against."

Arun adds, "On a technical level, pair colors on the opposite side of the color wheel. That is what will make it pop out. Try using purple with yellow, or red with green. The thumbnail should also highlight the positive aspects of the video content. If you are excited about the topic, showcase a frame of you super excited. If you are reviewing a piece of technology, then make it a really big element on the thumbnail. Or, if you are interviewing a well known guest, make them stand out! But it is important to note that there's a fine line between making a thumbnail clickworthy, and deceiving viewers.

"Do not represent something on the thumbnail that is not in your video. At the end of the day, the most important thing, all else being equal, is that if the content is great, your video will be recommended to more people."

One last thing . . . If you feel you can produce video much better than you can write, you can flip the script around. Instead of writing a story and turning it into a video, you can make a video, transcribe it with a transcription service, and then clean up the text. This way, you will have both a video and audio. When you have all your assets, make sure to post them on as many platforms as possible. Remember how I will put my Facebook Live video onto YouTube, LinkedIn, and Twitter, and then embed the video into a written story on Quora, Medium, LinkedIn, and my website? You can do that too, to make sure you take advantage of every platform. You got this! In Chapter 14, we will teach you how to stay on top of the pack.

CHAPTER 14

STEP SIX: BE CONSISTENT WITH CONTENT

Leonard taught me something simple and powerful when I first started building my brand. "The market is perpetually changing, just like my mom's hair," he said. And it is true. Every time I see his mom, she has a new hairdo. And as you start to grow your brand, you must understand that there are always new participants, new competitors who are seeking to claim your space. But if you keep too much focus on what your competitors are doing, you will never be in the lead.

RYAN

In this chapter, you will learn how to stay top of mind with the people who are consuming your content. As a side benefit from staying top of mind, your content will also begin to take on a life of its own so you can stay at the head of the pack. When you are creating content, it's easy to get stuck and confused about what to continually produce, especially when you are making content on the fly. The solution to that is to create a plan where you figure out exactly what to share on each day of the week. Set themes that allow you to have peace of mind when it comes to content development and stay consistent in your content creation habits, and you will propel your content to get more eyeballs as you feed the platform algorithms. In other words, you will be able to stand out from the crowd and create new relationships, while your career and your business continue to propel forward.

KEEP YOUR EYES ON YOUR LANE

The cardinal rule of content is this: don't pay attention to what others are doing. When you pay attention to what others in your space are doing, you will feel like you are being left behind, worried that you aren't getting the same types of results they are, and possibly second-guessing your instincts and following the herd. It is an easy trap to fall into, but if you make it a rule not to pay attention to the competition, you will see results.

The truth is, successful people don't do what others can't do. Successful people do what everyone can do, but not what everyone does. They figure out how much content they can push out comfortably, whether that's one piece of content a week or one a month, and then push themselves to improve upon their output.

That brings us to Step Six of the Expose Yourself Process: nourish streams of content to stay foremost in people's thoughts.

When you share a one-time exposure, it is not enough to drive brand growth and loyalty. If it's a masterpiece, it will make a spark, but it is not enough to keep the attention of your target market. There are countless amounts of people who have created one piece that has resonated with many people, and then stopped. You may have encountered some of these pieces in your life and can recollect them by memory. Others are a distant haze that you will never remember again. Regardless of whether or not you can remember the content that resonated with you, chances are that you can't recollect who created the pieces or what these people are doing now.

In order to get around that, you need to understand that one blockbuster hit isn't enough to make your career. And if you are only making a few pieces of content, it may be quite difficult for you to create a piece of content that will be readily appreciated around the world. The only way to get to this level—and to maintain it—is to keep producing new content that keeps your message fresh.

In order to do this, you first need to pay attention to certain people that you already look up to. Are you on their email list, and do you look for their daily emails? Think about how you interact with their content, and if you are waiting to consume it every time they release something new. Think about what you do when you miss something that they sent you and how you react to that as well, and whether or not you are searching for more content they produce through your search engines and social media networks.

The reason you are so engaged with these people and are looking for the content that they continually produce is because they have built a relationship with you. A relationship in which they will continue to produce content as long as you continue to consume it. You need to do the same thing, so you are constantly in front of the customer's or employer's mind.

That means you need to turn your content creation into a daily routine and habit. If you're thinking that you don't have time to go out there and create content daily, it's okay. It's a normal feeling. And it might even feel a bit overwhelming.

In order to overcome this, first you need to find your baseline. Time how long it takes for you to create one story that is 1,000 words, or four minutes long on video. Whether that's a few hours, a day, a week, or a month, you need to know your baseline. Then, you begin to break your content down to different levels.

After you figure out how long it takes to make content, you need to examine how many different pieces of content you can create out of that single piece, by dissecting it. For example, you could expand your single piece of content into a few social media posts, segment the story into smaller stories to share on social media, or clip the video and share different pieces of it. Then, once you do this, you need to challenge yourself to continually improve your ability to produce stories in less time.

Winnie has a fun formula that keeps her content volume high. She calls it her social media breakfast, lunch, and dinner. She makes sure to do 15 minutes in the morning, 15 minutes in the afternoon, and 15 minutes at night. And much like how Michael spends over 40 hours on a single article, Winnie plans out her pillar content. She does this by clearly defining her activity, like her weekly tweet chat, her daily videos, and her livestreams.

For some people, an easy hack is to look through your Quora feed and then immediately think of answers. Others who can't think of content on the fly may need a Content Calendar that outlines different themes based by day so they can keep on track to hit their daily content output.

Use the Content Calendar Worksheet that follows to start working on creating your own content outline.

Content Calendar Worksheet

*Think through what you will post
and on what platforms.*

Step 1. Pick your themes.

Coming up with story ideas on the fly is hard. To make it easy, come up with themes. These make it simple for you to plan out your content for either the next week, the next month, or the next year. An ideal Content Calendar is filled out with content for five days each week. However, set your own pace with what you are comfortable with.

If you plan to share content Monday through Friday each week, make sure at least two of your posts include stories taken from your Exposure Bank, two posts are derived from positive experiences, and one post is related to your business or career. As you continue to share content, get braver and share higher-level exposures.

Your themes could be related to finance (or lack thereof), personal setback, childhood, relationships, how you were raised, being picked on, feeling stressed out, and many other topics. Reflect upon our stories and check the Exposures Ranked by Level Worksheet to start thinking of more ideas. You can also place stories from your Exposed and Authentic Bio Worksheet into the slots below.

WORKSHEET

Pick and choose a theme for each day of the workweek. As an example, here is what a week might look like:

Monday	Tuesday	Wednesday	Thursday	Friday
Personal story about childhood.	Personal-related exposure (personal setbacks).	Business-related story discussing a unique problem I solved at work.	Personal-related exposure (financial struggles).	Positive story about overcoming a struggle.

Now you can try to practice building out a daily theme for each day of the workweek.

Monday	Tuesday	Wednesday	Thursday	Friday

Step 2. Based on your overarching topic, brainstorm what kind of story you want to share for each workday of the month.

Here is what a full month could look like:

	Monday	Tuesday	Wednesday	Thursday	Friday
Theme	Personal story about childhood.	Personal-related exposure (personal setbacks).	Business-related story discussing a unique problem I solved at work.	Personal-related exposure (financial struggles).	Positive story about overcoming a struggle.
Week 1	The first time grandpa took me out for fast food.	Having difficulty getting a girlfriend for 10 years.	Saving employer $100,000 annually by implementing a new process.	Not being able to afford rent when I was 22.	Standing up to my childhood bully.
Week 2	Getting my first pet.	How I failed my driving test the first time and how it crushed me.	Growing work's revenue stream by identifying new market.	When I bought a car I couldn't afford.	My path to college and how I almost didn't make it.
Week 3	First day of school.	When all my luggage got stolen in Costa Rica.	Launching boot camp across campus with significant attendance.	Being broke and trying to date by planning picnics, but it always rains.	What I learned after 10 years in a committed relationship.
Week 4	Teacher that made an impact.	How I broke my ankle and was bedridden for three months.	Solving a significant problem for client that the client didn't know he had.	When I tried disputing my credit card bill only to find out I spent that much.	Internal battle with depression and how I came out ahead with a new perspective on life.

WORKSHEET

Step 3. Create your own Content Calendar following the overarching theme for each day.

Use a short sentence in each box to spark what the story is about. Use the calendar template below, or a digital calendar, an Excel spreadsheet, or a calendar for your desk or wall.

	Monday	Tuesday	Wednesday	Thursday	Friday
Theme					
Week 1					
Week 2					

Week 3				
Week 4				

Great job! Now you have a Content Calendar. Follow it as closely as possible and repeat each month.

You need to create a content calendar so you can stay top of mind with your audience. With the stories you create, figure out where you can place them in your calendar. Regardless of what platform you are posting your content on, your goal should be creating a consistent stream of engaging content. It's what drives exponential growth. The more you produce for any one particular platform, the more that platform wants to push out your content. And as long as you are following the ditch the act model and exposing your true self, people will continue to engage with your content. The more they engage with you, the more people who will continue to see it. But you only get engagement by sharing what you are scared of.

When Leonard started sharing content daily, the platforms continued to push his content so much, that he was able to take almost a two-year hiatus from writing. In those two years, he wrote a total of only 10 articles. However, since platforms like Quora and Medium saw so much engagement from his content, they continued to push it out to long-tail in another 1 million views, after he stopped writing. Then on top of that, he landed close to 200 media features in one year, when he wasn't even producing content anymore. When I put in the same input, I ended up with a similar output. In the year Leonard landed almost 200 media features, I spoke at three times as many events than the year prior, and three times as many events the year prior to that. That's because once you get the cycle going, it will take on a life of its own, then continue to grow and flourish.

As long as you keep maintaining your content production, this cycle continues to repeat until you end up at the top. And when you do that, you will build more relationships with people who were once far out of your network. If your dream is to one day get to know a *New York Times* bestselling author, someone who gave an amazing TED Talk that you can't stop talking about, a philanthropist who changed the world, or an influential figure that may have shaped your childhood, know this: all these people become within reach once your content starts to rise to the top, and some of these people may even reach out to you.

We've had many, many people reach out to both of us, telling us about an article or a talk by us that impacted their way of thinking, made them see the world in a different way, helped them when they were down and lonely, saved their life, or made them want to meet us and share a beer together. We constantly have people reaching out to us, saying that they saw us in *Forbes*, or came across us on Twitter, or read about us in *Entrepreneur*, stating that they want to hire us for our expertise. And time after time, they pay us to hold workshops at their companies, to work directly on building their personal brands, or to enroll in our courses, and are ready to get to work.

Get ready to put in the work, because when you dive straight in and follow the Expose Yourself Process to the T, you will get the results you are looking for, and more. In the next chapter, we will show you how to translate your content production into deep relationships and new business.

CHAPTER 15

STEP SEVEN: KEEP IT SOCIAL

Brands thrive when they really connect with their customers. After years of being fed cliché messages, consumers want brands that feel authentic, relatable, and driven by a mission. Yet so many brands and experts still play by the old rules and try to exude perfection and surface messaging.

When I wanted to become a renowned speaker, I was taught to try to be the biggest, most amazing person in the room. The person that everyone looks up to and wants to devour knowledge and insights from. The one who doesn't just have everyone's attention, but has their respect. For the longest time, I felt I needed to keep up the facade of being completely together, strong, and bold about what I do. While that image fueled me to drive brand growth to a certain degree, it was also the same limiter that prevented me from moving past this invisible ceiling that I couldn't figure out how to break through.

RYAN

When I asked Leonard about what was keeping me from getting over this hurdle, he asked me a really interesting question—whether I was interacting with the people who were following me. I didn't want to tell him truthfully that I was just clicking "like" on replies to my content and not even checking my DMs, but that was exactly what I was doing. When I did admit it, he explained that my approach was only going to hold me back.

If your desire is to build an engaging personal brand, launch a product, find a new job, land a speaking engagement, or drive more customers to your business, you can't keep preaching from the pedestal. Instead, you need to build a community.

ENGAGING WITH YOUR AUDIENCE

When it comes to building your intentional brand, just posting content and pushing it out there is not enough. You need to take it another step further by keeping it social.

When I asked Leonard about why I was having so much difficulty in outperforming his success, he didn't say it was because he started sooner. In fact, he told me that I do have a clear path to get past where he is. But I needed to put in the effort to get past standing on a pedestal, spreading ideas, and educating others. I needed to engage with my audience too.

I knew how this worked in person. When I would go to a conference or an event, I would seek others out and start conversations with them immediately, then double down into building a deep relationship with them by emailing them regularly, calling them, and meeting them in person. Even thinking of them on holidays and their birthdays. Because I did this, I built a network of many people I could call upon, but I never felt the same way about my digital networks. I wondered if it was possible to get the same types of results with my digital community.

It was a difficult concept for me to grasp, but Leonard showed me how digital connections and in-person connections were actually the exact same thing. When I began to strike up conversations online, the dynamics of my digital relationships changed. Respondents went from just followers to actual people who were a part of a new community that I was making a conscious effort of creating, and more importantly, maintaining.

CREATING A VIRTUAL TRIBE

That brings us to Step Seven of the Expose Yourself Process: fostering camaraderie in new relationships. Camaraderie isn't something that happens overnight. It doesn't just come to you because you respond to someone who is engaging with your content either. Camaraderie is created through building deeper relationships with the people who become a part of your community.

If you've been following the Expose Yourself Process to a T, you will have already posted a story and shared it. And if you haven't, you need to try doing that as soon as possible, because consuming the information within this book without taking action renders what you have learned up to this point useless. This process only works when you do.

Now that your story is out there, there are a few different scenarios of what could happen. People could consume your content, they could like or upvote your content, they could comment on your content, or they could share it with their colleagues. If you've already been receiving engagement from others, then that's great! If you have yet to receive any attention on what you are producing, that is great too. No one is expected to start creating content and receive worldwide attention on the first day. That attention is something that you build up to. And that attention is only created when you begin establishing your relationships.

Relationships are the key to success in your life, no matter what it is that you do. Relationships are what will land you a better job, get you into the C-suite, get customers knocking at your door for your product, and create partnerships that could propel you further in your career. The best way to start these relationships is to give appreciation to get appreciation. When you begin to show appreciation, that is what transforms your content from being a broadcast message promoting only yourself, and evolves it into becoming true engagement.

CHANGING YOUR WORK RELATIONSHIPS

At the University of California, Irvine, my boss, Iain Grainger, meets with each of us, individually, every Tuesday to go over our objectives for the week. He starts each meeting with the normal pleasantries and asks us to share stories of our weekend. The culture that Iain has created is that of trust and support. When the two of us meet, if there is something that is not going right in my life even if it is outside of work, I share it with him. He listens intently and usually has an anecdote or story from his past that he shares with me that helps provide an additional perspective on my situation.

The meetings are a highlight of my week because I know Iain is not there to judge me, and because I know that it is a safe space for me to be me by sharing what is really going on. There are also times when he has things to share about his life outside of work, and I am there to listen and be supportive however I can. Going past the pleasantries and sharing how I really feel and really getting to know him has strengthened our working relationship to the point where I see him not only as a boss, but as a friend.

At Keck Medicine of the University of Southern California, Leonard's boss, Christopher Bazin, holds a similar type of meeting with the entire digital marketing team, once every two weeks. When Leonard first started working at USC, he would ease into his stories with a high-light reel, but after he built comfort with the team, he started sharing how he really felt about his weekends and included the good, the bad, and the ugly. As time progressed, the digital marketing team felt a deep affinity for Leonard and treated him with not just respect, but compassion and empathy as well.

Those relationships that went deeper than surface-level feelings happened because Leonard revealed his whole self to his colleagues. But how do office relationships look for normal people?

The reality is that at work, many people are hiding who they truly are, and oftentimes they simply mirror the sentiments of those around them. Have you noticed that office pleasantries tend to go like this:

BOSS: Good morning, how is everyone doing today?
EMPLOYEE 1: Great, thanks.
EMPLOYEE 2: Very well, thank you.
EMPLOYEE 3: I'm great too. How about you?
BOSS: Great. I'm good. Thanks.
(Awkward silence)

BOSS: Okay then, talk to you later.
EMPLOYEES: Bye!

When conversations stay at surface levels, not much happens, and you won't form real bonds with people. It is amazing how we work in close proximity to people for years, yet sometimes never really get to know them.

STARTING PEER GROUPS

If you want to change the entire culture of your work and bridge the gap between your relationships, start by sharing a low level of exposure. Think of it as making the first move toward stronger work relationships. When it comes to being real with your coworkers, no one wants to make the first move. The problem is that when no one goes first, the conversation never moves past pleasantries. To change the workplace culture, it just needs to start with one person willing to open up past saying that everything is great. The person who lets their guard down and shares that they are not having a good day because of any number of reasons, whether they are personal or work related, opens the conversational door for employees to open up and share the similar challenges they are facing. This then starts to create a real bond from shared experiences.

Consider starting a Ditch the Act (DTA) Peer Group or Party to connect with, bond with, and transform your team. Think of it as a book club that meets a mastermind group. A DTA Peer Group is when you gather a group of people together who have similar interests, to support each other in working through the concepts you are learning in this book on a recurring basis. The difference between a DTA Peer Group and a DTA Party is that the party would be a one-time event.

Surrounding yourself with people who want to start working through the elements and steps in this book will create a safe and supportive way to refine your new skills and build your brand with support. If you are a business owner, consider starting a DTA Peer Group for your employees.

You could invite people from your work, friends, family, or people from the DTA community that you meet online. By organizing events to bring people together in real life, you put yourself in a position to meet new people and practice how you communicate your exposure levels to the world. The group you become a part of could be as few as one or two other people, or you could start your own group and see how large it grows.

The Ditch the Act Peer Group Charter Starter Worksheet will help get you started.

Ditch the Act Peer Group
Charter Starter Worksheet

Organize events that will build your community.

Take the lead and organize a Ditch the Act Peer Group or Party to connect, share, and practice ditching the act. This worksheet will help you get started in six easy steps!

Step 1. Pick a location.

Secure a location to meet. You might meet in a conference room, in a coffee shop, on a digital meeting platform like Zoom, or even in your own home.

Step 2. Decide whom to invite.

Write down a list of people whom you would want to invite to your group. They could be friends, family members, coworkers, or people you have met digitally.

WORKSHEET

WORKSHEET

Step 3. Invite and organize.

Once you know whom you want to invite, the next step is to reach out via email, phone, social media, and/or face-to-face with people in real life. At times, it may be difficult to coordinate schedules between multiple people, so consider using a polling app that helps to determine availability for deciding the best time and day for your group to meet.

Great attendance to your group is achieved by inviting people early and following up with those who are invited. Here are sample scripts that can be modified for a phone call, a text, a direct message, or an in-person conversation.

In person or via phone

> Hi _____ ,
> I hope you are doing well. I wanted to invite you to a group I am forming based on a book I recently read. The nature of the group is informal, and the idea is to get some friends together to meet on a regular basis to practice revealing their whole selves. Are you interested?

Text/DM

> Hi, I am gathering a small group of friends to meet up and work through some concepts from a book I just read and wanted to see if you were interested in joining. The idea is to form a mastermind group where we help each other reveal our whole selves. Would you like to join?

Step 4. Narrow the focus of your group goals.

The great news is that this book can be used as the basis for your individual meetings. Make a list of goals that you want people to be able to achieve as a result of joining and participating in your group.

Step 5. Create your meeting topics.

In each meeting, you should take a deep dive into one of the concepts, activities, and/or worksheets. List which ones you would like to use as the starting point of conversation in your group meetings.

```


```

Step 6. Create your meeting agenda.

Now that you have all the pieces, you just need to put them together into an agenda and send it to the people you invite. Make sure you include the:

- Time
- Location
- Group goals
- Topic(s) to be covered

At the end of the day, whether you form a group in your town, join an international group online, or do neither, forming bonds with people can be as simple as looking for opportunities to make the first move and be real about how you feel. You can do this by sharing lower-level exposures to spark more meaningful conversations. If you start to look for opportunities to ditch the act, they will naturally start to appear.

WORKSHEET

PAY IT FORWARD

There are a few different ways for you to go out there and spark up conversations that lead to camaraderie. When you are out and about, you can do what I did at events—meet others and start conversations with them; then when they give you their business card, actually keep in touch and follow up with them to see how they are doing. If you're browsing through, closely reading, or watching content created by others, you can "like" their content and let them know what you appreciated about what they are doing, or explain how you felt it related to you, and even go as far as sharing the content with your network with an introductory statement of what you took away from the piece. You can also follow people who have similar interests as you or send DMs (direct messages) to others.

When you begin to engage with the content of others, they will begin to feel appreciated for the content that they are producing. They will feel valued, and when people feel valued, they tend to want to get to know who they are talking to. This could potentially motivate them to check you out even further, read your bio, find your content, consume it, and appreciate what you are doing as well. When a person begins to appreciate your content back, you begin to form a bond with the other individual, and that bond lays out the foundation of what could become a deep relationship.

Once people begin to engage with your content, you can send them a message stating that you appreciate their support; you can follow them to show that you aren't looking to preach, but to actually build relationships; and you can respond to their comments to start a conversation. When you begin to truly produce content that is engaging to others, you will begin receiving emails from others and also DMs on the platforms you are creating content on. These DMs could be from people who want to know you at a deeper level, from people who want to work with you, or from people who want to offer you opportunities. It is highly unlikely that you will receive a public comment from someone who wants to hire you for a project or recruit you for a new job. The money, opportunity, and career growth you are looking for are in the DMs, so don't overlook them, because this is where you will begin to actualize your greater success.

If you're a representative of your company and you begin to build deep relationships with the community, the company you work for is able to stand out and shine, instead of being just another company with a product to push. Building those relationships doesn't just help you; it helps the bottom line of your company as well. An infographic on social employee advocacy created by MSL, a public relations group, indicates when sharing brand messages on employees' platforms, there is a 561 percent further reach than on the brand's official channels. Imagine how much more reach your company receives when that content isn't just a brand message, but a humanized message that your customers are seeking.

TAKING IT TO THE NEXT LEVEL

Once you converse with others, don't stop at the surface level by keeping these new contacts at an arm's distance. Your entire livelihood and success depends on these relationships, so take it even further. Figure out how to bring these people into your community by being easily accessible and there to help, or by building support systems where you can all grow together. When you are creating dynamic, responsive relationships, they start to take on a life of their own and continue to grow. This is how you foster camaraderie and is exactly what you need in order to boost your brand's growth.

Is there a template for how this works? In 2013 when Leonard first started using Quora, he was full of curiosity. He wasn't a voracious reader. He wasn't that social. He didn't even have much confidence in himself either. But after discovering the platform and reading content on the site for about a month, Leonard gathered up the courage to write his first post. After he wrote his first post, he received a few upvotes and followed the six or seven people who upvoted him. When people like your content, you should follow them too to show that you acknowledge them.

Leonard then went around the site, reading other pieces of content he felt were insightful and leaving comments on those. He would say things like, "Wow, I can't believe that happened!" or "I never looked at things this way. I'm so glad you shared your perspective because it has changed my outlook too!" or "That was so brave of you to share your story. I'm inspired!" When you encounter content you like, engage with the person who created it. After perusing the site for a month and leaving comments, Leonard drew the attention of a Quora user by the name of Erin Paige Law. Leonard had written and commented about Erin's content. After reading what Leonard wrote, Erin shared it with 1,000 people. That's what propelled Leonard into writing daily.

When Leonard wrote daily, it didn't stop him from reading the content others were creating either. He still continued commenting on content that touched him, and as others commented on his posts, he responded to them as well. When people would upvote Leonard's content, he would show his appreciation by following other users and reading their content, if they had any. If you are receiving acknowledgment from others, show them your appreciation by engaging with their content too.

As Leonard's Quora presence continued to grow, he didn't just receive public comments. His DMs began to fill with people who were sharing their own personal stories and struggles, or asking him for his advice for particular situations. Some people would DM him purely because they wanted to become his friend, while others sought out mentorship. As time progressed, people began DMing Leonard, stating that they wanted to pay him for his services. At the beginning of Leonard's writing career, he read every single message he received, and he responded thoughtfully to each person he spoke with. Because of the influx of inbound requests, he has had to change his process a bit. He still takes the time to read messages, but he segregates people into different areas. For work-related activities, he asks for people to fill out a form prior to DMing so they get filtered to the top of his priority list. For requests from the media, he asks for a specific headline. For requests in general, his highest priority is email, then the social media platforms he is most comfortable with. Leonard won't respond to someone who just messages him and says hi. For others, he chooses to respond on a case-by-case basis. He will look over each DM and respond, or not, depending on how much the message resonates with him.

When people DM you, make sure to read their message and as long as the message is not derogatory, spam, solicitation, or illegible, respond.

That is what led to Leonard fostering camaraderie with James Altucher, a renowned author who inspired Leonard to start writing. And it led to Jason Chen, a former McKinsey consultant who worked in private equity, offering to invest with Leonard in any business he wanted to create. That was also what attracted me, drew me into his life, and became the foundation of our business partnership.

It wasn't all perfect though. Leonard regrets losing a few close friends he made, like Ellen Vrana, who he felt was like a sister, and Dave Cheng, who offered to hire Leonard on the spot if he decided to leave Los Angeles to live in Taiwan. That's because he dropped the ball in nurturing and maintaining these relationships that meant a lot to him, due to his personal insecurities.

If Leonard didn't take the time to go out there and focus on Step Seven of the Expose Yourself Process by investing in his relationships, I highly doubt he would have had the same success he does now. In fact, he might still be working at Honda, earning $16.24 an hour, as opposed to being named a top marketer, year after year. Isn't it a little crazy how relationships are what truly drive people to success, as opposed to what you may have imagined to be the magic formula? But it's the truth.

It's not just Leonard who succeeded with DMs either. Winnie landed eight-figure deals while creating a network of avid supporters; Iman created an entire tribe of people who share their stories and support each other; Hai has friends reconnecting with him that he hasn't spoken with in years; Michael bonded with people who have similar beliefs to his; Mark has had the opportunity to encourage others to go out there and overcome their fears; Aaron's conversations led to people jumping in to support his bigger efforts in a heartbeat; and I've landed multiple speaking engagements and media features and built friendships in the DMs too.

When you invest in your relationships, hold onto them. Give value to them, and they will give value back to you. As long as you continually invest in the people you meet, they will continue to invest back in you. And at the same time, your career will continue to flourish. Now in the next chapter, we will teach you how to stack your successes upon each other to . . . You guessed it, stack more success.

CHAPTER 16

STEP EIGHT: SEQUENTIAL STEPS CREATE SUCCESS

Congratulations! You are at Step Eight of the Expose Yourself Process. You are about to get the final components of a formula that outlines the exact method for building an intentional brand that will reshape your career and life. However, you have to understand one crucial fact that is

RYAN & LEONARD

the key to your success—a large social media following doesn't do nearly as much for your career as you may have assumed it does. A large volume of followers that you don't have connections and ties to means nothing unless they feel connected to you at a human level. On the other hand, a large volume of followers who feel deeply connected to you will help you achieve your goals at a breakneck pace.

WHAT WILL (AND WON'T) DRIVE YOUR SUCCESS

The truth is, having a million followers isn't going to change your life. Being sought out like a celebrity isn't as glamorous as it sounds either. If this is what you are picturing for your future, then you might be out of luck, because it probably won't happen; and even if it does, these results aren't what truly brings you the success you are looking for. What does bring amazing results is the relationships that you create through your platform.

When you view your social media efforts, your writing, your video creation, your imagery, as more than just a number—but as fostering camaraderie—you will create the solid connections you need to move forward. You will build the lasting friendships you are looking for. You will sign on new clients. You will get a better job. You will be promoted at your company. And most importantly, all this happens because you have positioned yourself for career growth in both the job and the business world.

BRING EVERYONE ALONG

Our society has come to the point where people begin relationships with a transactional mindset, thinking what the other person could do for them. Yet so many people see right through that, and that is why so many people have their guard up when making connections with other people. If you know someone who has this mindset, you may feel put off when this person messages you or calls you asking for another favor. Or if you yourself are this way, that could be the reason why others avoid speaking to you.

What if you were to take that expectation away? If you were to expect nothing in return from your relationships and instead you approached your newfound relationships by offering to help others first. Would they be grateful and give back to you? Chances are that they will, tenfold. When you give from the bottom of your heart and with no expectations of something in return, there are no limits to how far you can succeed.

When you begin receiving professional recognition, you won't be growing by yourself; you will be growing together with the people who surround you and your company. Use the attention to bring more success to your job and your business. Sol Orwell, founder of Examine, a company that does independent analysis on supplements and nutrition, embeds an attitude of giving into everything he does. He holds events where he invites people he has both loose and strong connections with to connect over desserts, and he donates the proceeds (well over 400,000 CAD to date) to charity through what he calls his Cookie Offs. On top of that, he gives value each chance he gets, having an insatiable desire to help others either by providing referrals or by responding directly to those who ask for his advice.

Ryan uses every chance he gets to include his employer, the University of California, Irvine, in his media features. In return, UCI shares those accomplishments in its weekly recognition emails to the entire faculty, staff, and students. And sometimes, UCI even shares the good news on its social media platforms too.

As Ryan built relationships with members of the media, he was able to help out more than just himself. When Michael Dennin, the vice provost of teaching and learning at UCI, shared a few insightful thoughts based on his expertise in education with him, Ryan felt that some of those thoughts should be shared with his media contacts and helped Michael grow his intentional brand as well. Don't keep all the success you receive to yourself. Spread it around to help those around you—especially the people you care most about.

#WINNING

When you picked up this book, you may have thought that this was your solution to win at the game of social media, but it's so much more than that. It's your formula to win at all aspects of business and life. Your personal brand stays with you forever. It doesn't matter if you end up at a crossroads in your life and you are thinking of switching careers, or starting a new business, or pursuing your passions; your brand will always follow you until the day that you die. And if you build your intentional brand properly by giving back and contributing to improving society, it will even live long after your death.

In Step One, you established your positioning. In Step Two, you focus on the problem you solve. In Step Three, you exposed your true self. In Step Four, you expanded upon the types of content you create and homed in and focused on what worked the best. In Step Five, you learned how to incorporate video into your content. In Step Six, you built a consistent flow of content to stay on top. In Step Seven, you dove deep into fostering your relationships and keeping things social. And that brings you to adding the last step of the Expose Yourself Process: success stacking.

As long as you stick to doing the first seven steps of the Expose Yourself Process, your content will get consumed. People will connect with you. You will grow a following. You will be given opportunities you may have never even imagined were possible.

You will begin to experience wins—wins that will continually grow to become more and more substantial. At first, someone may start quoting you on their social media platforms. Then someone will reach out to you and ask you for your expertise. Then someone will want to interview you on their personal blog. A publication will syndicate the content you create onto its platform. Podcast hosts will begin to interview you. Trade publications will ask you to share your expertise. You will end up being talked about in major media publications. You might find your name on the list of the top people in your industry. You may find yourself front and center, speaking on a stage, or even being on TV. And who knows, that may even be in another country with a tropical paradise.

But all this only happens when you start success stacking. This is how it works: You get a win; then you use that win to get another win; then you use that new win to get another win. This may sound like it would take years upon years to establish yourself and achieve your goals, but we both did it in a short amount of time. The Success Stacking Worksheet will walk you through the process.

Success Stacking Worksheet

Stack small successes to build bigger successes.

Why do you stack successes?

You stack successes so you can build bigger successes. Once you have the first success, everything else becomes easier.

How do you stack successes?

There are three steps in stacking each success:

1. Find the opportunity.
2. Do the work needed.
3. Share the work you did.

And if you achieve a success that is "bio-worthy," like being featured in a publication, make sure to include the information in the very first section of your bio. Then as you achieve more noteworthy successes and get into higher-level publications, replace the older lower-level accolades in your bio with your new achievements!

Following this format, you can stack your successes on each other to build momentum to achieve bigger and bigger successes. See the Success Stacking chart below to see how the process works:

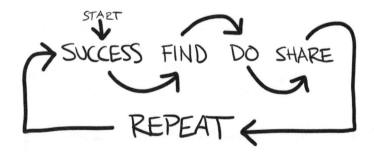

WORKSHEET

Let's look at a realistic example of success stacking when you are just starting out building your brand.

Success 1	Find	Do	Share
Being featured in a blog as a result of reaching out to people you respect and pitching why they should feature you in their blog.	Identify people who would want to interview you based on your experience, contact them, and make your ask.	When you find someone who wants to write about you, prepare and do your best to showcase your expertise.	Share the blog everywhere you can, and get others to like, comment, and share.

Success 2	Find	Do	Share
Becoming a guest on a small podcast.	Identify podcasts that are newer and cater to your target audience. Share your site with them, highlighting stories that performed well.	Land a spot on the podcast and share your story.	Share the podcast episode everywhere you can, and get others to like, comment, and share.

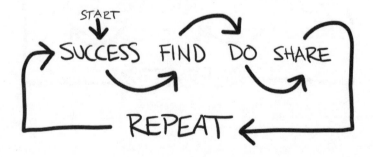

START
SUCCESS FIND DO SHARE
REPEAT

Success 3	Find	Do	Share
Becoming a guest on a medium-level podcast, or a Facebook Live interview, or a radio show.	Identify podcasts that have a mid-range following and that cater to your target audience, sharing your previous podcast with them and highlighting how many times it was shared.	Land a spot on the podcast and share your story.	Share the podcast episode everywhere you can, and get others to like, comment, and share.

Success 4	Find	Do	Share
Getting a media feature in a small publication or industry blog.	Identify and contact writers at desired publications, highlighting previous blog and podcast interviews.	Successfully pitch article ideas and get writers sold on your story.	Share the featured article everywhere you can, and get others to like, comment, and share.

WORKSHEET

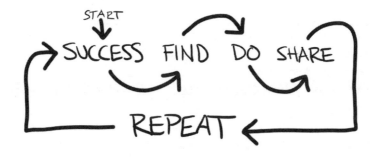

Use this worksheet to identify and track small successes that can lead to bigger ones.

Success 1	Find	Do	Share

Success 2	Find	Do	Share

Success 3	Find	Do	Share

Success 4	Find	Do	Share

Remember: Use your highest accolades (as you earn them) to update your bio as you build your brand!

What are you waiting for? Start small and start stacking those successes!

WHAT SUCCESS STACKING LOOKS LIKE IN REAL LIFE

Leonard's Success Stack

A few months after writing about failing and about all his personal set-backs, before Leonard ever wrote a book or had the massive platform he does today, someone asked Leonard if they could interview him on their blog. A few months later, he was invited as a guest on a podcast called the *QuoraCast*. Right after that, another blogger wrote about him, then another one, and then Leonard began to get a few more interviews on other podcasts. He shared these interviews, then updated his bio to include them. About six months after landing his interview on the *QuoraCast*, James Altucher invited him to be on *Ask Altucher*, the podcast he renamed *The James Altucher Show*. Leonard shared the interview with his network and added it too into his bio.

A few months after being on *The James Altucher Show*, one of the articles Leonard wrote was syndicated by *Inc.* magazine. He then sent the article that he had in *Inc.* to the writer submission email, and because he already had written one article for *Inc.* magazine, he started writing for *Inc.* regularly with his own column. Leonard used his *Inc.* column to land a column in *HuffPost* and *Entrepreneur*. Then as his brand continued to grow, someone who wrote for *Inc.* wrote about Leonard's expertise. Leonard also added that into his bio. Then publications like *Entrepreneur*, *HuffPost*, and *Forbes* wrote about him as well, including in the print publication. Now, Leonard began to be featured in specialty publications that focused on branding and marketing, including *CMO*, a publication for chief marketing officers.

Leonard continued to stack those successes, which led him to be interviewed on television. The success continued, as Leonard became recognized as a top marketing influencer, top personal branding expert, and top digital marketer in these same types of publications. Shortly afterward, Leonard had over 300 media features, spoke at events across North America and Europe, was on the TEDx stage at UCI, was on a television show, and has released this book. By the time you've read this book, you will probably have seen him doing interviews on multiple television networks, holding workshops, and giving keynote speeches about this exact book and the processes described within it.

Ryan's Success Stack

Ryan went from blogging to writing for *TechDay News*. These articles gave him credibility, which he used to go from emceeing to doing speaking gigs. This led to being featured in many of the same prominent publications Leonard has been in, starting with *Inc.,* then *Entrepreneur,* then *Forbes,* and more. He continually reshaped his bio as he success-stacked, and then he went from being an unpaid speaker to a paid speaker.

As Ryan continued to build his intentional brand, he decided to launch his radio show so that he could sharpen his speaking skills. Then he was invited to keynote in Portugal, and then he began to get invited to speaking engagements all across the world. Then he launched his *World of Speakers* podcast. Because all this happened, he was named as a personal branding expert, and that helped him get two big promotions at UCI, as well as many of the same accolades as Leonard. He was also on the same television show as Leonard and has made appearances on the news too. Ryan also stacked his TEDx Talks and leveraged each TEDx he did to land another, and another, and another. If you've picked up this book, chances are it's because you have seen Ryan (or myself) sharing the lessons in this book at a conference, through a media feature, on the radio, on one of his podcasts, or on television.

How Our Experts Success-Stack

Success stacking comes in various forms:

- Iman's media connections led her to being featured in major media publications and to having a seat at the media table for industry decisions.
- Hai leveraged writing for *TechDay News* to get a job at UCI part-time, then secured a full-time position, and then got an internal promotion.
- Aaron used a scrappy website and a dozen or so blog articles to pitch media publications his content, and now has articles

in nearly every major media outlet, along with the top writing position at Shopify Plus.

- Winnie went from slowly growing her social media following, messaging one user at a time, to being called to speak across the United States and be interviewed by *Forbes*, *Barron's*, FinCon, and many other outlets. She even was named the #1 top female finance influencer by *US News & World Report*.
- Pansy supported others around her in the office, one person at a time, until her departments helped push her toward success.
- Dana went from working in a business that left her completely exhausted, to getting a few people to buy into social marketing with her, to being able to run a charity.
- Rahfeal went from living in poverty and growing up around crime, to writing one book, to writing a total of 16 books, and then to being on TV and speaking across the world.

Sara Bliss:

When I launched my Instagram account four years ago, I focused on putting up gorgeous pictures. At the time, I was writing profiles along with lots of stories on hotels and design. Instagram seemed like the best outlet to showcase gorgeous travel shots. My feed featured gorgeous beaches, beautiful hotel design, and snowy peaks.

I pretty much never put myself in the picture. I didn't want to be posing all the time; why would anyone want to see me? Better to showcase the way I see the world. Right? Actually no.

The truth was even though I was writing about beautiful things and interesting people, writing *New York Times* bestsellers as a ghostwriter, writing stories on Yahoo that got millions of views, doing cover stories for the *Wall Street Journal*—I was totally behind the scenes—both on Instagram and in terms of my professional reputation. The editors I worked with loved my work, and readers were responsive, but I kept myself out of the picture. And my career reflected that. It was easy for me to get work as a ghostwriter. Getting books in my own name? Impossible for many years.

Two years ago, I was able to sell a book I had dreamed about writing for over 10 years—*Take the Leap: Change Your Career, Change Your Life.* It is all about people making big career leaps and inspiring life changes. I interviewed Leonard about going from failed job to failed job to bankruptcy before hitting his stride as a social media guru. So much of his wisdom resonated with me. "Who needs a brand?" he said. "It is really, who doesn't need a brand."

I hung up the phone and realized I needed to brand myself. I needed to start sharing more of me with the world. I needed to put myself in the picture and talk about what I'm doing, and why I am doing it. Not just spotlighting everyone else. I've been doing it slowly. It felt weird at first, but now it just feels like a natural extension of my work. Readers reach out to me now. My followers have almost tripled (they were pretty low to start!). I just launched my own *Forbes* column.

When the book came out, I posted a lot about it on Instagram. That self-marketing led to editors reaching out. I also used Instagram to connect with editors I had lost touch with. With a quick glance at my feed, they could see what I was doing. The book has been featured in *Shape, Money, Girlboss, Forbes, Yahoo Finance,* and the *New York Times* . . . so far. More to come.

My leap has really been going from being a behind-the-scenes person to being out in the world, promoting my book, sharing my leaps, and yes, putting myself in the picture. I spent the past month editing this amazing book! And I've learned so much, and am realizing how much more I need to do. I'm ready and inspired.

Think it's unreal to get these kinds of results? We thought it was too. But much like a snowball that is rolling down a mountain, the momentum of success stacking continues to move forward unless it hits a brick wall. As long as you continue to success-stack, the successes will continue to come.

HOW TO MAKE STACKING WORK FOR YOU

As you begin to connect with others, people will begin to follow you. Make it a best practice to look up who is following you. Some of these people may be a part of the media, work at companies that you may want to do business with, or work in positions where they can onboard you onto their teams. Whenever members of the media take an interest in you and what you are doing, add their names into a spreadsheet and keep track of what they are doing. Engage with their content, get to know them even further; then when you have something that they may find intriguing, ask them what they think of your idea. They may highlight what you covered in one of their articles, and when they do, you will continue to see your brand grow through validation. As you invest in these relationships, you can call upon them in the future when you are working on something big, much like how we called upon our media contacts to garner a lot of attention to this book at the time of release.

If you work in an office, you have opportunities to share your accomplishments with your colleagues in company newsletters, social media, and meetings. Inform your boss about your recent achievements, and ask if your boss can help you share your wins throughout the company's network. Outside the office, as you network with colleagues at events, after you break the ice with your personal stories and build rapport, you can talk about some of your insights and achievements from these media features too. This way, others are aware of what you are doing, and you can position yourself for promotions or better opportunities as they arise.

Whenever Leonard has an exciting moment occur, he shares it with his boss, Christopher. Christopher then shares the exciting news with the department through an email. Whenever Ryan lands a new speaking engagement, he shares that moment with his boss, Iain. Iain then gets excited because he understands that the opportunity will also benefit UCI.

THE BRAND HALO

When you think of a corporate brand and a personal brand, most people fall under the misconception that they are unrelated. However, the brand halo works multiple ways. Prestigious companies and universities usually hold their reputation because they bring in the best of the best to work at their organizations. Their brand is leveraged by the reputations of the most successful names in their field. And these successful people work at these organizations because these organizations are known for bringing the best into their respective enterprises. Then, as new recruits begin their careers, they are able to leverage the company's brand halo.

As most companies and universities are looking to bring in the best, as you become more well recognized as the leader in your space, the opportunities for career growth open up exponentially. Dr. Ashley Wysong, a California dermatologist with Midwest roots, worked as an assistant professor of clinical dermatology at the Keck School of Medicine of USC. She made a point to connect with the media relations team and became easily accessible whenever quotes were needed by the media. She also did outreach and community service activities, conducted and published novel research to get herself out there in the academic research communities, and volunteered to be on committees for several national dermatology organizations to expand her professional network. She appeared on television and in a multitude of publications. Because her reputation continued to grow, when the University of Nebraska Medical Center was opening up a new department of dermatology, the university recruited Dr. Wysong to become the chair and lead the entire program, and she was open to change and new exciting challenges. That kind of situation can happen to you when you let your company know that you are available to speak on behalf of the company leveraging your expertise.

AVOIDING PITFALLS

As you begin to increase your visibility and are featured in national publications, you will face two difficult challenges that could knock you off track. The first is suffering from impostor syndrome, where you feel that you do not deserve the attention and recognition that you are receiving. The latter is becoming egotistical and feeling that the media attention defines who you are. Both of us have personally faced both situations, where at times we felt we weren't as great as the media was making us out to be and at other times felt we deserved opportunities based on our reputation. And both situations changed us and ultimately began to affect the success we had developed. As time progressed, we both had to learn how to stop belittling ourselves and stop feeling as if we deserved more than what we had. We both had to adopt an attitude of gratitude and return to our roots.

You will face these two challenges as well. You will feel that you are inadequate and may even feel like a fraud. But you cannot discount yourself. You made it this far because of exactly who you are. And at other times, you will feel that you deserve the entire world. But you don't. You need to maintain an attitude of gratitude and be thankful for all that you have, or you will begin to lose what you've worked so hard to earn. In order to avoid either pitfall, which can ultimately strip away your career, you need to stay true to your roots. Don't let the achievements get to your head. Instead, remember your bio. Remember your stories. Remember who *you* truly are. As long as you maintain your foundation of being your true, authentic self, everything else will continue to grow.

MARKETING YOURSELF

As your intentional brand continues to flourish, there will come key moments in your life where you need to call upon the power of your peers. As long as you have built up a solid network of people you have established camaraderie with, you can call upon them when you are in need of a helping hand. This could be to nominate you for a TEDx Talk, to support you at the launch of a new book or product, or to vouch for you as a reference for a new position.

When people think about the word "marketing," or getting something that is important out in front of others, they usually freeze up and don't think that it is something that they can do. But you can. Think about the significant moments in your life—your wedding, your graduations, your birthdays—you may have had no problem spreading the word and celebrating. For your business, you will need to follow the same format. That is the only way those activities will be brought into a bigger light. When both of us did our TEDx Talks, we told everyone we knew about what was going to happen. As we shared, many members of the media decided that they wanted to see the talk and share the talk with their audiences. From the moment we gave our talks, there was so much buzz around what we said, that once the videos were released, they were featured in nearly a dozen publications in the first week the videos went digital.

Success stacking works no matter who you are. But that success . . . It's only half the story . . .

USE WHATEVER YOU HAVE — MICHAEL HOULIHAN

CHAPTER 17

YOUR SUCCESS IS HALF THE STORY

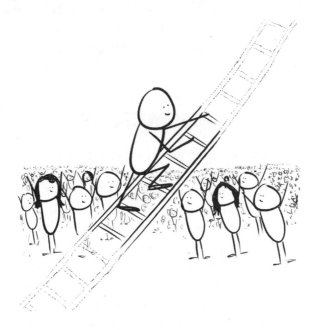

By exposing our failings and fears, we create points of connection between our intentional brands and others. What's more, we control the message of our brand and are able to demonstrate our unique contributions and areas of expertise. Exposing ourselves helps us reclaim our identity and be our whole selves, our true selves. In this final chapter, we'll challenge you to join us on this journey of exposure, but not only to build a healthier more robust brand. We'll challenge you to expose yourself, growing a healthy and authentic personal brand that is an extension of your own health and authenticity.

RYAN & LEONARD

You may have picked up this book because you want to go out in the world and attract greater success in business. However, you will end up with much more success in your overall life. You may have assumed that the ultimate result would be attracting more social media followers or becoming the most sought-after expert at your craft. But there's so much more to the equation than meets the eye. You will have pushed yourself to go beyond the self-imposed limitations that have continually held you back throughout life.

EXPOSE YOURSELF

It is our hope that by sharing how we used exposure to overcome our struggles, and how other people overcame their own hurdles, and how you can use exposure to break free, that you will say goodbye to the worry and anxiety that inhibits your ability to do what your heart truly desires. We hope that you realize that the feeling that you are the only one who has experienced a multitude of setbacks in your career and personal life is exactly what many others feel too. We hope that you say goodbye to feelings of inadequacy where you continually believe you aren't good enough.

Exposure is the key to freeing yourself of these constant limitations that we and society in general push into people's faces. It will take away the feelings of embarrassment and shame that have held you back for so long and allow you to truly become who you always wanted to be. Exposure is the singular solution that will allow you to live a life feeling comfortable in your own skin.

Go out there and expose your stories. Share your stories with your friends. Share your stories with the public. Share your stories with us. Let us know what you have gone through to get to this point in life. Let us know what has reshaped you into becoming the person you are now. Let us know where you aspire to go as you continue onward in your life. We will all be rooting you on, as the only way to true success is to all band together and work to eliminate the falsehoods of our society—when we all ditch the act together.

THE LIFE-CHANGING BENEFITS OF SHARING EVERYTHING

Authentic exposure is, ultimately, a matter of brand choice. Sure, if you don't go and share stories that scare you, you can still attain some success. If you go and strictly share content based on your business or profession, you can gain some traction as well. However, you will not stand a chance against the true mavericks who are able to expose their entire lives in a congruent manner. Imagine just how much happier you will be as you live each day as your true self, in the office, at home, and on social media. You won't be overlooked, because both what you have failed at and what you have achieved are documented. You won't be ashamed of hiding who you truly are. You won't be scared that people may discover a deep, dark secret that they can use against you. Because it's already out there; you have already gotten ahead of it and controlled the narrative.

You have taken your future back into your own hands. The gate-keepers that have always prevented you from moving forward, such as the hiring managers, your superiors at work, the members of the board, the investors, and the other groups of people who hold the ticket to your future, are no longer in charge of your life. You are. And you alone. The more you expose your whole self to the world, the more opportunities will come knocking at your door.

Your best content will include exposing your fears and your failures. These will drive the deepest connections to the people consuming your content. And it truly is what will spark the camaraderie that will fuel the life you are meant to live. But don't feel that you need to only share your scariest moments. We push you to grow more comfortable in sharing, and as you continually share, to get more and more vulnerable until you are sharing your Level 4 exposures.

But remember, the happy and good stories matter too. Your stories aren't limited to your own personal life either. They can be stories of what you've experienced at work or in a relationship, what you learned from someone else, or what you gained from an insightful conversation that you were a part of. Stories surround you, and the stories are all a part of you and your life. At first, these stories will heavily resonate around you and your experiences, but as time goes by and you pivot a few times into figuring out what you truly want to do, they will start to be more centered on your areas of expertise.

When following your Content Calendar, make sure to take time to share your personal and business stories, but also gather up all your courage and let your fear guide you when it comes to sharing those dark moments that have had a grip on you for so long. Once you let go of your fear and let it become public, it no longer controls you. You control it.

Before exposure was a means to earn more revenue, exposure was the key to Leonard overcoming abandonment and suicidal tendencies and to Ryan overcoming bullying and a debilitating federal investigation.

POSTING AND PUTTING EVERYTHING OUT THERE

What can you do daily? Weekly? Monthly? Set your cadence. Get into a rhythm. Then push yourself to improve upon what you are already doing by 10 percent, then 10 percent again, and again and again and again. Continue improving upon and pushing out your content, and you will be at the head of the pack. Then dive deep into creating those connections between yourself and others, as you will have a community that will stick by your side even after the going gets tough.

As time progresses and you begin to pick up more eyeballs on the stories you are sharing, start to sprinkle in your unique contributions, content that is based on your expertise. Recall your intentional brand, your 3-1-3, your talent discovery, and share your message in a way that makes it unique by including the real you within the content.

GOING FOR IT

Do you want to get a raise? A new career opportunity? Start a company? Make a side income? Become a public speaker? Help a worthy cause? It doesn't matter what it is that you want to do; now is the time for all of us, including you, to ditch the act and be our whole selves, our true selves.

Are there risks involved? Of course there are. The risks of not moving forward with exposing yourself include staying at the same job forever, not being promoted, not pursuing the business or career of your dreams, not working in the industry you want to work in, not being able to quickly find a job after being laid off, not attracting new customers to your business, not getting your team to create a strong bond and form as a unit, and the list goes on. The only thing that will happen if you don't expose yourself is that you will stay stagnant in the exact position you are in now. And staying in place leaves you open to the most vulnerable position of all—being complacent and losing what you have worked so hard to build.

When you do begin to expose your whole self, your true self, you do still face some risks. You become accountable for what you say and do, but you have always been held accountable for that. You can become a role model for others, so you may need to give up on some of your vices. You may even have a few people who are jealous of what you are becoming—but these people who try to put you down were never your true friends to begin with. Your world image will evolve, and the true natures of the people you surround yourself with will be brought to light, and you will need to make choices of whom to keep and whom to let go of. It may be hard to give up friends that you've known for years, but if all they are trying to do is sabotage you and keep you from becoming who you are destined to be, are they truly the great friends you thought they were?

On the other hand, you will start to see the world through a new lens. Your reality of how the world works will evolve further outside your current bubble, as you start to see how various cultures from across the world operate, learning about how people communicate in other cities, states, and countries. With a more global perspective, you will come to find that most of the world is just like you and me; we are all just looking for love, compassion, and a sense of belonging.

BREAKING THROUGH

Come with us on this journey of exposure. We challenge you to expose yourself. We want you to grow a healthy and authentic personal brand that is an extension of your own health and authenticity. Exposure has helped us build our unique and personal brands to the point that we were able to shed our fears that held us back, like the thought of being in an entry-level job forever or of being on the edge living in fear that we were going to lose everything we had. It's what has helped us build stronger personal and professional relationships. And it's what has helped us make such a deep connection with our personal and professional networks, which include you as well—a connection, we hope, that will allow you to feel a sense of trust if you ever meet us on the street, at an event, or even when we are on vacation.

Remember, just because we have a significant social media following and all these accolades, it doesn't mean anything. That doesn't change who we are. We are still ourselves, one of us a dork with a weird personality and a unique perspective on life and the other an overly curious ginger who gets excited about new ideas. And those accomplishments and milestones won't change who you are either. It will help propel you further to the success you're looking to achieve, but it won't change the fact that all along, you have always been yourself.

As long as you've followed the Expose Yourself Process, continue onward. Keep doing what you are doing and don't stop. That's the easiest way you will achieve success—by turning everything you are doing into daily habits. Stay humble and true to who you are. Show your vulnerabilities and your weaknesses, so they no longer can hinder you or hold you back. Instead, let them shine, because people resonate with this. And when they resonate with what you have felt and gone through, they will be driven closer and closer to you.

Do you know what the only thing that separates successful people and unsuccessful people is? Successful people don't do what people can't do. They do what everyone can do but nobody does. They do simple things, like working on a Sunday at 9 p.m., or finishing a chapter for a book when they could be at a Super Bowl party with their friends, or starting their day earlier by waking up at 5 a.m., or being vulnerable and sharing something that scares them, like we shared our skeletons of being suicidal or dealing with the FTC. All the answers you've been looking for are right here. You already have them. They're laid out in this book. But we both know that having all the answers means absolutely nothing.

You need to start doing what no one else is doing. You need to go back over the Expose Yourself Process and go through each step over and over and over again. All that's left for you to do is take action and execute. And that execution is what will lead you to the top. And when you think you've made it, you need to keep going. We thought we hit the top of where we could go many times, only to find a new pinnacle, then a new one, and a new one again. We've done so many things that we once deemed impossible, only because we kept moving forward. You may not be able to envision it yet, but the same thing will happen to you.

If Ryan stopped going through the Expose Yourself Process, he would stop getting keynotes. If Leonard stopped writing (which he did for a really long time), he would stop getting media features (which did happen).

If you are an entrepreneur, you will connect more with your employees, investors, and clients. Your company culture and bottom line will also grow. If you're working at a company as an employee, remember that you aren't the only one who benefits from building an intentional brand; your boss, colleagues, and direct reports also benefit. You evolve from being just treated as an employee to building the company culture of having each other's back. And as you grow your digital presence, your company starts to benefit from the halo effect, as the company begins to share some of the positive reputation that you yourself are cultivating.

Ditching the act isn't meant to be held onto like a secret. It isn't meant to be your secret superpower that no one else has access to. It's more than just an idea or philosophy; it's a way of life. And a way of life is meant to be shared with others. Can you see how friends, family members, or colleagues may be able to benefit from ditching the act? Share this book with them.

If you're a manager or executive at a company, can you see your coworkers benefiting if they had the opportunity to read this book? Or what would happen if your entire office began to create a new culture of ditching the act?

Share *Ditch the Act* with people who matter to you by letting them know how this book has impacted you on your own personal journey, and by sharing what you feel they will learn as well. You can even leave a review about the book, so others can get an idea of what to expect once they flip through the book for themselves.

You've pushed yourself to get through the book. You've read through all the philosophies within. You've questioned whether or not they are valid, but you see how they play out in real life, through all the examples and research. You've faced fear head on as you've brought up some of your past skeletons. You've held onto that feeling in your gut that someone may judge, mock, or ridicule you.

But it's time to let all that fear go. It's time to recognize your fear and do something about it. And what you are about to do is execute. Take action. Because the only way this all works is if you work.

So make your Exposed and Authentic Bio public. Share your low-level exposures. Start telling stories. Get braver and share the scarier moments of your life. Stay on top. Communicate with others and foster camaraderie. Start stacking your successes. And we will watch you grow from where you are today to reach new peaks.

We encourage you to choose the path of exposure for the sake of building an engaged, energetic, and authentic business and career, as well as a healthier, happier life. Why? Because you deserve it.

This is much more than a book on branding. Ultimately, it's a book about being confident in, and accepted for, your whole self. Now go share your whole self with the world.

NOTES

Chapter 6

Power, Rhett. "Trust Is as Important as Price for Todays [sic] Consumer." *Inc.* March 30, 2018. Accessed February 12, 2019. https://www.inc.com/rhett-power/trust-is-as-important-as-price-for-todays-consumer.html.

Bernhardt, Boris C., and Tania Singer. "The Neural Basis of Empathy." *Annual Review of Neuroscience.* Vol. 35:1–23 (July 2012). Accessed February 12, 2019. https://doi.org/10.1146/annurev-neuro-062111-150536.

Schawbel, Dan. "Brene Brown: How Vulnerability Can Make Our Lives Better." *Forbes.* April 21, 2013. Accessed February 12, 2019. https://www.forbes.com/sites/danschawbel/2013/04/21/brene-brown-how-vulnerability-can-make-our-lives-better/#5d3a4a7636c7.

Chapter 7

Brown, Brené. *Dare to Lead: Brave Work. Tough Conversations. Whole Hearts.* Random House, 2018.

Brown, Brené. "Myth: 'Vulnerability Is a Weakness.'" March 14, 2013. Oprah.com. Accessed February 13, 2019. http://www.oprah.com/own-super-soul-sunday/excerpt-daring-greatly-by-dr-brene-brown.

Chapter 8

DiMenichi, Brynne C., Karolina M. Lempert, Christina Bejjani, and Elizabeth Tricomi. "Writing About Past Failures Attenuates Cortisol Responses and Sustained Attention Deficits Following Psychosocial Stress." *Frontiers in Behavioral Neuroscience.* Accessed February 13, 2019. https://www.frontiersin.org/articles/10.3389/fnbeh.2018.00045/full.

Chapter 12

Schwartz, Mel. "The Problem with Perfection: Why Would You Seek Being Perfect?" *Psychology Today*. November 30, 2008. Accessed February 14, 2019. https://www.psychologytoday.com/us/blog/shift-mind/200811/the-problem-perfection.

Chapter 13

Bradford, William C. "Reaching the Visual Learner: Teaching Property Through Art." *The Law Teacher*. Vol. 11 (2004). Accessed February 15, 2019. https://papers.ssrn.com/sol3/papers.cfm?abstract_id=587201.

Chapter 15

MSL Group. "Infographic: Social Employee Advocacy." MSL. December 11, 2014. Accessed February 15, 2019. https://mslgroup.com/insights-thought-leadership/infographic-social-employee-advocacy.

INDEX

Accolades, showcasing, 145–146
Altucher, James, 22–24, 267, 277
American Honda, 21, 22
Amplify What Is Working Worksheet, 222–227
  choose your budget (step 4), 226–227
  explore analytics (step 2), 223
  pick a platform (step 1), 223
  promote/boost (step 3), 224–226
Analytics, 223, 233
Any Given Sunday (movie), 209
Appreciation, 257, 264
Artbound, 104
Ask Altucher (podcast), 277
Attention:
  building, 257
  feeling defined by, 283
Attitude of gratitude, 283
Attracting clicks, to videos, 242
Audience:
  being relatable to, 92
  committed, 83–84
  engaging with, 256
  relationship with, 245
  using "you" in speaking to, 240–241
Audio, with videos, 233, 241
Authenticity, 7
  of bio, 182
  in brand building, 8
  defined, 82
  Exposed and Authentic Bio Worksheet, 131–148
  results of, 9, 10
  in Ryan's speaking style, 48
Authority, earning, 129

Bazin, Christopher, 45, 52, 63, 121, 258, 281
Be consistent with content (step 6), 243–253 (*See also* Content)
Being different, fear of, 81
Being real:
  Leonard's story of, 11–24
  in videos, 239–240
Being relatable, 92
Being yourself:
  and authors' partnership, 41–45
  by being real, 11–24
  ditching the act as, 80
  Leonard's story of, 11–24, 41–45, 50–55
  by owning your whole story, 3–10
  and running farther with imperfect friends, 41–55
  Ryan's story of, 25–39, 41–49, 54–55
  by speaking your truth, 25–39
  (*See also* Ditching the act; Putting yourself out there)
Beliefs:
  losing followers when sharing, 84
  standing up for, 81
Bennett, Dan, 162–163
Bernstein, Gabrielle, 107
Bios:
  authenticity of, 182
  creating, 86–87
  Exposed and Authentic Bio Worksheet, 118, 131–148
  revealing yourself in, 86
Bliss, Sara, 55, 81, 279–280
Body language, in videos, 240

Boy, Soulja, 181–182
Bradley, Joseph M., 86, 87
Brain, rewiring, 8
Brand halo, 46, 282, 291
Brand process, 61, 272
    be consistent with content
        (step 6), 243–253 (*See also*
        Content)
    discover what makes you stand
        out (step 2), 161–183 (*See also*
        3-1-3 Method)
    focus on form, not force (step 4),
        213–229 (*See also* Intentional
        brand)
    keep it social (step 7), 255–267
        (*See also* Community building)
    make eye contact with camera
        (step 5), 231–242 (*See also*
        Videos)
    overcome fear and share (step 3),
        185–211 (*See also* Overcoming
        fear)
    positioning is an art form (step 1),
        129–160 (*See also* Positioning)
    sequential steps create success
        (step 8), 269–284 (*See also*
        Success stacking)
Branding/brand building:
    authenticity and exposure in, 8
    based on Exposure Résumé, 117
    neglecting, 181
    order of activities in, 41–42 (*See
        also* Exposure Résumé)
    sharing only your good side in, 6–7
    what consumers look for in
        brands, 76
    (*See also* Intentional brand;
        Personal brand)
Braun, David A., 82
Break Through the Crowd (TV show),
    53–54
Breathing exercise, 237–238
Bringing everyone along, 270–271
Brown, Brené, 82, 92

Bryant, Chris, 232–233
Budget, choosing, 226–227
Buffett, Warren, 76–77, 92
Busch, May, 24
Bush, George W., 197–198

Cal State Fullerton, 49
Call to action, 145, 291
Camaraderie, fostering, 257, 264, 270
    (*See also* Community building)
Careers:
    day jobs while starting side
        business, 44, 45
    recession-proof, 62
    sharing early careers, 18
    (*See also* Work)
Changing how others see you, 62–64
Chaos Makeup, 83, 84
Cheadle, Don, 46
Chen, Jason, 24, 267
Childhood moments, sharing, 18
Community, growth vs., 49
Community building, 255–267
    changing work relationships,
        257–259
    creating virtual tribe, 257
    Ditch the Act Peer Group Charter
        Starter Worksheet, 260–263
    engaging with audience, 256
    paying it forward, 264–265
    starting peer groups, 259–260
    taking it to the next level, 265–267
Competition:
    authenticity vs., 82
    not paying attention to, 244–245
    on Personal Brand Positioning and
        Strategy Worksheet, 154–155
Confidence, 124–125
Connection:
    digital and in-person, 256
    to flawed people, 92
    honesty and exposure for, 76
    from sharing firsthand experience,
        93

through content, 215–215
through exposing fears and
    failures, 285
through exposing your whole
    self, 7
through following brand process,
    291
through intentional brand, 215
through video, 231
(*See also* Relatedness)
Content, 243–253
    best platforms for, 221–222
    connection with others through,
        215–215
    Content Calendar Worksheet,
        246–252
    cycle of, 252
    exposing fears and failures in, 287
    form, not force, in, 219
    frequency of, 244–246, 288
    of other people, 244–245
    ratio for personal content,
        228–229
    10 commandments of sharing for,
        119–120
    for videos, 234–235, 238–239
    written vs. video, 232
Content Calendar Worksheet, 246–252
    creating, 250–253
    pick themes (step 1), 247–248
    stories to share each workday
        (step 2), 248–249
Conversations:
    leading to camaraderie, 264
    polarizing topics of, 92
    taken to the next level, 265–267
    transcribing, 141
Cracking the Curiosity Code
    (Hamilton), 55
Creating your brand, 75–89
    discomfort with self-exposure in,
        85–89
    goal in, 77–79
    honesty in, 82–85

secret of success in, 78–82
and trying to hide shortcomings,
    75
(*See also* Branding/brand building)
Credentials, 6
Credibility, 38
    cultivating, 131
    in the market, 85
    from size of following, 187
Culture, 87, 89, 258, 259
Custom interview questionnaire,
    134–139

Dare to Lead (Brown), 92
Decision Points (Bush), 197
Dennin, Michael, 46, 271
Digital connections, 256
Digital footprint, 62, 182
Digital realm, putting yourself out
    into, 218–222
Direct messages (DMs), 264, 266–267
Discomfort, in revealing your flaws,
    85–89
Discover what makes you stand out
    (step 2), 161–183 (*See also*
    3-1-3 Method)
Ditch the Act Peer Group Charter
    Starter Worksheet, 260–263
    create meeting agenda (step 6),
        263
    create meeting topics (step 5), 263
    decide whom to invite (step 2),
        261
    invite and organize (step 3), 262
    narrow focus of group goals
        (step 4), 262
    pick a location (step 1), 261
Ditch the Act (DTA) Peer Group/
    Party, 259, 260
Ditching the act, 107–125
    avoiding negativity in, 124
    benefits of, 82–83
    building confidence in, 124–125
    Exposure Résumé for, 109–118

Ditching the act (*continued*):
　how sharing works in, 122–123
　individual meanings of, 79–81
　as lifestyle, 11, 79, 291
　sharing stories in, 118–119
　and sharing that goes too far,
　　121–122
　10 commandments of sharing,
　　119–121
　whom to start sharing with, 123
　(*See also specific topics*)
DMs (direct messages), 264, 266–267
DTA Peer Group/Party (*see* Ditch the
　Act Peer Group/Party)
Duning, Evan, 85

Early careers, sharing, 18
Egotism, 283
Emotional transitions, in stories,
　143–145
Employers:
　brand halo for, 282, 291
　company benefits from employee
　　brands, 49
　company benefits from
　　relationships with community,
　　265
　deciding to stay with or change, 63
　helping employees build their
　　brands, 63
　included in your media features, 271
Engaging:
　with audience, 256
　with content of others, 264, 266
　with followers, 281
The Entrepreneur's Book of Actions
　(Power), 76
Ethics, in intentional brand, 215
Examine, 271
Expertise:
　authentic, relatable basis for, 7
　failure to connect through, 6–7
Explaining what you do (*see* 3-1-3
　Challenge Worksheet)

Expose Yourself Process, 11, 13, 61,
　118, 125, 130, 131, 162, 186,
　189, 200, 216, 232, 244, 253,
　257, 267, 269, 272, 290, 291
Exposed and Authentic Bio
　Worksheet, 118, 131–148
　build custom interview
　　questionnaire (step 2),
　　134–139
　build intro to showcase accolades
　　(step 11), 145–146
　clean up text (step 7), 142
　conduct life story interview
　　(step 3), 140–141
　include call to action (step 10),
　　145
　include what work you do
　　(step 13), 146–147
　let personality shine through
　　(step 12), 146
　make emotional transitions at end
　　of stories (step 9), 143–145
　make headlines for sections
　　(step 8), 142–143
　organize your stories (step 5), 141
　pre-interview questionnaire
　　(step 1), 132–134
　pull best stories together (step 6),
　　141–142
　transcribe conversation (step 4),
　　141
Exposure(s), 285
　avoiding, 188–189
　as brand-building tool, 8
　challenge for, 289–290
　connecting with audience
　　through, 7
　discomfort of, 85–89
　discomfort with, 85–89
　for freedom from limitations, 286
　and impossibility of hiding
　　shortcomings, 75
　levels of, 8 (*See also* Exposure
　　levels)

as lifestyle, 11, 79, 291
magic of, 78–79
risks of, 289
single, 244–245
so things can't be used against
    you, 47
before someone else exposes you,
    197–199
to take control of narrative, 7, 199
(See also specific topics and people)
Exposure Bank, 8, 115–117, 119,
    200, 201
Exposure levels, 8, 92–98
    becoming comfortable with,
        189–195
    Exposures Ranked by Level
        Worksheet, 92–98
    Level 1, 93, 94, 190–192
    Level 2, 95, 192–194
    Level 3, 96
    Level 4, 93, 97, 195, 196
    Level 5, 93, 98
    in starting peer groups at work,
        259
Exposure Résumé, 8, 109–118
    building brand based on (step 6),
        117
    designing story behind "skeleton,"
        114
    fictional elements of perceived
        truth in (step 2), 112–113
    funneling skeletons into line items
        (step 6), 115–116
    questions to answer in (step 1),
        110–111
    repeating steps for each "skeleton"
        (step 4), 115
Exposures Ranked by Level
    Worksheet, 92–98
    Level 1, 93, 94
    Level 2, 95
    Level 3, 96
    Level 4, 93, 97
    Level 5, 93, 98

Failures:
    avoiding talking about, 6–7
    exposing, 285, 287
    writing about, 123
Fear(s):
    of being called a fraud, 46–47
    of being different, 81
    exposing, 285, 287
    fighting through, 186
    of full exposure, 188–189
    of judgment, 199
    letting go of, 292
    in making videos, 237–238
    overcoming *(see* Overcoming fear)
    of putting yourself out there, 99
    value of sharing, 186
    of your story, 209
Federal Trade Commission
        investigation, 5, 37–38, 46, 47,
        99, 195–197
Feeling(s):
    avoiding negativity, 124
    of being undeserving, 46
    like a fraud, 35, 46–47, 283
    sharing, 26
Ferrazzi, Keith, 3, 4, 9, 79
Fey, Tina, 46
Fight Club (Palahniuk), 198
Focus on form, not force (step 4),
        213–229 *(See also* Intentional
        brand)
Fraud:
    being called a, 46
    feeling like a, 35, 46–47, 283
Frequency of content, 244–246, 288
Frontiers in Behavioral Neuroscience, 123
Fun, in making videos, 241

Gates, Bill, 92
Geico, 76–77
Ginger MC, 48
Goals:
    in creating your brand, 77–79
    for Ditch The Act Peer Group, 262

Goals (*continued*):
    of employees, supporting, 63
    going for, 288–289
    going through steps to achieve,
        129–130
    for personal brand, 148–151
    in Personal Brand Positioning and
        Strategy Worksheet, 153–154,
        159
    in preparing for videos, 239
Gordon, Rahfeal, 80, 182, 188, 220,
    279
Grainger, Iain, 45, 257–258, 281
Growth, community vs., 49

Habits, 290
Hamilton, Diane, 55
Headlines:
    for bio sections, 142–143
    for social media, 178–179
Honesty, 37, 76, 82–85
Hrudey, Kelly, 28
Huawei, 48
Huie, Kevin, 72
Humanizing yourself, 80
Humans 2.0 (podcast), 89
Humor, in videos, 236–237

Image(s):
    on social media, 87
    that you present to the world,
        85–86 (*See also* Personal
        brand[s])
Impostor syndrome, 41, 46–47,
    282–283
InfluenceTree, 6, 42, 43, 49, 54–55
Information regurgitation, 236
Insecurity, overcoming, 80
Intentional brand, 213–229
    Amplify What Is Working
        Worksheet, 222–227
    in digital realm, 218–222
    elements of, 215
    engaging with audience, 256

    finding your personal space,
        228–229
    longevity of, 271–272
    why sharing truth matters, 216–218
Interviews:
    custom interview questionnaire,
        134–139
    life story interview, 140–141
    pre-interview questionnaire,
        132–134
Intro, to showcase accolades, 145–146
Invisible line for sharing, 121–122

Jokes, in videos, 236–237
Judgment, 83
    fear of, 199
    towards wealthy people, 92

Keck Medicine of USC, 24, 44, 52,
    63, 258
Keep it social (step 7), 255–267
    (*See also* Community building)
Kelley, David E., 31
Keywords, for videos, 238–239
KUCI, 48

Lady Gaga, 186
Law, Erin Paige, 266
Lawrence, Jennifer, 78
Lee, Pansy, 63, 81, 102, 121, 150–151,
    187, 216, 279
Leonard's story:
    career success, 54–55
    childhood and early career, 11–24
    commenting on others' content,
        265–266
    early content writing, 219, 252
    early partnership with Ryan,
        41–45
    exposure levels, 102
    growth of personal brand, 52–55,
        266–267, 277–278
    and perceived personal brand,
        59–60

relationships, 50–54, 267
  success stack, 277–278
Level 1 exposure, 93, 94, 99, 118,
    119, 190–192
Level 2 exposure, 95, 119, 192–194
Level 3 exposure, 96, 119
Level 4 exposure, 93, 97, 99, 118, 119,
    195, 196
Level 5 exposure, 93, 98
Life story interview, 140–141
Lifestyle, ditching the act as, 11, 79, 291
Lin, Mei, 213–214
LinkedIn, 88, 123, 219

Maini, Arun, 242
Make eye contact with camera (step 5),
    231–242 (*See also* Videos)
Market, changes in, 243
Marketing yourself, 283–284
Martinez, Megan, 83–85
Medium, 123, 219, 252
Messaging:
  to connect with customers, 76
  control of, 285
  core, defining, 158
  direct messages, 264, 266–267
  fresh, 245
Metry, Mark, 81, 87–89, 183, 221, 267
Midson-Short, Daniel, 237
Mistakes:
  avoiding talking about, 6–7
  in making videos, 239–240
Mrwhosetheboss, 242

Narrative, controlling (*see* Taking
    control of your narrative)
Narrogance, 16, 60
Neary, Eduardo, 27
Negativity, avoiding, 124
Netflix, 77
Network(s):
  in marketing yourself, 283–284
  power of, 187–188
  public, 123

"The Neural Basis of Empathy," 77–78

Obama, Barack, 197–198
OC Tech Happy Hour, 48
Omission, lying by, 83
1 Million Cups, 48
Orange County Transit Authority
    workshops, 49
Orendorff, Aaron, 80, 101, 150, 182,
    187–188, 220–221, 228, 267,
    279
Orwell, Sol, 271
Oshri, Hadari, 196–197
Oubou, Iman, 80, 101, 150, 182, 188,
    209–210, 221, 228, 267, 278
Overcoming fear, 185–211
  of being different, 81
  easing into, 190
  examples of, 190–194
  exposing yourself before someone
    else does, 197–199
  fighting through fear, 186
  Overcoming Fear and Sharing
    Worksheet, 189–194
  power of your network, 187–188
  of sharing, 185–211
  standing out, 188–189
  taking control of your narrative,
    199–208
Overcoming fear and share (step 3),
    185–211
Overcoming Fear and Sharing
    Worksheet, 189–194
Owning your whole story, 3–10
  attractiveness of, 7
  and biggest branding mistake, 6–7
  life change from, 8–10
  by revealing skeletons, 197–199
  rewiring brain and social
    platforms for, 8

Palahniuk, Chuck, 198–199
Pause test, 120
Pauses, power of, 241

Paying it forward, 264–265

Peer groups:
  Ditch the Act Peer Group Charter
    Starter Worksheet, 260–263
  starting, 259–260

Perception:
  asking others to describe you,
    67–68
  changing how others see you,
    62–64
  by others, trying to control, 85–86
  reality vs., 59–61, 64
  of truth, 112–113

Perfection:
  customers' rejection of, 76–77
  of image, 86
  people put off by, 91
  trying to give appearance of,
    214–215

Personal brand(s), 59–73
  as being your whole self, 186
  changing how others see you,
    62–64
  creating (see Creating your brand)
  effectiveness of, 62
  of employees, company benefits
    from, 49
  knowing goal for, 148–151
  need for, 61–62
  perception vs. reality of, 59–61, 63
  "pillars" of, 71–72
  portraying only good side in, 6
  Rapid Reflection Discovery
    Process Worksheet, 64–72
  reliance on, 109
  website for, 180–181
  why customers relate to, 76–77
  (See also Intentional brand)

Personal Brand Positioning and
  Strategy Worksheet, 151–160
  competition, 154–155
  defining core messaging, 158
  primary platforms, 157
  self-evaluation, 156–157

  where you are today, 152–153
  where you want to be featured, 159
  where you want to go, 153–154

Personal space, claiming, 229

Personality, expressed in bio, 146

"Pillars" of personal brand, 71

Platforms, choosing, 221–223

Playing it safe, 84

Polarizing topics of conversation, 92

Positioning, 129–160
  Exposed and Authentic Bio
    Worksheet, 131–148
  knowing goal for personal brand,
    148–151
  Personal Brand Positioning and
    Strategy Worksheet, 151–160

Power:
  of pauses, 241
  of putting yourself out there,
    102–103
  of your network, 187–188

Power, Rhett, 76

Pre-interview questionnaire, 132–134

"The Problem with Perfection"
  (Schwartz), 214

Professional masks, 6, 7

Public networks, 123

Putting yourself out there, 91–105, 288
  being relatable from, 92
  in digital realm, 218–222
  getting over fear of, 99
  levels of exposure in, 93–98
  power of, 102–103
  in real life, 103–105
  success stories of, 100–102

Quora, 22, 24, 123, 219, 252, 265

QuoraCast, 277

Raaf, Dan, 79, 199–200

Rapid Reflection Discovery Process
  Worksheet, 64–72
  ask others to describe you (step 2),
    67–68

categorize responses (step 7),
    71–72
collect all answers (step 3), 68–69
identify characteristic traits
    (step 1), 65–66
look at assortment of traits
    (step 5), 70
look at traits you can work on
    (step 4), 70
remove all boxes with only one
    color (step 6), 70
for taking control of the narrative,
    72
Real life:
    new perspective on, 289
    putting yourself out there in,
        103–105
    success stacking in, 277–280
    3-1-3 Method applied in, 178–180
Reality, perception vs., 59–61
Rejection:
    for exposing vulnerabilities, 104
    of perfection, 76–77
Relatedness:
    of Buffett vs. Geico, 76–77
    creating relatable brands, 77–79
    to good stories, 87
    from putting yourself out there,
        92
    through sharing mistakes/failures,
        6–7
    (See also Connection)
Relationships, 257
    accessibility in, 265
    with audiences, 245
    with the community, 265
    with followers, 281
    in success stacking, 270
    transactional mindset in, 270
    at work, 257–259
    (See also Community building)
Revealing your whole self (see Brand
    process)
Robbins, Tony, 77, 220

Ryan's story:
    career success, 54–55
    childhood and early career, 25–39
    early content writing, 252
    early partnership with Leonard,
        41–45
    exposure levels, 99, 103
    FTC investigation, 5, 37–38, 46,
        47, 99, 195–197
    growth of personal brand, 45–49,
        53–54, 278
    keeping a facade, 255–256
    media relationships, 271
    and perceived personal brand, 60
    steps missed toward achieving
        goals, 129–130
    stick figures, 219–220
    success stack, 278

Schwartz, Mel, 214
Scripts, for videos, 238–239
Seacrest, Ryan, 107
Selfies, 213–214
Sequential steps create success
    (step 8), 269–284 (See also
    Success stacking)
Shalit, Dana, 80–81, 103–104, 183,
    279
Sharing, 118–119, 286
    building confidence in, 124–125
    in ditching the act, 122–123
    of feelings, 26
    with friends vs. with public,
        122–123
    identifying platforms for, 159
    of information from this book,
        291–292
    life-changing benefits of, 287–288
    limits for, 98, 121–122
    overcoming fear of, 185–211
    public networks for, 123
    Story Creation Worksheet for,
        201–209
    10 commandments of, 119–121

Sharing (*continued*):
  timing of, 122–123
  whom to start sharing with, 123
  at work, 118–121
  of your truth, 216–218
  (*See also* Exposure levels)
Shatner, William, 32
Shortcomings:
  revealing, 79–80
  trying to hide, 75
Simmons, Michael, 24, 79–80, 100,
  149, 182, 188, 220, 246, 267
"Skeletons":
  being forthcoming about,
    197–199
  designing story behind, 114 (*See
    also* Taking control of your
    narrative)
  fictional elements in perceived
    truth about, 112–113
  funneled into line items, 115–116
  questions about, 110–111
Snapp Conner, Cheryl, 76, 80,
  101–102, 199, 221
Social anxiety, 81, 88
Social marketing, 104, 271
Social media:
  building/growing following on,
    118, 187
  crafting headlines for, 178–179
  images presented on, 87
  and real identity, 290
  size of following on, 269, 270
Social Media Marketing World, 48
Social platforms, rewiring, 8
Speaking:
  on camera, 235–236
  your truth, 25–39, 216
Spotify, 77
Standing out:
  discovering traits for (*see* 3-1-3
    Method)
  overcoming fear of, 188–189
Standing up for your beliefs, 81

Stories:
  appealing to emotions in, 238
  behind "skeletons," 114
  defined, 201
  developing, 201
  drafting, 123
  emotional transitions at end of,
    143–145
  essential components of, 204
  Exposure Bank of, 115–117, 119
  organizing, 141
  pulling best stories together,
    141–142
  questions to spark, 202–204
  to share each workday, 248–249
  sharing (*see* Sharing)
  sources of, 287–288
  Story Creation Worksheet,
    201–209
  template for, 205–208
  that create camaraderie, 87
  in your content calendar, 252
  (*See also* Taking control of your
    narrative)
Story Creation Worksheet, 201–209
  essential components of stories,
    204
  questions to spark stories,
    202–204
  template for stories, 205–208
Success:
  creating habits for, 290
  in creating your brand, 78–82
  culture of, 87
  from doing what others will not
    do, 244, 290–291
  drivers of, 270
  lifelong, 107
  and polarizing topics of
    conversation, 92
  in putting oneself out there,
    100–102
  putting yourself out there in
    stories of, 100–102

showcasing, 86
steps in creating (*see* Success stacking)
Success stacking, 26
   avoiding pitfalls in, 282–283
   brand halo, 282
   bringing everyone along, 270–271
   making stacking work for you, 281
   marketing yourself, 283–284
   in real life, 277–280
   Success Stacking Worksheet, 272–276
   what will and won't drive success, 270
   winning, 271–272
Success Stacking Worksheet, 272–276
Sun, Winnie, 80, 101, 149–150, 182, 188, 220, 228, 245–246, 267, 279
SWAAY, 209
SWOT analysis, 156–157

Take the Leap: Change Your Career, Change Your Life (Bliss), 55, 280
Taking control of your narrative, 46, 199–208
   exposure in, 7
   Rapid Reflection Discovery Process Worksheet for, 72
   and Ryan's FTC investigation, 195–197
   Story Creation Worksheet, 201–209
Taylor, Dave, 28
TEDx Talks, 48, 50, 52, 241, 278, 284
Themes, for content, 247–248
Thought leadership, 62
3-1-3 Challenge Worksheet, 163–177
   explain what you do in one sentences (step 2), 171–173
   explain what you do in three sentences (step 1), 164–171
   explain what you do in three words (step 3), 173–177

3-1-3 Method, 162–180
   applied in real life, 178–180
   3-1-3 Challenge Worksheet, 163–177
Top of mind, staying, 243
Toyota, 213–214
Traits:
   characteristic, identifying, 65–66
   as foundation for your brand, 71–72
   looking at assortment of, 70
   that you can work on, 67–68, 70
Transcribe conversations, 141
Transparency, 76, 80 (*See also* Exposure(s))
Truong, Hai, 81, 100, 149, 187, 220, 228, 267, 278
Trust, 76, 131
Truth:
   exposing, 189
   hiding from, 199
   importance of sharing, 216–218
   perceived, fictional elements of, 112–113
   speaking your, 25–39, 216

UCI (*see* University of California, Irvine)
UCI Antrepreneur Center, 37
Undeserving, feeling, 46
Uniqueness, identifying (*see* 3-1-3 Method)
University of California, Irvine (UCI), 37, 44, 45, 48, 52, 63, 257–258

Values:
   giving and receiving, 267
   in intentional brand, 215
Varvaro, Chris, 102–103
Videos, 231–242
   attracting clicks to, 242
   being real, not perfect in, 239–240
   body language in, 240
   creating scripts, 238–239
   dealing with fears, 237–238

Videos (*continued*):
  finding content, 234–235
  first InfluenceTree videos, 44
  having fun with, 241
  importance of, 232
  power of pauses in, 241
  speaking on camera, 235–236
  tips for creating, 232–234
  using humor in, 236–237
  using "you" in, 240–241
  writing content from, 242
  written content vs., 232
Virtual tribe, creating, 257 (*See also*
      Community building)
Visibility in the market, 85
VoiceAmerica Influencers channel, 52
Vrana, Ellen, 267
Vulnerability(-ies):
  in brand-building, 8
  in creating relatable brands,
      77–79
  and customers' rejection of
      perfection, 76–77
  for relatedness, 92
  sharing, 3–7
  society's support for, 82

Washington, Denzel, 46
Website, 180–181
Whitman, Meg, 78
Who you can become, imagining, 88
"Why You Should Let Your Fears
      Guide You" (TEDx Talk), 53
Winfrey, Oprah, 77
Wins, 271–272

Work:
  changing relationships at,
      257–259
  in Exposed and Authentic Bio
      Worksheet, 146–147
  including bio information about,
      146–147
  incorporating videos in, 235
  sharing stories at, 118–121
  (*See also* Careers)
Worksheets:
  Amplify What Is Working,
      223–227
  Content Calendar, 247–251
  Ditch the Act Peer Group Charter
      Starter, 261–263
  The Exposed and Authentic Bio,
      132–147
  Exposures Ranked by Level, 94–98
  Exposure Résumé, 109–117
  Personal Branding Positioning and
      Strategy, 152–159
  Overcoming Fear and Sharing,
      190–194
  Rapid Reflection Discovery
      Process, 65–71
  Story Creation, 201–208
  Success Stacking, 273–276
  The 3-1-3 Challenge, 164–179

World of Speakers (podcast), 48, 278
Wysong, Ashley, 282

"You," used when making videos,
      240–241

ABOUT THE AUTHORS

At first glance, Leonard Kim and Ryan Foland seem like two people who would never work together, since their personalities are on the opposite ends of the spectrum. Leonard is an introvert who expresses himself best through the written word, while Ryan is an extrovert whose sharpest tool is speaking. One fateful evening on Saturday, September 12, 2015, they met at a dinner party at the house of the inventor of co-elevation and number one *New York Times* bestselling author Keith Ferrazzi, where they quickly discovered that they needed each other's help. Fast-forward to today, and people are amazed at how their stark contrast creates such a congruent balance of ideas, philosophies, and processes.

Leonard is a marketer who not only is great at marketing companies, but does extremely well within the niches of marketing people and professional development, most commonly referred to as personal branding.

Ryan is a keynote speaker, hosts multiple podcasts, and has a passion for helping his audiences harness the power of simplicity, vulnerability, and belonging.

Both Leonard and Ryan are TEDx speakers whose talks are named on top TED talk lists, are recognized by *Entrepreneur* magazine as top Personal Branding Experts, are named as Top Marketers by *Inc.* magazine and Brand24, and have been featured in almost every major business-related publication in the United States (and a few in Asia as well).

Through their company, InfluenceTree, Leonard and Ryan hold workshops at companies, speak at conferences, work hands-on with executives and entrepreneurs who run eight-figure-plus businesses, provide consulting, and teach their crafts through online courses. Outside of work, Leonard spends his time with his beautiful wife, Angie, and their adorable chihuahua, Roo, while taking vacations at The Parker New York Hotel, and Ryan sails the seven seas with the love of his life, Cyn, on their 1977 Cal 34' sailboat named *BINGO*. If Ryan is not speaking and Cyn is in between science experiments, there is a good chance you can find them anchored off the coast of Catalina Island, their home away from home.

What brought Leonard and Ryan to where they are today is a mixture of transparency, vulnerability, and authenticity—being their true, authentic selves. So many people talk about the importance of these things, but how many people really know how to implement this way of living, let alone teach others how to do it? Leonard and Ryan do, and they share all their secrets here in *Ditch the Act*.